The Hero Trap

Most companies today are firmly on the social and environmental issues bandwagon like bees around a honey pot from oceans plastic to diversity. People are increasingly distrustful towards these efforts viewed as cheap marketing stunts meant to wow people into buying more. "Try to fly like a superman, and you will come down like a tin of soup." Internationally recognised purpose pioneer Thomas Kolster takes a hatchet to his earlier beliefs and warns organisations and leaders to stop putting themselves first when it comes to purpose. Drawing on top-line marketing case studies and in-depth interviews, Kolster demonstrates how people are truly motivated to act when they're in charge of their own life and happiness. 'Who can you help me become?' is the one essential question you need to be asking and acting on to chart a new course for your organisation, changing behaviours at scale and unlocking sustainable growth that benefits all.

Thomas Kolster is a marketing activist on a mission to make business put people and planet first. As a seasoned branding and sustainability professional of more than 18 years' standing, he's advised everything from Fortune 500 companies to small start-ups. He's a globally experienced keynote speaker, author of the book *Goodvertising* (2012) and a columnist for Adweek and several other publications. Thomas's belief is simple: change begins with you!

The Hero Trap

How to Win in a Post-Purpose Market
by Putting People in Charge

Thomas Kolster

Routledge
Taylor & Francis Group

LONDON AND NEW YORK

First published 2020
by Routledge
2 Park Square, Milton Park, Abingdon, Oxon OX14 4RN

and by Routledge
52 Vanderbilt Avenue, New York, NY 10017

Routledge is an imprint of the Taylor & Francis Group, an informa business

British Library Cataloguing-in-Publication Data
A catalogue record for this book is available from the British Library

Library of Congress Cataloging-in-Publication Data
Names: Kolster, Thomas, 1978– author.
Title: The hero trap : how to win in a post-purpose market by putting people in charge / Thomas Kolster.
Description: Abingdon, Oxon ; New York, NY : Routledge, 2020. | Includes bibliographical references and index.
Identifiers: LCCN 2019052667 (print) | LCCN 2019052668 (ebook) | ISBN 9780367242701 (hardback) | ISBN 9780367242695 (paperback) | ISBN 9780429281457 (ebook)
Subjects: LCSH: Organizational behavior. | Organizational change. | Marketing.
Classification: LCC HD58.7 .K644 2020 (print) | LCC HD58.7 (ebook) | DDC 658.8—dc23
LC record available at https://lccn.loc.gov/2019052667
LC ebook record available at https://lccn.loc.gov/2019052668

ISBN: 978-0-367-24270-1 (hbk)
ISBN: 978-0-367-24269-5 (pbk)
ISBN: 978-0-429-28145-7 (ebk)

Typeset in Avant Garde
by Apex CoVantage, LLC

Contents

Acknowledgements

I promise, I will keep trying.

Art enables us to find ourselves and lose ourselves at the same time.

– Thomas Merton, American Trappist monk and social activist

Thanks for pushing me further

This book is the fruition of more than three years' challenging work and there are so many people and organisations along the way that I'll be forever thankful because you supported me, inspired me and believed in me. There were also countless people who didn't, but here it is: love or hate the book, but don't ignore it! Love, gratefulness and *tusind tak* (Danish: "thanks a lot") in no specific order of appearance: Mum, Dad, my brother, Klara (Keep inspiring the next gen!), Indy, B. Joseph Pine II, Saša Leben, Mojca Randl, Henry Mason, Martin Nørgaard Furze, all the hospitable people at uitchiscratch, Octavia Francis, the whole team at Trendwatching, Alex Batchelor, Didem Sekerel Erdogan, Luca Petruzzellis, Bari University, Maria Dalskov, Alexander Silva Lopera, Greta Valvonytė, Dorte Gjerrild, Søren Christensen, Justin Kirby, Radu Nechifor, Saba Nejatallahi (again), Sally Phelps, Hend Raafat, Elena Rodriguez Benito, Jacqueline Lew, Nicolas Fuhr, Virginie Helias, Koann Skrzyniarz, John Izzo, Mathias Birkvad, Christiane Dolva, Joanna Yarrow, Jonathan Yohannan, Cyrus Wadia, Marc Pritchard, Marie de la Croix, Ulrik Feldskov Juul, David Hall, Dave Hakkens, Marcello Leone, Maja Rosenstock, Søren Ejlersen, Valérie Hernando-Presse, Daniel Lubetzky, Michael Lee, John Schoolcraft, Jaime Pla, Jukka Peltola, Tom Daly, Max Vallot, all the inspiring people at Sustainable Brands, Etienne White, Christine Bihlet, Valentina Mazzoli and Luigi Piper from the University of Bari, Will Gilroy, Marie Risum Stryhn, Martin Jørgensen, Edel Rodriguez, Michael Langhoff, Mathias Wikström, Ines Gergoric, my freelance editor Tree Elven, Paul White (again), Barbara Kutscher, Siena Parker and everyone at my publisher. If your name is not here, it should've been: I say thank you nonetheless from the bottom of my heart.

Cover artwork by Edel Rodriguez

I met Edel at an event in Prague and his work instantly struck a chord with me. I couldn't wait to find a project where we could work together. Edel has helped translate my words into a simple, iconic cover. Forever grateful.

Illustrations by Martin Jørgensen

I've known Martin since we both worked at the ad agency DDB in Copenhagen. His pen has shaped the visual storytelling throughout the book and I'm thankful for his time and effort. If you like any of the nine quirky chapter introduction portraits by Martin, you can get your own poster here: martin-j.dk.

Behind the title

Naming this book was like naming a child. Honestly, just take a look at this long list of almost-there, could-be, maybes before I finally settled on one title. Guess that's part of the lifelong struggle of creating anything. Embrace trying.

Change in a heartbeat; No lip service; Superbrand is dead; Buying means less, being is everything; From living bigger to living better; A war on self-actualisation; Dear brand, challenge me; Pass the recipe; Pass the starter pistol; Brand catalysts; Butterfly brands give people wings; It's people's business; Honestly, this is for my own sake; From reaching people where they are to reaching who they are; The untold story of what truly motivates us; The untold carrot story; To the best I can be; Brands do not matter, people matter; If not you, who?; Nothing beats the finish line; Nothing beats, I did it; Done is best; In your customers' shoes; Walking in your customers' mind; The catalyst; The power of clay elephants; The great human potential; Finding your own stick and carrot; Empowerability; The perfect human being; Flawless being; Possible being; Change starts with who?; Caterpillar brands; Butterfly brands; The butterfly trigger; Life triggers; Breaking better; The personal code; The change diary; Ask who; Pass the steering wheel; and Post-purpose.

About the author

Hi, let's create change together!

Thomas Kolster is a marketing activist on a mission to make business put people and planet first. As a seasoned branding and sustainability professional of more than 18 years' standing, he's advised Fortune 500 companies, small start-ups, governments, agencies and non-profits. He's the founder of the global Goodvertising movement that's inspired a shift for the better in advertising. He's also the author of two books: *Goodvertising* (2012) and the one you're holding in your hands now.

He's an internationally recognised keynote speaker who's appeared in more than 70 countries at events like TEDx, SXSW, D&AD and Sustainable Brands. He is a columnist for the *Guardian*, *Adweek*, *The Drum* and several other publications, as well as a regular judge at international award shows such as Cannes Lions and D&AD. As a passionate entrepreneur and change agent, he's launched several impact platforms like Cph:Change and Wheregoodgrows. Thomas's belief is simple: change begins with you!

thomaskolster.com

THOMAS
KOLSTER

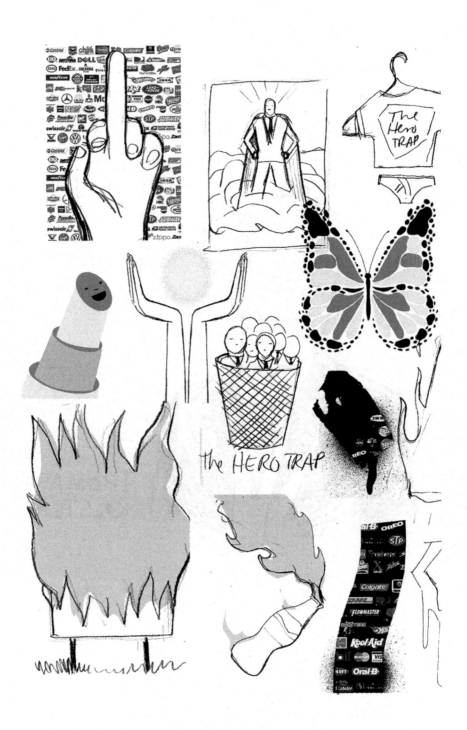

The HERO TRAP

Introduction
Change begins with who?

Brands as a force for good and a force for growth have become mainstream. There is no alternative for brands than to behave more responsibly.[1]

- *Marc Pritchard, Chief Brand Officer, Procter & Gamble*

MARC PRITCHARD

Life is a labyrinth: it's easy to lose focus

I was wrong about purpose. All these years I had been asking the wrong questions. Let me ask you this: who do you want to be? And I'm not talking about that inquisitive question from your mother or dad, when you as a child could simply say fireman, pilot or doctor. I'm talking about "who" you see yourself as becoming. "Who" do you aspire towards being? "Who" embodies a good life for you? It can be smaller "who's" or roles in your life, like a more considerate boyfriend or girlfriend, a better vegan chef or a better runner, right up to passions like a hotshot creative director, a skydiver or simply a great mum or dad to your children. We all go through life struggling to find our "who."

Often, we lose focus on what's important in our lives, or we prioritise wrongly; the same can be said about marketing and building purposeful brands. Our dreams, fears and aspirations are the building blocks of great, long-living brands that matter to people. The organisations that get this are touching the very core of people's being, the very top of Maslow's Hierarchy of Needs – people's urge to fulfil themselves through sports, arts, work or whatever rocks their boat. Think of the sense of safety you feel when driving a Volvo: you are a responsible mom or dad. Or think about the unhindered creativity when working on an Apple MacBook: you are truly a creative. It's not about the product, it's about who you become.

Admittedly it's easy to get lost in the fast-paced world of marketing, with all the talk of artificial intelligence (AI), digital transformation, real time and whatever else is trending, but the answer is right in front of you – people. Yes, people like you and me. In a post-consumerist society, the cost of ignoring people's urge to reach self-fulfilment is brutal and, in most instances, fatal. It's time to refocus. Market economists have made us believe we're driven by green bills or status, but the inherent human truth that goes across age, culture and gender uncovers a stronger force: we want to be in charge of our own lives and our own happiness. You're truly motivated to act when you're calling the shots or chasing that dream. The organisations that get this win by making people become more, do more.

My own story of transformation

In my early twenties, I started working as a copywriter in an ad agency in Denmark. I liked writing and I guess I always had a creative edge, but I didn't feel a burning purpose, and quite bluntly, I was getting paid for what most of the time seemed like a hobby. But something within me didn't feel right. It took me the better part of ten years of advertising agency life – from copywriter to creative director to owner of an agency – to realise that I had to change.

It wasn't an easy journey and, in hindsight, it probably wasn't even a conscious one. More of a spontaneous outburst, a rallying cry against my industry and the unhinged capitalism and consumerism it stood for but, maybe more importantly, an alignment of my work life and my values.

My wake-up call happened when politicians from all over the world gathered in my hometown of Copenhagen in 2009 to agree on a climate treaty to curb rampaging carbon emissions. I had high expectations because all the big guns of politics were there: Merkel, Obama, Sarkozy, Blair, Putin. But as you know . . . nothing happened.

Frustrated, I couldn't help but think that I'm selling cars, burgers and quick loans people really don't need. How can I make a difference? How can I make marketing people realise that their voice and work truly matter in shaping a better world? How can I make them realise that creativity and communication are powerful tools that can be used to serve human and planetary betterment?

My mission was shaped, and it formed the springboard for my first book, *Goodvertising* (Thames & Hudson, 2012). So I slowly developed a voice and a conviction, which was ultimately to give others a voice, give others a platform. I grew from feeling I was getting paid to use my passion and creativity on something I didn't believe in to waking up energised and ready to spark change.

From "Why" to "Who"

I've been in the hurricane's eye of the purpose revolution the last decade and have been a vocal advocate. Today, I've lost my belief in putting organisations or leaders on that purpose pedestal rallying for change. If you try to fly like superman, you'll fall like a can of soup. If we are to create change, we have to put people first. I'll argue that organisations have to chart a different course, where they instead help people to follow through on their needs and their ambitions in life. It's a move from "why" your organisation matters in the world to understanding how you as an organisation can help me to achieve "who" I want to be: making me matter. It's a move from being a self-obsessed evangelist to a real leader. We're at a tipping point, and although a sustainable narrative is becoming more commonplace, there is still far to go in pushing people to live better, more sustainable lives. This can only happen if organisations truly motivate people to act.

A real change story about personal development

No parental supervision. Lower middle-class family.
Had to be brave enough to change majors after 3.5 years of study.[2]

– Rich Faber, Innovation Manager at Fortune 250 Company, on Quora.com

Great leaders make you grow

Michael Jackson hit the nail on the head in the classic hit song "Man in the Mirror": "*I'm starting with the man in the mirror, I'm asking him to change his ways.*"[3] No doubt about it, we are our own biggest enemies of change. That's why organisations should look to people as the agents of change. Everyone has the potential to change at any point in his or her life, from small goals like eating healthier to bigger aspirations like living with your heart first. We just need the right motivation. Very few organisations have been able to bridge the purpose gap and get people to move from buying in to the purpose to actually buying the product or changing behaviours for the better. The intention is there, but action doesn't follow. Through years of advising leaders and organisations on purpose, I finally realised what the missing link was: the very people you are supposed to serve and consequently motivate. I looked to coaching methodologies and psychotherapy to understand how to move people from inaction to action, from unfulfilled to fulfilled. One simple but essential question helped spark the needed change: "Who can you help me become?" When you dare to ask "who," you motivate people to make that jump across their own personal gap from aspiration to action. You become a gardener of change and prepare the soil for people's growth. Ultimately, you have to help people grow – not directly control or lead them. You have to light a fire in everyone not by passing it on but by helping them to make it! The best leaders I have come across in my life have been those who made me grow, who made me better. The "why" of an organisation has to be found in the individual's "who."

Mass-marketing, mass-production and the other "masses" are dying, as people are gaining control. Organisations are faced by smaller, more agile challengers, and there are plenty of those – potentially eight billion ordinary people armed with great ideas and a burning passion, Davids with a sling. Across industries, the big players, the Goliaths, have felt the impact, and some have been brought down. It's the many Davids who are taking over the very creation of marketing, the very creation of business. It's unavoidable to put people first.

The transformation toolbox: begin with "who"

I want to set a new agenda for leadership, a new agenda for brand growth going forward, that's bottom-up, inclusive, diverse, democratic, sustainable, open, life improving – everything that's so far from how organisations, businesses or marketing programs traditionally behave.

My goal is to write a practical, hands-on book, one that's not just left on the bookshelf to gather dust but is being applied again and again to transform people, organisations and leaders. It's goal oriented. A book that enables you – and your stakeholders. We all need a friendly push from behind sometimes, that reminder not to leave going for that run till tomorrow. Your "push in the back" for crafting organisations that are not dumb, irrelevant, self-centric or outright harmful is now. I believe that together we can create a wave of change for happier, life-improving growth, and it all begins with truly putting people in charge of their own change. The aim of this book is to provide you with the tools for that transformation, and it begins with that one simple question: Who can you help people become?

1   Me is the new mass

For an organisation like IKEA it can be very scary to be open, because what if our customers think that sustainable living is boring or what if they think that IKEA moving into this space is bullshit? And my point was well, if they're thinking and talking about it anyway, wouldn't it be better that IKEA be part of that conversation? 1

– Joanna Yarrow, Head of Sustainable & Healthy Living, INGKA Group (IKEA)

JoANNA YARRoW

No CEO is "Uber" the new rules

When power balances shift, revolution or transformation happens. "*The power of the people is greater than the people in power!*" exclaimed Egyptian Internet activist Wael Ghonim[2] during the Arab Spring. This rings especially true today. Everything we know about marketing, business and leadership is changing, as individuals challenge the long-held monopoly on power, storytelling, manufacturing and distribution. No matter what type of communication you work with – journalism, politics or advertising – what you say holds no power in itself. It's truly about becoming people-first, from how organisations are built to how they behave.

The top-down model has been turned upside down. The era where market shares or opinions were won by domination has come to an end. From shelf space to the commercial bloc to tying customers to phone contracts, the modus operandi of retaining control by hiding important information in the small print or impossible-to-read nutritional facts and stealing people's precious time by bombarding them with advertising is no more.

Now, one individual can challenge an entire organisation or leader. Take the case of Travis Kalanick, CEO of Uber, a company with a valuation of $60 billion. He was confronted by one of his own Uber drivers during a ride. "*People do not trust you anymore,*" the driver said, blaming the low-fare prices for practically bankrupting him. Instead of taking the criticism on-board, Kalanick unleashed on the driver: "*Some people don't like to take responsibility for their own shit*" and gave him a one-star review.[3] The driver recorded the exchange, and it quickly became a public shit-storm, fuelling the already blazing bonfire of Uber's controversies.

Dinosaurs versus dynamism

He's not the only one. CEOs from billion-dollar companies are increasingly hitting the headline with apologies to individuals and society at large. Complacency and being stuck in their ways have become real dangers for leaders and organisations. Power, privilege and money are no longer a shield, as Hollywood blockbuster producer Harvey Weinstein – famous for films such as *Pulp Fiction*, *The Crying Game* and *Shakespeare in Love* – experienced when he was confronted with a tirade of sexual harassment allegations. His lawyer termed it "*an old dinosaur learning new ways.*"[4] Perhaps Weinstein should have spent more time in history class – we all know the fate of the dinosaurs.

I share these stories because many organisations are still stuck in the old mass-marketing, mass-production, mass-movement mindset. You can see it on a daily basis, with news organisations struggling to adapt to a new reality where everyone is a content producer. In the United States, Google and Facebook command more revenue than all newspapers combined.[5] The marketing industry has become an ignored stalker trying to get out of its imaginary glass cage – your average 12-year-old girl is a savvier marketing machine as she promotes her latest yummy-one-minute-chocolate-chip-cookie on Insta (read: Instagram).

Regrettably, most companies simply don't get that people aren't just waiting around to buy their bland, industrialised, generic products. Today, people have choices and can opt for the bakery on the corner that serves freshly baked bread every three hours, rather than purchase a vacuum-packed brick of bread that'll outlast the Great Wall. Research in 2018 revealed that half of the companies listed on Fortune 500 have declining revenues or declining after-tax profits.[6] The big question to ask yourself as an organisation, as the power balance is tipping, is, "*What is it you can do for people?*"

Everything you can do, I can do (better)

There has never been a time when individuals can do so much, express themselves or showcase their talent (or lack thereof) to the world. Everything has changed – how we as a society communicate with each other, look for love, do our work, start a business. The structure that used to demand big teams, expensive equipment and somebody with a big pay check has crumbled. Now, everybody with a laptop, a phone and a big chunk of passion can be her own moviemaker (iMovie), music studio (Songtrust), craft shop (Etsy), hotel owner (Airbnb), taxi company (Uber), coffee store (Wheelys), teacher (Skillshare), cleaning company (Handy) or whatever floats her boat. The market no longer belongs to the big brand household names but to José, Christine Raj, and the many other talented people out there.

Organisations are failing because they lose focus of what's important. They are narrowly focused on growth – winning market shares or customer acquisitions – rather than on developing, evolving and thinking, "How is our organisation meaningful to people's lives?" Innovation from big companies seems to be at a standstill as anyone can come up with an innovative approach. Ideas are cheap. Hey, ideas often happen in the shower or when you're doing nothing – how's that for cheap?! Couple that with the fact that today, there's almost nothing you can't do yourself as the cost of putting ideas into action plummets. For big companies with unwieldy, costly and often bureaucratic departments, the challenge is real across the whole marketing spectrum – from research and development to positioning to marketing and distribution. How is your organisation adjusting its marketing mix or brand to cope with a people-powered marketplace?

Hey, who's telling this story?!

With business becoming everybody's business, there's increasing pressure to cut through the noise of conversation and communication. The business of storytelling is a very gratifying business, whether it's a Hollywood script, a piece of investigative journalism or a 30-second commercial. As always, it's about the narrative, the good story. But, like the teenage girl retaking selfies until it's pose-perfect, we have all become storytellers trying to amplify the right story about ourselves to the world. It's critical to be aware of this: the monopoly of storytelling is challenged when everybody armed with a smartphone can spread a good story that contests the social, cultural or economic elite at lightning speed. This surge in quantity and quality of content undeniably reveals real gold nuggets that stand up to the power elites, such as the #MeToo movement in 2017, rightfully dubbed the most influential communication campaign of that year. Or the resounding call for climate action from the young Swedish girl Greta Thunberg, who in March 2019 inspired more than 1.4 million students across the world to go on strike under the banner "School strike for climate."

Trust is at risk. According to an Edelman Trust Barometer in 2019,[7] 61% of people say that "a person like them" is a credible source of information, compared to only 47% who would say they trust a CEO. Even the power elites seem to circumvent the traditional media channels and opt for social media or whistleblower sites when they have an agenda that goes against the institutions, with no better (or worse) an example than the US President Donald Trump. One man or woman with a phone is like David's staff and sling, ready to take on Goliath – be that a company, organisation or government.

People worry about surveillance, companies misusing data, states spying on their own citizens and Big Brother watching. For every one government, spy or company, we the people, in our millions and billions, are the ones watching these institutions. Every time the state or a company crosses the line of its authority or commits any other wrongdoing, there's a concerned citizen with a phone – from the Taksim Square to Ferguson protests and rallies; from #blacklivesmatter to #chapulling (Prime Minister Erdogan's use of the word *çapulcu*, meaning "looter," to describe demonstrators was adapted to "chapul" meaning "fighting for one's rights").

As an organisation, you can't treat people as a target group or the next customer in line. You have to converse with them like people, peers, friends. Their voice equals your voice. Their Twitter update equals your Twitter update. And in many instances, their voice(s) might even outdo your best efforts! When people are the megaphone amplifying or decrying your efforts as a leader or an organisation, how can you keep them aligned with your communication? We're entering a new era of communication, where it's not about what you say but about how you can enable others to sing your praises.

Important lesson in parenting and marketing

"*It's like you're always stuck in second gear. When it hasn't been your day, your week, your month, or even your year.*" I'm sure that feeling sometimes overruns you, with everything around you changing so fast. No, the quote is not by the oft cited Mark Twain, it's the *Friends* theme tune, "I'll Be There for You" by the Rembrandts – you have most likely clapped to it at some time in your life. Growing up in Denmark in the 1980s and 1990s, I, like many families around the world, watched American-bought TV shows such as *Seinfeld* and *Friends*. It was the Golden Age of TV, unbeaten in at least a decade, according to a Nielsen measurement of Top 20 most watched TV epi-sodes.[8] The *Seinfeld* series finale in 1998 is still the most recent episode to reach the Top 100. That is testament to a change in the very notion of mass-communication.

With the world becoming flatter, as Thomas Friedman proclaimed in his 2005 *The World is Flat*,[9] digitalisation and globalisation are bring-ing us closer together as one big village. Internet memes – today's version of small town gossip – travel around the world in a couple of hours. At the same time, it is tearing us further apart. As one screen becomes many, the Internet has fragmented mass-media as one-to-many becomes many-to-many and individuals move from being con-sumers to creators.

In his essay "Death to the Mass,"[10] Jeff Jarvis sets out the challenge to any organisation stuck in a "mass" mindset: "*What has died is the mass-media business model – injuring, perhaps mortally, a host of institutions it symbiotically supported: publishing, broadcasting, mass marketing, mass production, political parties, possibly even our notion of a nation. We are coming at last to the end of the Gutenberg Age.*"

The average organisation is now akin to parents desperately trying to cope with an independent teenager daughter or son questioning every message or action and craving control and independence. If you have a teenager, you've probably been confronted with a chal-lenge of your previously sovereign expertise, along with rolling eyes and disdain: "*Mum, I know how to do that, ok!?*" That's your consumers, customers, people of today. It's important to observe this change in the power relationship as it unveils the level of transformation.

I see the loss of power from organisations to individuals in three dis-tinct phases, with the power of the mass and the power of the indi-vidual still interchanging:

The Three Power Shifts

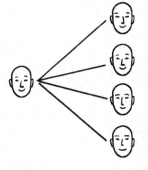

The power of the organisation:
Power-centric – one to many –
"We do."

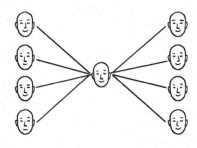

The power of the mass:
Power-sharing – one to many
and many to one – "We do
together."

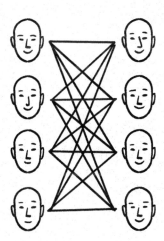

The power of the individual:
Enabling – many to many – "I do."

Let's take a closer look at those shifts and at how the positioning of brands has changed within them.

Poster boys and USPs: the power of the organisation

What happened with the Golden Age of TV is now happening with marketing. The opportunity to influence a whole conversation has toughened up compared to the mass-media days of advertising hits like Budweiser's "Whassup?" from 1999, which shaped the language of a whole generation. I've been shouting my fair share of highly con- tagious "Whassups" and am sure you have as well. Or just think how a cleverly crafted ad depicting the Volkswagen's Beatle with the head- line "think small" underneath captivated the American public in 1959 and encouraged them to embrace smaller German cars, challenging the heartland of US car manufacturing, Detroit.

The advent of mass-communication and mass-production commod- itised and industrialised everything and everyone, creating a system where people were organised by mass-demographics, such as income, sex, age and postcode, and targeted accordingly.

McDonald's was the poster boy of a well run engine designed to ensure quick service, clean surroundings and uniform products, its marketing machine churning out campaigns bigger and more fre- quent than any other competitor. Today, the assembly line–inspired Big Mac still astonishes – an historic symbol. In the 2017 biographical drama *The Founder*, Ray Kroc, played by Michael Keaton, portrays the early days of McDonald's, where he times how long it takes to assemble a Big Mac, showing how no detail was left unattended. In the mass-marketing and mass-production era, it was about unique selling propositions (USPs) based on the idea of a qualitative differ- ence between product A and product B – and it was advertising's role to enhance and dramatize this difference. McDonald's has become one of the most criticised symbols of that era in popular culture, a "superbrand" built by mass-marketing. Hated or, as Justin Timberlake's McDonald's jingle cries, "I'm lovin' it."

#SomethingGate: the power of the mass

The early cracks in the power monopoly began with the widespread use of the Internet and a tsunami-building wave of user-made content. In 2000, the baby video *Charlie Bit My Finger*[11] (yes, a video of a baby biting his younger brother's finger) surpassed what professional market- ers could only dream about. The video was simply uploaded by the charming young brother's mum and dad. They allegedly made over $1 million in advertising revenue off a video with more than 850 million views at the time of writing, not to mention remixes, parodies, and a ten-year anniversary version.[12]

Pepsi and Burger King shaped other early indications that the land-scape was changing. In 2004, Burger King arrested slipping sales and outsold its arch-rival McDonald's by inviting customers to play along with the "Subservient Chicken," an interactive game illustrating that you could get your chicken any way you liked it at Burger King: on a dedicated website, users could write commands, and a chicken character would perform pre-made actions of the commands, often in humorous ways. And in 2010, Pepsi abandoned their traditional celeb-rity-endorsed campaigns, featuring the likes of Britney Spears, to launch Project Refresh, which asked Americans to decide what community project they should support with $20 million.

Suddenly mass-communication opened up and became more interactive and engaging. Everyone could shape or co-create the advertising.

But it didn't stop there. What people had come to expect from the Internet in terms of having a say quickly changed the product offering. Nike was one of the brands quick to embrace co-creation on a large scale with the launch of Nike iD, where people could customise a pair of Nike sneakers online or in one of multiple dedicated Nike studios and get the shoes shipped to their homes. This wasn't just about organisa-tions giving people more choice – they were increasingly demanding it. This was no longer about one-way communication; people could talk back – and they did. Now, no company was safe from the explo-sive social media update #SomethingGate – anyone witnessing unjust actions to themselves or others could become everyday activists, even taking a hard hit at an organisation's share prices. It was a tug of war, with organisations on one end of the rope and a mass of people on the other, each fighting for their say.

But it also saw organisations rising to meet the challenge of the changed landscape, to converse and engage people around shared interests or common good – what marketing guru Seth Godin dubbed "tribes": "*a group of people connected to one another, connected to a leader, and connected to an idea.*"[13]

Real beauty and the purpose revolution

As I mentioned, in early 2010, I started doing research for my first book, *Goodvertising* (Thames & Hudson, 2012), detailing an emerging marketing trend which required brands to aim beyond profit to doing good for people and planet. Across markets, people were beginning to search for more than the mere performance or affordability of a product or service: they bought into a "value alignment," as Simon Sinek famously coined in his book *Start with Why* (2009).[14] No longer are people convinced by the old mass-market approach, instead looking out for like-minded peers, a brand reflecting their values: "*I like that . . . I am like that.*" People want to drive the car that aligns with their values, eat the ice-cream that's the best personal match.

As purpose moves centre stage, people look for authentic brands they believe in. Suddenly, the personality and beating heart of those brands are important. Does the brand act with integrity? Is it authentic in what it says and does?

Research by Edelman[15] from 2018 across 14 countries and 14,000 people revealed that 64% of those asked said they would buy or boycott a brand based on the brand's position on a social or political issue (a remarkable increase of 13 points since 2017). Purpose is becoming the main differentiator for people looking for an authentic brand experience as purpose transforms from niche to the mainstream and research points to a strong correlation between brand purpose and profitability. The increasing focus on brand purpose was pushing brands to compete on something bigger than product narratives.

One of the time-encapsulating examples of purpose and movement building is the Unilever Dove Real Beauty campaign from 2004: It kick-started a conversation around society's view of women and beauty with a simple billboard campaign asking people to vote on whether the women pictured were "fat or fit?" or "wrinkled or wonderful?" Among many other powerful executions, one of the campaign's early hits was "Evolution," showing a woman being Photoshopped into a supermodel.

All this was in the early days of digital and one of the first truly blockbuster viral advertising hits. The campaigns stirred up mould-breaking conversations around issues like beauty ideals, Photoshopping, and body size. The Dove campaign was mimicked by many other brands, but no other beauty campaign has done so on such a truly global scale. The campaign is still alive today, winning hearts and minds.

What makes one brand stand out from another is its ability to convey its story in an authentic manner, so that people perceive the brand as true to its values: you are, as a brand, what you say you are and how you act according to those values. That's when people buy into the brand purpose. By no means is it over. Purpose is still very much on everybody's lips (and minds). It is a continuous dialogue and power play among the organisation and you and me – one to many and many to one as the rope gets tugged back and forth.

You're the activist: the power of the individual

This tug of war is developing into a losing game for brands, leaders and organisations that fail to get people to pull the rope for them. Traditionally, a movement is led by a value-driven leader, an evangelist, whereas a new kind of leadership is appearing that's about enabling individuals. Let me share a campaign from American Express (AmEx), which understands how to enable its customers. On their website, American Express describes how since 1850, AmEx "*has worked to make a difference in their customers' lives in ways that matter most to them.*"[16] They also mention how they "*promise to understand, respect and back their customers, and help them on their personal journeys.*" One such example was initiated in 2010 in the aftermath of the financial crisis in the United States, where many small store owners were struggling to turn a profit. American Express created the initiative Shop Small with a simple rallying cry just after the echoes of Black Friday: support your small local businesses with "Small Business Saturday."[17]

The campaign turned the mass-marketing playbook on its head early on and created a platform for both passionate people in the community and small business owners to voice their support and to not only take part but to co-create the campaign. A bottom-up, almost grassroots approach, it involved social media toolkits, a YouTube video maker, logos, posters and digital assets where cities, towns and communities could create Neighborhood Champions to support their local stores. AmEx even bought Facebook ads for small businesses.

This was not your average mass-marketing approach: while a movement requires energising people to take part, this campaign gave them the tools and support to turn into campaigners themselves. Shop Small was a platform for people to participate on many levels rather than just a campaign, and its empowering message was not only adopted as an official shopping day by US legislators but also endorsed by former President Barack Obama himself when he visited a local store to "shop small." When did your efforts inspire a president to join the cause? Or get mentioned by one of the world's most recognised marketing papers, *Ad Age*, as one of the 21st century's most influential campaigns? The campaign continues to break local spending records year after year and was replicated in the UK in 2013, where it is also growing and delivering revenue to small business owners and to American Express as well. A thriving small business means better business for American Express. At the centre of this campaign were passionate individuals who wanted to do something for their local community. American Express enabled them to not only support but also to rally their friends and neighbours, creating a snowball many-to-many effect as people took over the creation of the campaign. Turning individuals into campaigners and amplifying the reach beyond any traditional campaign made the scale of this initiative possible. For American Express, it's been one of their most successful campaigns ever, and I'll share more about the results in chapter 10.

Here for your life goals

For the Canadian sportswear brand RYU (Respect Your Universe), it's not simply about a campaign but about the whole mindset of the organisation that aims to transform an individual. RYU was founded in 2011 on a simple idea of getting people to reach their goals: "*We're here to help you achieve more than your gym goals, RYU is here for your life goals.*" The organisation is taking a backseat and cheering for its customers' success. It's not empty words or a brand-centric "We care about you" but a promise to its customers – and a difference their customers can feel as RYU pushes them towards realising their goals, whatever they may be.

Unmass-marketing

One of the organisations that's witnessed this transformation in the marketing space from the power of the organisation to the power of the individual is the world's second biggest consumer goods company, Procter & Gamble (P&G), known for brands like Always, Gillette, Head & Shoulders, Oral-B, Ariel, SK-II and many others. A company founded in 1837, which is in itself a testament to its ability to adapt. I was curious about how to stay agile in a world of constant change. I and organised a call with P&G's Chief Brand Officer Marc Pritchard,[18] who's responsible for a portfolio of brands with the world's biggest advertising spend, estimated at $10.5 billion, which is equal to the GDP of a country like Panama or Cyprus.[19]

Marc instantly challenged my assumption about people being in power:

> I would say consumers always have had the power. From when we made Ivory soap in the 1890s to Tide in the 1950s to the products we're selling today, consumers ultimately have the power to buy or not to buy our products. What has changed in recent years is that technology has enabled us to be even closer to the people we serve, and in the near future, we'll have the ability to be in constant contact. That's why we need brand builders to operate as brand entrepreneurs with their "hands on the keyboard" erasing any distance between our brands and the people we serve.

The continuous connection with people, the dialogue, is something I picked up in conversations with other brand leaders and CEOs: the market is talking, which ultimately puts the individual at the centre. P&G is focusing increasingly on the roles these brands can play in people's lives rather than on focusing on product advantages. We all remember how P&G's products were blasting their superiority with loud jingles and catchy slogans, such as Gillette's singing chorus, "The best a man can get"? Marc views this change as a must: "We've chosen to use our voice in advertising as a force for good because our brands reach so many people, and what our brands say can spark important conversations, change perspectives, and ultimately change behaviour."

It's evident across the portfolio, from washing powder to high-end beauty cream. Ariel's campaign "Share the load" in India challenges gender stereotypes and encourages men (and their sons) to "share the load" of washing; the Always campaign "Like a girl" changed the meaning of the sentence "Like a girl" from being an insult to a statement of pride; SK-II empowers women; and recently Gillette asked men to go up against toxic masculinity and become "The best a man can be" – and the list goes on.

"*We take action and we express these views to change behaviour – and enable people to have constructive conversations,*" says Marc. "*If you look at the Gillette ad, it shows men stepping up to stop harassment, bullying and actually shows good behaviour and how to do it.*" Marc explains how P&G takes a problem-solving approach to stay relevant:

> *We're looking at consumers' problems that we can solve, and we're taking a more holistic view of the entire consumer experience. We have found that when our brands are focused on solving consumer problems and we quickly invent something that is irresistibly superior – product, package, communication, retail experience, and value – then we're able to grow. The small emerging brands have made us better at being more focused on the complete human experience and caused us to get better at bringing it all together in a more effective way.*

Change is unavoidable

Marc shares the case of the fast-growing Asian high-end beauty brand SK-II and how they're using big data, meeting people on a one-on-one basis, creating and co-creating content with people to reinvent the advertising. SK-II is taking a start-up approach to marketing with smaller, faster-moving, competing teams; even the titles are different than what you'll normally come across in a marketing organisation like a "*hacker*" being the data scientist and the "*hipster*" being the marketing creative.

Change is unavoidable, says Marc: "*We are re-inventing marketing for brands to be good citizens of the world, which means we're re-inventing brands to be both a force for good and a force for growth.*"

As we ended the call, it was clear to me that when the world's biggest advertiser is trying to behave like a start-up, the market has changed: mass means less. It's like P&G is Goliath trying to mimic David's every move but with the strength of a giant.

The built-in bullshit detector

"Purpose" might be a word that gets too big for its own good as people challenge the notion of unselfish interests from leaders and organisations. Although younger generations are buying into values and appreciating companies with values, they're also critical because they've grown up at a time where they're the doers. As Shane Smith, CEO of Vice, the youth-focused media house, rightly states: "*Young people have been marketed to since they were babies. They develop this incredibly sophisticated bullshit detector and the only way to circumvent the bullshit detector is to not bullshit.*"[20]

Instead of sitting around and waiting for brand XYZ to talk about how much "*We care,*" young generations rather start their own business aligned with their values on Kickstarter.com or create and sell their own products on Instagram or Etsy.com. They want to be in control, and the usual brand-pursuing purpose can quickly become that parent hot on the tails of a teenager who is thinking: "*Please stop, I can do this myself.*"

What younger generations have come to expect from digital experiences where they're in control is a new status quo for brands. Crying out your organisation's hopefully heartfelt purpose "*We care*" is not enough. Young people want to be part of the change, and change begins with "I," not "we."

Selling dreams or enabling dreams to come true?

There is no room for fooling around in this new landscape. People want to participate, and brands will have to open up for people's creativity and passion. It's a move from the mass-market approach "*We create*" to giving individuals a platform to unlock their "*I create, I realize, I want to*" aspirations. It's people who ultimately grow the brand; now it's about time brands also grow people and make them realise their dreams, aspirations and needs. This is not only about telling your organisation's story – the product or service is no longer "*yours only*". Big, global organisations are witnessing the change and trying to move away from a mass-marketing model to a more personalised, faster and digital reality.

Marc Pritchard from P&G shared the response they're implementing:

> *We are innovating how we innovate. We took lessons from the lean innovation start-up approach from the tech world, and we have created more than 130 small teams, that are basically operating like new-to-the-world start-ups. Taking this approach has helped us innovate faster to be able to solve consumer problems and meet the needs of consumers more effectively.*

One of the lean approaches we use is what we call 'GrowthWorks.' We focus on a consumer problem that needs to be solved, then we engage with the consumers in a real-time, one-to-one basis. We make a minimal viable prototype, or MVP, to quickly test in the market.

That's no mean feat: 130 teams innovating and doing real-time tests with people is like an army of entrepreneurs but with access to P&G's muscles in research & development, marketing and data and insights – taking the best from the start-up space and mixing it with global marketing capabilities to chart a new way forward.

Mass-production, ironically enough, was what lowered the prices and made products available to the masses, like Volkswagen bringing affordable cars to the market in the 1940s and 1950s, which fuelled the rise of the middle-class family. But today, democratisation has shot a hole in the mass-produced plastic bucket, making it possible for people to be producers, makers and business owners themselves. Businesses could traditionally uphold a certain leadership within an industry secured through years of experience, manufacturing advantages, patents, lobbyists, distribution, consumer trust and so on. The call for change cannot go unanswered.

Dave vs Goliath: Dutch designer goes against the grain

Meet Dave Hakkens, a young Dutch designer. Upset with how quickly phones were being built to become obsolete as the hardware became outdated, he came up with the idea of a new, modular phone. Phonebloks allowed you to swap parts or improve your phone as you like, as if it were built out of LEGO bricks.[21] For a better camera or a longer battery time, for instance, you could swap in a bigger camera or battery block. Dave envisioned the hardware platform like software, so you could always update the hardware to the newest version and every company could take part and make the best possible phone. Rather than one company making the camera block, several different camera companies could compete to deliver the best possible solution. For Dave, it was simply an idea conceived almost straight out of university, but he created a video outlining the idea with visualisations of how the phone could potentially look, gauging whether people out there really wanted a phone that was worth keeping. And indeed they did. In less than two months, Dave's idea had sparked the imagination of 20 million people, and he quickly landed a development deal with Google's Motorola brand.[22]

Some years ago, I invited Dave to speak at an event, Sustainable Bottom Line, I arranged in Copenhagen. Following Dave's keynote, I was curious to ask him how he felt about working with Google (Google, now Alphabet), which for many people is a very attractive workplace. His answer really resonates with how Gen Zs in many ways feel about companies and to some extent about ownership: "*Phone-bloks is not a Dave Hakkens phone, it is not a Google phone, it's the community's phone.*" The mission of the crowd-powered phone enabling people to turn a phone into their very own individual tool was more important than working with some big corporation. Phone-bloks shows just how cheap it is to come up with an idea that challenges the old powerhouses with their often slow-moving research and development departments, at the same time enabling people to do more – a powerful story that spreads.

A real change story about home

I feel most at home in Virginia where I grew up. My Grandma raised me. I feel most at home when I visit there & in her presence. I just returned home from a month-long visit to Virginia and it literally revived my soul. Home is where there is LOVE. Genuine LOVE.[23]

– Tiffany Hornback, Behavioural Health Technician, on Quora.com

The lowering of barriers

The barriers for you and me to turn ideas into actions get lower every day, and no territory seems to be off-limits. You may remember the story of Cody Wilson. On the face of it, he was your average guy in his mid-twenties, who decided not only to make the world's first 3D-printed gun, the Liberator, in 2014, but also to make the blueprint available for everyone to download on his website, Defense Distributed. More than 100,000 people chose to do so in just two days, before the US State Department removed them.

Even space is no longer the domain of powerful governments, with big business entering the space race, led by deep-pocketed billionaires like Elon Musk's Space X and its Falcon 9 rockets, Jeff Bezos's Blue Origin and its New Shepherd rocket and Richard Branson's Virgin Group aiming for suborbital tourist flights. Three-quarters of the money being invested in space today comes from commercial activity – not governments. One of the challengers to big money is Peter Beck and Rocket Lab's Electron rocket, built mainly of carbon fibre with its engines all 3D-printed, bringing the average cost of a satellite launch down from $200 million to a mere $5 million. He wants to provide a reasonably priced test bed in Space, and, rather than the 22 space launches of 2016, he aims for weekly launches. As he touts: "*Now you can just go online and click a few buttons and you've bought one.*"[24] The sky is the limit no longer! No industry will be untouched.

Making goes mainstream

Some organisations understand the power shift and experiment with new models to serve this need. Nike's much heralded launch of its customisation effort Nike iD has expanded and turned into a thriving business, with their physical Nike iD Studios enabling individuals to create their own shoes, across more than 102 outlets in Canada, Europe, China and the United States. Since then, many other organisations have followed, and today being the creator or maker of a product or a service has become mainstream and you most likely have played your part. Maybe you have turned your room into a hotel through Airbnb, become a car rental company by lending out your car – or embraced the maker or creator in yourself by brewing your own beer, turning your window into a vegetable garden or making your own table out of an old pallet.

This shift spans online through programming and platforms like the development platform GitHub, rendering World of Warcraft characters or weapons to APIs (application programming interfaces) and open source; and it's happening offline for everything from baking, brewing, woodworking to sewing.

It's also happening between the digital and physical spheres, through 3D printing, robotics, drones and Internet of Things. This is no small fad. Etsy is a digital platform that brings the maker community together and enables them to connect with buyers around the world, involving everything from eco-friendly crayons to handmade jewellery, all in all generating revenue of $3.9 billion in 2018,[25] almost a quadrupling of its sales in 2013 of $1 billion.[26]

People can more easily follow their dreams, and most cities today boast at least a couple of food trucks or artisan food stores where passionate citizens can live out their maker/creator/foodie dream.

From consumer to creator

Not long ago, our relationship with companies as "consumers" was cold. But today you and I can take on several roles from promoter, creator or maker to distributor and investor. An obvious entrant into this maker field is Swedish furniture giant IKEA. You probably have wrestled with one of their furniture flat-packs at one point in your life and experienced that ultimate sense of accomplishment when proudly showing off your creation to your better half, a friend or family. In 2016, IKEA created an open-source do-it-yourself flat-pack spherical garden that grows plants, veggies, and herbs called the Growroom that enables people to grow their own food locally. In many countries, people felt inspired and transformed the designs into living gardens with people daily sharing their own home-built Growrooms with the community. The fascinating part is that the designs are given away for free to foster and encourage an already flourishing IKEA DIY and maker/hacker community and to make people think differently about food production. In 2018, more than 100 Growrooms had been built around the world.

Another example is denim fashion company Levi's turning people's passion into pieces in their collection under the "Levi's Makers" tag. One of their designers is 29-year-old Alice Saunders, who makes custom totes out of salvaged military fabrics. Jared Everett, who is responsible for the Levi's tailor shops explained to *Adweek*: *"For Levi's, the Makers program celebrates those who are still making things by hand while providing an outlet to tell their stories to inspire others,"*[27] Like IKEA, Levi's is bringing its community of makers closer and giving them a platform to experiment – their fans become the creators not only of the brand story but also of the actual product.

Make or break

These are no longer fringe examples. The global DIY market has increased by around 7% over the past few years – predicted to reach $43.7 billion in 2018 (from $31.9 billion in 2013).[28] Organisations are opening up to people's urge to create and can also be viewed as early experimentation to better understand the challenges and opportunities that customisation, 3D printing and mass democratisation of manufacturing will bring tomorrow. Without doubt, what you make yourself or when you're having a clear say brings more and lasting joy than the quickly fading happiness of the swipe with a credit card – at least in the well-off Western world.

The disruption is clear. Since 2000, over half of the companies in the Fortune 500 have gone bankrupt, been acquired or ceased to exist. That trend doesn't seem to be stopping as it is projected that another 40% of the companies will be gone in the next ten years.[29] It's not surprising that every CEO these days talks about innovation, but how do you innovate against an army of talented individuals and enable people to become creators rather than just consumers?

Growth is reciprocal

Ultimately, power rests in the hands of the people that organisations serve or should serve. Today it feels like an insult when a leader or an organisation insists on its way rather than my terms. As the phrase regarding any relationship goes, no tree grows in another tree's shadow. It's about time to realise that growth is reciprocal.

People today are the biggest producers of content, outnumbering professional content by who knows how many times, a trend that's projected to grow exponentially, outcrying and outnumbering the old media institutions. The old power grip is being shaken across the marketing mix, and organisations need to adapt to a model which is about being a facilitator or coach helping people to achieve what they want and embracing more collaborative models.

This is a real power struggle, but it's also an illustration of how people are viewing everything with "mass" in a different light. As an organisation, you need to respond to people's cry: "*How can you help me do more, live more, feel more or be more?*" Airbnb turned their users' homes into guest houses. American Express turned a whole community into advocates for local shopping. Andy Warhol famously foresaw individuals' rise to fame: "*In the future, everyone will be world-famous for 15 minutes.*"[30] In my years in advertising, companies have spent billions to get people to wear a T-shirt with their name and logo on it; now it's changing, and people can proudly wear their own accomplishments on their chests. The challenge cannot be ignored. What's your response?

Key takeaways

1   The mass-production and mass-marketing era is losing its power to the democratisation of everything from businesses to media.

2   Power is shifting from an organisational power-centric, one-to-many model ("*We do*") to the individual, where the role of the organisation is to enable a many-to-many model ("*I do*").

3   People are taking over the creation across the marketing mix from products and services to campaigns. Organisations can, with advantage, turn people from passive recipients into active (co-)creators.

4   Organisations have to serve people and give them a say.

5   Anything you can do, people can and want to do (better).

Questions to ask yourself

1   Do you feel more or less in control over your marketing activities today than five years ago?

2   How is your organisation adjusting your marketing mix to cope with a people-powered marketplace?

3   What is it actually you can do for people that they can't do themselves?

4   How can you enable people to do more, live more or feel more?

5   How can you with mutual benefit turn people from passive recipients into active creators across the marketing mix?

2 Catalysts of the good life

Everybody has dreams and things they want to do like go to the beach, travel the world, earn lots of money. It wasn't up to Wheelys to dictate anything, but simply make those ambitions possible for people.[1]

– *Maria de la Croix, Co-founder, Wheelys Café*

MARIA DE LA CROIX

Less about buying than being

There is a change in the relationship between companies and people that's less about buying and more about becoming. When I was a teenager, my biggest wish for my 14th birthday was a Boombox – yes, I was a nineties kid. Boombox? You might remember one of those portable music players featuring double cassette tape players and an AM/FM radio. I really wanted to be part of the cool club or, as Pepsi would call it at the time, "the new generation." Eventually after a lot of nagging, my parents bought the Boombox and it was time for some loud, pumping "*Jump, The Mac Dad will make you jump, Daddy Mac will make you jump, Kris Kross will make you jump jump.*"[2]

Fast-forward to my brother's oldest daughter, Klara, and her birthday in 2017. Her list of wishes wasn't the latest fashion dress, a new iPhone or something Bieber (musician Justin Bieber). She was looking for an experience that added meaning to her life, something that would really challenge her and make her confront her fears. Her parents and grandparents were petrified, but, as her uncle, I had to keep my cool. She wanted to jump out of a moving plane 12,000 feet above the ground with a parachute. That was 13-year-old Klara's biggest wish.

I share this story to illustrate the radical change in perception among youth. When I was a teenager, a good life was still defined by consumption. It was about owning cool stuff to show "who" you were: a skater, a pop kid or an Indie fan. When today's young generations look at meaning, they don't buy what you as an organisation produce but what that specific product or service can make them experience, do or become. Identity can be bought off the shelves like a cheap cap with a label, but a personality must be earned through experiences or personal accomplishment. The same goes for products or services claiming to serve a higher purpose or a cause. There is not much generosity or, for that matter, status in flashing yet another T-shirt decrying ocean plastic as it demands little to no effort. Being generous cannot be bought; it's something you earn by giving time or effort. For leaders and organisations, the "who" you can make people become moves centre stage.

Post-material values

An independent Finnish fund, Sitra, initiated by the Finnish government, has studied trendsetters in North America, Europe and Asia[3] to understand how they view consumption and the rise of post-material values. For younger generations like Millennials, status is no longer obtained through buying traditional status symbols such as cars or designer handbags but rather by a quest for what Sitra calls "symbols of distinction." It's not about telling a story about personal wealth or success but rather one where the story distinguishes one through personal gain of knowledge, experience and acquired skills – a bottle of wine bought at a home stay on a farm in Portugal, for example. Sitra identified a number of different patterns, and two of them are interesting in this context (I quote the report's definition):

Better me

People seek goods as a way to focus and regain a sense of control in a fast-moving environment. Some goods also express the individual's quest for non-materialistic self-improvement or "betterment."

Better World

Goods can connect to a larger narrative, whether environmentally or socially. Therefore, people see their choices as carrying a long-term impact.

From villa and Volvo to personal transformation

For my parents' generation, the post-war generation, a good life was defined by material security and a steady job. For new generations, that is giving way to a definition where self-development, self-actualisation matters more, where meaning trumps pay, where story beats stuff and where ownership of things is just one of many options. We don't buy stuff; we buy, rent, share or loan a better me. This poses an all-important question to your organisation: what are you really selling? These tendencies are not just beginning to show in the curious, open-minded, always-on segments but are increasingly turning mainstream as people are pivoting away from owning stuff to sharing. According to Statista,[4] the numbers of adults in the United States using sharing economy services such as Uber or Airbnb in 2016 was 44.8 million and are forecasted to reach 86.5 million in 2021. Projections from PwC[5] show a similar rise across five key sharing sectors – travel, car sharing, finance, staffing, and music and video streaming. These sectors, combined, have the potential to increase in global revenues from roughly $15 billion today to around $335 billion by 2025. In general, we're redefining our role with things, with ownership, which is a sign of a bigger change in what we perceive as a good life.

Through the years, I've been part of the community around Sustainable Brands. It's a like-minded global organisation sparking conversations and change in the cross section of marketing and sustainability. In 2017, they launched what they called "Enabling The Good Life" report[6] to try to understand changing consumer aspirations. The report found that 71% of people believe their parents' definition of The Good Life is different from their own. Dear reader, I don't know what generation you're from, but I can definitely relate to the findings of the report, can you?

In developed markets, the tendency is clearer: people are valuing the pursuit of a simpler, balanced life that is rich with connections to people, community and environment. Across generations, genders, and political affiliations, 36% of Americans ranked Balanced Simplicity as the most important element of The Good Life, followed by Meaningful Connections (28%), Money and Status (26%) and Personal Achievement (10%). The findings weren't as strong in developing markets such as in Turkey where money still took the top score, though closely followed by better health.

As materialism takes more of a backseat in the developed world and among younger generations, what we're seeing is that people are increasingly looking for meaning within themselves.[7] A general rise in people's average wealth is pushing the development towards self-actualisation further as materialism isn't delivering the happiness once promised in glossy ads.

Take the world's richest guy as an example: Mark Zuckerberg has all the money in the world to do whatever he wants but happiness is not bought, it's earned. Since 2009 Mark has given himself a new personal transformation challenge each year. His challenges have varied from wearing a tie every day (2009), learning Mandarin (2010), only eating animals he kills himself (2011), coding every day (2012), meeting a new person every day who doesn't work at Facebook (2013), writing one thank-you note a day (2014), reading a new book every two weeks (2015), coding an AI assistant (2016), visiting all states to "get out and talk to more people" (2017) to "Fix Facebook" (2018) because of the increasing criticism around privacy. In 2019 Mark announced he wanted to retire the challenges altogether and instead host a series of public discussions about the future of technology in society." The personal challenges give meaning: they're about learning, personal growth, pushing oneself further and ultimately, when succeeding, getting that "*I did it!*" rush of accomplishment.

Can one buy happiness?

And it's not just Mark. People are looking for happiness in other places than their wallet or shopping baskets. According to Harris,[8] consumer spending on experiences and events has increased by 70% since 1987. Millennials are quickly reshaping the market, and in 2018 US Millennials already accounted for an estimated $1.3 trillion in direct annual spending. Let's not fool ourselves, the change we're seeing is gradual, but as an organisation you have to aim a lot higher than just plugging product.

Estonian neuroscientist Dr Jaak Panksepp has looked at human emotions and identified a strong driver of fulfilment: seeking. It's an emotion we share with other mammals. Take a rat sniffing around and looking for food. When Dr Jaak took care of the rat's nutritional needs in a lab, something interesting happened: The seeking impulse didn't stop, but the rat began to gnaw on wood, bite itself, eat its own faeces. The search continued.[9]

The body rewards this searching behaviour with dopamine, a neurotransmitter linked to reward and pleasure. We humans are on a similar search. When we fail to seek to live because our material meets are need, we become less happy. This explains why achieving major goals or even winning the lottery doesn't cause long-term changes in happiness. Seeking is in itself a fulfilling activity.[10] We don't need to envy Mark his billions, but he's on to something with his annual personal challenges.

Jaak Panksepp's neuroscience-based work builds and proves what earlier scientists like Maslow famously coined with his pyramid of physiological needs: the basic needs of food, water and sleep, then safety and economic resources, health and so on form the lower layers, whereas the top of the pyramid represents self-actualisation, which is about creativity, problem solving and lack of prejudice.

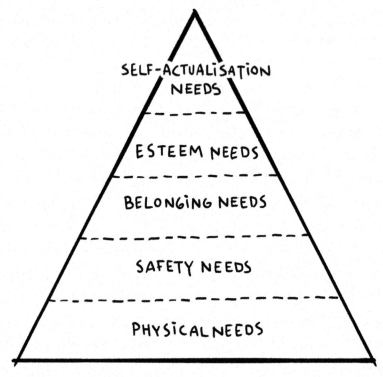

HIERARCHY OF NEEDS
MASLOW'S PYRAMID

SELF-ACTUALISATION NEEDS

ESTEEM NEEDS

BELONGING NEEDS

SAFETY NEEDS

PHYSICAL NEEDS

With our material needs fulfilled, it's "self-actualisation," as Maslow would call it, that's beginning to step into its place. If you as an organisation are looking to play a bigger role in people's lives. You have to change the focus. Ultimately, you are not buying a pair of running shoes or the running company's mission or higher purpose but instead how the organisation can help you towards "self-actualisation." Like friends, some leaders or organisations bring out a better side in you, and those that get you to experience new things, explore new sides of yourself or bring you to achieve what you always wanted build stronger bonds and a sense of accomplishment.

Buying the recipe for a good life, not the ingredients

Let me give you one example. I'm a foodie to such an extent that when I travel, I always bring home local food as my souvenir. For me it's about reliving the experience through my taste buds, but more importantly, it's about challenging myself to cook and explore new ingredients, new recipes. When it comes to cooking, I still have a lot to learn and I'm really passionate about learning how to cook more plant based. Frankly speaking, it's also a way for me to lower my climate impact and getting a slightly better conscious. In Denmark we have a company called Aarstiderne; they deliver fresh produce in a box to your front door from their own farms and a network of farms. The boxes come with recipes by their own chefs and the ingredients needed meet your specific food craving like, for example, vegetarian, quick cooking in 15 minutes, traditional Danish food, low-carb and the like. Their mission is about spreading "*the joy of organic produce and great tasting meals,*"[11] something they call "*an Earth connection.*" The result is that I'm improving my cooking skills and learning how to make great tasting organic vegetarian meals. I feel thankful for the new-found cooking skills, which I can enjoy and share with friends. I don't buy their organic produce – I can buy that many other places. I buy who Aarstiderne helps me become: a better plant based cook. And I tend to share my vegetarian cooking joy, at least when things turn out well, with friends or my digital following, thus spreading the "*Earth Connection.*"

From living bigger to living better

Other surveys back up our inherent quest for self-actualisation. The World Business Council for Sustainable Development (WBCSD), a global, CEO-led organisation of over 200 leading businesses and partners working together to accelerate the transition to a sustainable world, did a report in 2017 with advertising group Havas into what US youth prioritise.[12] The finding correlates well with The Good Life report findings because US youth prioritised being with family (64%), experiencing new things (54.9%) and spending time with friends (54.9%) as their Top 3.

For anybody who's familiar with surveys and statistics, I'm sure you'll agree with me that one thing is what people say they do – and another thing is their actual behaviour. Or, as Prime Minister Benjamin Disraeli said about statistics: "*There are three kinds of lies: lies, damned lies, and statistics.*"

What I liked about the WBSCD work is that they actually went on to observe Millennials' social media updates to see if there was a shift in the lifestyle portrayed by them, showing peers an aspiration or a highly curated perspective on how they want to be perceived. As mentioned earlier, I do the same; when I proudly share my colourful vegetarian casserole, I project an image of myself as both a great cook and a conscious eater although admittedly, I do have the odd craving for a really, really good beef burger.

Although not a substantial body of research, the WBSCD report pinpoint how Millennials paint a good life, from realising themselves through simple pleasures such as reading a book or contemplating in a hammock to growing their own food, cooking, bicycling, doing sports or meditation to hanging with friends. What the report from Sitra called "Symbols of Distinction" or "Better Me" or "Better World."

These social media posts show us how the old marketing mantra of bigger, better, faster is giving away from living bigger to living better. One of the posts that stuck with me was the Instagram user @hausbar-farmsatx, who chose spending time with family over watching football: "*Wonderful dinner with our parents last night at Dai Due while the rest of the world was watching football.*"

Happiness is being redefined every day, and organisations will have to stay ahead to stay relevant. You don't go to a gym to get muscles; you go there to exercise. As an organisation, you'll have to re-evaluate what you promise people. I'm on a search to becoming a better version of myself – I'm looking to realise myself.

Door waiting to be kicked open

A 2017 CSR Study from Cone Communication into the US population of Millennials and Gen Zs shows a beginning shift in people's mindset.[13] Young Americans don't see organisations as world-saving superheroes but increasingly view themselves as the change agents. Expectations to companies and governments are still ranked highly. 70% believe companies have an obligation to take action to improve issues that may not be relevant to everyday business operations, but increasingly the young expect change to be happening by their own hands, voices or whatever other means. 45% believe individuals are most effective at solving today's pressing social and environmental challenges. These trends will probably only rise, as the trust in business is, to say the least, troubled. According to a Millennial and Gen Z study by Deloitte[14] from 2018, only 48% believe that corporations behave ethically (down from 65% in 2017). Nearly two-thirds say companies have no ambition beyond wanting to make money (up from 50% from the year before).

People's aspiration towards taking matters into their own hands also fits with an increasing curiosity to know more about how they can make change happen: 36% want to know how their personal actions will make a difference. This is a door waiting to be kicked open by organisations. It also cements the increasing number of people willing to either punish or reward companies who are doing the right thing: 87% would purchase a product because a company advocated for an issue they cared about, versus 76% who would refuse to purchase a company's products or services upon learning it supported an issue contrary to their beliefs.

People want to be part of the change, and it's up to you as a leader or organisation not only to make them part of the journey but even, more importantly, to put the needed change and responsibility in their hands. Let people play a bigger part. The carrot is there. The Good Life report found that 65% believe they can influence companies to do better through purchase, yet only 28% followed through and purchased the product or service. For you as an organisation, it's important to help people bridge that gap between intention and action, between aspiration and realisation.

Catalysts of a happier life

Although people's expectations of themselves as agents of change are lower than their expectations of companies, there is an increasing self-reliance. And I think there is ample reason to believe that this will only increase going forward as the barriers for self-actualisation and self-sufficiency are becoming lower while trust in governments and companies is fading – and even turning hateful.

The lower numbers for individuals might also show some self-insight on behalf of the respondents. Guess we all know how changing behaviour is difficult in a time-constrained day. It's easier to point fingers at others (read: companies and government) than to do anything about it yourself. But the want for desire is there, and it's up to organisations to make it easier for people to take change into their own hands. According to The Good Life report, the majority of Americans believe brands can help them live more meaningful lives, yet two-thirds don't believe companies currently are providing products to help them do so. There's an untapped potential for organisations.

Four in five Americans state they would be loyal to brands that help them achieve that "good life." The organisations who can create platforms to enable this change for people can potentially feed people's desire to realise themselves and be the catalyst behind more happiness and better living. It's not enough to point to a societal problem; brands have to help people be part of the solution.

A real change story about romance

I would have given up if not for the support of my wife, on whom I lean heavily.[15]

– Larry Virden, Bachelor of Arts Computer Science and Sociology, Mount Vernon Nazarene University, on Quora.com

New work–life balance

The trend of people choosing meaning or purpose over pay is already challenging for some organisations and will be even more so when people put real self-actualisation over pay and a nice-sounding corporate purpose.

If we look at the discussion around meaning and work, then there's a clear trend that purposeful companies attract and retain staff better than their peers. According to the earlier mentioned Cone survey, 75% of Millennials would take a pay cut to work for a socially responsible company. And that matters because Millennials will make up 75% of the workforce by 2025.

But how you define that purpose is important. One thing is to work for a company that's socially conscious, but having a personal sense of meaning in one's work will always triumph in my book. Meaning reads differently to different people. Some might value a work that contributes to society, others might value work that allows them to improve their skills, and others again might value work and life balance. Don't forget Dr Jaap's finding; life is a constant search.

In the Western world, people now aspire to prioritise time off, time with family and freedom over pay. There are organisations out there that understand attracting new staff these days (especially Gen Z and Millennials) is not about an extra pay check but rather about a meaningful work–life balance.

One Danish agency, IIH Nordic, launched the four-day work week and after half a year, productivity rose, despite people working fewer hours, and job applications surged.[16] Similar results came out of Wellington in New Zealand where a company cut the working week from 40 to 32 hours as a one-month experiment. The employees reported a 24% improvement in work–life balance and felt more energised for work.[17]

Purpose sounds nice, but I want to be the boss of my own life

The seismic shift happens when neither pay nor corporate purpose is enough to make the new generations entering the workforce tick. Or, as Dr APJ Abdul Kalam cunningly frames it: "*Love your job, but don't love your company, because you may not know when your company stops loving you.*"[18] These new young minds want to feel empowered, part of the decision making, and sometimes even have a piece of the ownership pie. They are the I-want-to-be-the-boss-of-my-own-life generation, and they are not necessarily wrong to think so. They don't believe meaningful work comes from a production line with regimented tea breaks and clockwork-like efficiency. They know their worth because they view the world differently: to them, ideas are tremendously cheap and effortlessly made. They've grown up in a time where everybody can start their own company with the click of a button and get it funded on platforms like Kickstarter by everybody else. So why should they work for your company? Earlier generations' industrialist concept of blood, sweat and tears doesn't count; self-actualisation does.

Today all the young cool cats call themselves entrepreneurs, although the honest truth most likely is that they are unemployed and working on some start-up project. Today self-actualisation beats corporate security; being your own master simply weighs in higher than both corporate purpose and pay.

Let me share a personal example with you. I was doing a keynote at Copenhagen Business School in early 2019, not for the first time. Following my keynote, there was a panel with four different companies, and, to kick-start the conversation, the moderator asked the business students how many would like to choose a corporate career? I would say, of the 300–400 students in the lecture room, only 20–30 of the students raised their hands. This is obviously just an example, but it does show that even business students don't see the typical corporate career as especially attractive.

Freedom and self-development are important. It's become a career to be a traveller of the world, free of the constraints of corporate life or usual work hours. These professionals view themselves as what they call "digital nomads." They can work from everywhere, whenever. Younger generations are more likely to tell you everything that's wrong with your company than what's right. And who can blame them? They come from a generation experiencing change probably more rapidly than any before them. Just look at how a generation used to be the literal meaning of the word: a new generation born. Today several generational traits happen not in the span of 30 years but in simply 8–10 years: Gen Z, Gen X, Millennials and so on.

In a recent MBO Partners State of Independence Research Brief,[19] 4.8 million Americans described themselves as digital nomads. And the numbers are on the rise: the same survey finds that among traditional US workers, 27% said they "might" become digital nomads in the next two or three years, and 11% said they planned to.

For organisations, it can be dangerous to define purpose solemnly as a societal contribution. Meaning can mean many things to different people, and ultimately it's about enabling people to calling the shots themselves and offering the flexibility for them to grow and find their own meaning. A new type of leadership is needed that's not simply about blowing the corporate purpose trumpet but about being a platform for growth and personal development.

Work for our purpose or work for your own sake?

The change in mindset is showing across industries. Starbucks is the poster boy (or girl) example of a purposeful company, but today their way of living their purpose is being challenged by the likes of the fast-growing Swedish organic coffee bicycle company Wheelys Café. The co-founder Maria de la Croix had actually applied for a job in Starbucks because she initially bought into the company's purpose: "*To inspire and nurture the human spirit – one person, one cup and one neighbourhood at a time*"[20] – but she didn't get the job because at the time her hair was green, which apparently was not okay according to Starbuck's guidelines.

Maria set out to create Wheelys with a mission to enable people to start their own coffee business, and it's run by people who in Wheelys's words are "*a person with a heart and dreams.*"[21] Its customers can feel the passion because it's now present in 78 countries. When I sat down to talk with Maria one late evening over Skype,[1] she shared how people attracted to Wheelys are driven by very different passions. One of their first Wheelers (what they call their users or micro-franchisees) from Lebanon simply wanted to make a living, whereas a Danish couple are living out their passion for organic coffee. It's not a one-model-fits-all.

Maria is not in doubt that most people don't go to work to realise an organisation's corporate purpose but to realise themselves. "*Just thought that people should work less and do their own thing, like selling coffee on the beach, it wasn't planned initially, it just happened.*" For Maria, it simply makes sense that organisations are adapted to people's lives rather than the other way around. Personally, she wanted more freedom at the time to pursue her dreams, and she's very conscious how Wheelys fits into people's lives: "*When you own a Wheelys café, then you are your own boss. It's way more fun, because you do the things you want to do. And you can always decide if you want to make a lot of money and work a lot, which is fine, but if you don't want to do that, then you don't need to."*

But for the Wheelers and her, it's also clear that they are on a bigger mission as well: *"We will break the hegemony of the industrial fast food chains and pave the way for an organic revolution. Helping us do this are young hungry eco entrepreneurs from all over the world."*

When Wheelys launched, it put up a café in front of a Starbucks in Stockholm and counted how many coffees they each sold in an hour. The result: Starbucks 148. Wheelys 210. Obviously, Starbucks wasn't happy. For Maria, the dialogue between the Wheelers in the community is essential input to everything from products and marketing to design. *"People are threatened by the idea, that something is impossible to achieve,"* she says. *"But people enjoy this feeling of possibility that they are able to do something different. It feels more fun seeing a smaller fish doing something different that works out."*

I can feel a burning purpose in how Maria describes Wheelys, but it's a different strand of purpose, that's simply about creating a vehicle for people to do whatever they're passionate about. It's a powerful offering: the freedom to work for yourself, the freedom to define your own goals and dreams. And I wonder where you, as a customer, will feel the biggest burning purpose at a Starbucks or Wheelys? Or get the better service?

I'm the boss!

It's no longer just the few who go out of their way to avoid the established system. Call them conscious consumers, convenience driven do-gooders, or for that matter the activists who long ago said *"no way."* The choices (whether an illusion or not) that people have come to expect from the Internet and a simple search with the click of a button have put the power into people's hands. If you as an organisation can't offer business on people's terms where it's less about the product and more about their choice, you'll quickly be shutting the doors.

Across sectors, the change is visible. The media space has changed forever as search engines, citizen journalism and social media influence people more than ever before. The Internet is allowing people to become active participants, and people are mobilising, forming support groups and communities, collectively solving problems and holding organisations to account. And their voice is getting louder and louder. People are looking at the marketplace as a way for them to participate, create meaning and realise themselves rather than simply to buy.

One such company offering a new approach is Suop, a Spanish telecom provider. At Suop, users play an active part from running certain functions like customer service to helping innovate and suggest new products. The company takes a truly collaborative approach. On its webpage, Suop describes the core mission: "*Together, you and we can make things better, as they should be. That's why in Suop we do not want customers, we want collaborators.*"[22] Curious about the model, I jumped on the phone with one of the founders, CEO Jaime Pla, who explained:

> *Other phone companies are all about the offers, whereas we say that we collaborate with our users. We often turn to our users for small or big decisions. We have asked the users, if they want the voice of the messaging service to be male or female. Or when we have some issues in our community where some users are cheating then we ask the community; what actions we should take?*[23]

Suop's customers can feel the difference. It's not the typical phone company. The organisational structure is open, decentralised and collaborative, and, in a market that's so price driven, it's interesting to see a different promise. In Jaime's words: "*It's not about running a phone company, it's all about building trust.*"

And the model is working. Suop's users stay with the company for longer in a telecom market where everyone is shopping around for the latest offer. Jaime refuses to let quick growth win over the long-term satisfaction of customers; in his words, he's focusing on "*healthy growth, not exponential.*" The users are at the heart of the company. Suop is an example of an organisation on a mission to regain trust by reinventing how a company should operate and relate to its customers. From a corporate power model to a collaborative model. It's two completely different mindsets and ways of looking at people and behaving in the marketplace. In my dialogue with other companies enabling people, I saw a lot of similar characteristics, and not all of them are present in every company, but it does show a change in how we engage with companies from a hierarchical, centralised, shareholder structure to a decentralised, collaborative model that's all about giving people an active say.

Before – corporate power	Now – empower
Consumption	Transformation
Control	Empower
Centralised	Decentralised
Push	Pull
Hierarchy	Collaboration
Features	Choices
Campaigns	Platforms
Intellectual property	Open source
Experiences	Self-actualisation
Shareholders	Stakeholders

How close can you get to people?

Consumption is changing especially due to a new mindset among younger generations. They'll be grabbing a Kind cereal bar on the way to university while bicycling or using a ride-share program. At the university, they'll pop down to an organic communal kitchen run by Syrian refugees to grab some lunch. When going out, they'll be drinking a Mikkeller craft beer or opt for a Health-Aid kombucha. It's no longer the big fast-moving consumer goods brands that are winning their favour.

According to Bain & Company,[24] average revenue growth at the top 30 global consumer goods companies fell to just 0.4% annually in 2013–18, down from 4.5% for 2007–12. In the same period, the average growth in annual operating profits halved. More than $22 billion in sales moved from larger to smaller companies in the United States between 2011 and 2016, and the same trend is apparent in Europe. In the Group's analysis, they found that smaller brands in the United States are 65% more likely than large brands to outgrow their category. Slowly but surely, the smaller companies are winning turf with market shares up from 23% to 26% between 2011 and 2016 according to BCG and the IRI research group.[25] The market shift from bigger players to smaller, agile insurgents is a trend across most markets, according to Boston.[26]

These smaller, local brands are quickly closing the gap with their global competitors as they are much faster at adapting to market trends or local tastes. In 2017, the drinks sector was the only sector in which global brands were still taking the lead according to Business Insider.[27] In 2017, the local brands took 64.6% of all brand spend and left global brands with 35.4%.

In 2006, Paul Lindley founded Ella's Kitchen, motivated by his desire to feed his small daughter Ella tasty, fun and healthy organic food. The mission for Ella's (and Paul) is still the same: "*I passionately believe that Ella, my daughter, along with her generation, should have the opportunity to eat better food and also to discover that healthy food can be fun, tasty and cool.*"

This is not just another baby food brand, it's enabling a new generation to discover the pleasure of healthy food. Ella's understands the shift in the market place, and rather than blowing its own horn, puts its small customers first. After 12 consecutive years of plus double-digit growth Ella's has taken on global FMCG giants to become the UK's No.1 baby food brand with $116M[28] in global revenues. The success behind the brand is clear from the name: Ella's. The brand is putting little loved ones like Ella first.

These smaller, faster-growing brands have been better at being at eye-height with people. And rather than rolling out the mass-marketing machine, they've been talking directly to people in their own voice. The earlier domination of the media or shelf space no longer applies as these smaller players through digital can find and talk to people wherever they are.

Reach "who" they are, not where they are

How organisations position themselves and speak to people is becoming more like an intimate dialogue between friends – or, as many of the organisations I talked to phrased it, "*a community.*" The organisations are getting better at knowing more about their customers through data and speaking to them in a more individualised way and in channels that matter to them. That being said, the brand no longer stands unchallenged; the whole company is being scrutinised. People have a choice in the marketplace, and brand is simply one factor in the purchasing decision. As people are craving to realise themselves through the brands they use and to tell a story through those brands, it's all in the details. This puts even more focus on the company behind the brand – and going forward this will only matter more – as you could see from the preceding model and the move from company's exhorting "power" to "empower."

When you're shopping, it's not always easy to tell one brand from another. Who is walking the talk? Labelling efforts have as a consequence been on the rise, and even the company itself can today be certified on its commitments to society via a B-Corp certification. This is a growing group of companies that have come together to support a new direction for companies where profit is not enough. Each of the companies joining the program pledges and is being certified to maintain a certain level in areas such as the environment, ethical practice and corporate transparency. Since 2006, more than 150 B-Corps have joined in the UK, including high-profile names such as Ben & Jerry's, Pukka Tea and Ella's Kitchen, and more than 2,400 are operating globally with the bigger ones being the likes of Kickstarter and Brazilian cosmetic giant Natura. B Lab, the non-profit behind B Corp, released a survey in 2018 that looked at the growth of their members in the UK and found that they outgrew the national average by a factor of 28.[29] That's an impressive growth record. People want organisations that have a higher meaning and that behave sustainably, and the B Corp certification is one way for them to cut through the noise. The preceding surveys hint that the organisations acting to put a higher purpose first get rewarded at the cash register.

There is little to no status involved in buying when everybody can, and we're fast approaching a post-consumerist society where self-actualisation is valued higher than material success. This is, generally speaking, without ignoring the mounting economic divide between rich and poor and the many countries that struggle to deliver even a decent life for their citizens.

Everything from mass-media to mass-production is being challenged, and for advertising it's no longer about reaching people where they are but reaching "who" they are. The key takeaway is that brand is not enough; as an organisation, you have to have to help people live more simple, meaningful, independent and empowered lives, if you want to deserve people's trust. In other words, it's more about helping people go sky-jumping than selling them Boomboxes playing "Jump, Jump."

Key takeaways

1   People don't buy stuff, they buy a better me. Deliver personal distinction: a gain of knowledge, experience or acquired skills.

2   The definition of a good life is changing towards balanced simplicity (36%), meaningful connections (28%), money and status (26%) and personal achievement (10%).

3   Millennials increasingly see themselves as the biggest change agents; this offers a potential for organisations to become a catalyst of better lives.

4   Corporate purpose is not enough to create meaning in the workplace – people want to be the bosses of their own lives and realise themselves.

5   The growth of bigger companies is declining as smaller companies have been better at responding to people's expectations towards the marketplace where they can participate and create meaning.

Questions to ask yourself

1   How can your products or services deliver personal value through new knowledge, skills or experiences?

2   How are you portraying a good life in your communication channels?

3   Do you experience people asking more questions or being more critical towards your offering?

4   Have you seen your product category being challenged by new incumbents? What is your strategic response?

5   How close are you to your customers today?

3 Motivation

The untold story

We believe that the physical LEGO brick will always be relevant in the future as it stimulates creativity, unless humans suddenly didn't grow arms and fingers.[1]

– *David Hall, Senior Director, Brand, LEGO*

The IKEA effect

In 1956, Swede Gillis Lundgren was working at IKEA, which at the time was selling big, bulky furniture through mail-order catalogues. Obviously, furniture was expensive and demanding to ship, especially then. One day Gillis was heading to a photo shoot to take pictures of a new table called the Lovet, but he had difficulties cramming the leaf-shaped table into his small car, and he was said to mutter: "*Oh, God, then let's pull the legs off.*"[2] This was the idea that sparked IKEA's flat-pack business model. The flat-pack unintentionally delivered another secret sauce to IKEA's fortune by demanding assembly work from its customers. You've probably cursed at a Billy bookcase or Malm bed when trying to put it together, but there is a bigger lesson to be learned.

In a working paper by Michael I. Norton, Daniel Mochon and Dan Ariely, they describe how students at a university in the Northeast United States were tasked to assemble simple LEGO sets, origami and a piece of IKEA furniture. The study[3] showed that the participants placed higher value on their self-assembled creations and expected others to do the same – an increased valuation the researchers called the "IKEA effect," which was both apparent among Mac-Gyver-do-it-yourself participants and participants with little interest in handiwork.[4] If the task was too difficult or not finalised, the effect didn't materialise. The study shows how we simply value products higher when we successfully have invested our energy and time into them. Think about the business model behind toy giant Build-a-Bear that asks children to make their own teddy bears and charge people a premium for that little kick of creation. Adding a heart and giving the new furry family member a name finalises the labour of love that goes into creating a Build-a-Bear. You probably know that feeling of satisfaction or bond from when playing a part in the creation of something yourself.

It's time to unleash the IKEA effect and give people a chance to realise themselves through your organisation, through the brand and through the marketing mix. Great organisations don't just sell people the product. Or teach them how to use it. They help them become the best they can be. Social media turns every update into evidence of how healthy, smart, creative, travelled and entrepreneurial we are. It's less about what I *have*, which can easily be bought, and more about *who* I am and my achievements.

The best I can be

There's a saying that money can't buy happiness. The beauty cream promising you eternal, smiling youth, the car projecting a picture-perfect happy family or the shoe brand trying to make you feel good about yourself by donating a second pair to impoverished communities are increasingly falling on deaf ears because what we ultimately buy is in transition. In their book *Authenticity: What Consumers Really Want* (2007), B. Joseph Pine II and James H. Gilmore – the authors who coined the term "Experience Economy" – lay out four distinct economic periods, each defined by our reason to buy:

Agrarian economy: access to reliable supply (Availability)
Industrial economy: cost (Affordability)
Service economy: quality (Performance)
Experience economy: conforming to self-image (Authenticity)

Let me break each of these different periods down around a product I personally love: coffee. Coffee illustrates the value-added in each single step from a resource-based economy to an experience economy and how it's not the coffee bean at around one dollar a pound but the service or ultimately the experience that raises the price of a cup of coffee to often exorbitant levels.

The agrarian economy

The agrarian economy was an agriculturally based economy where farm produce was traded. Back then, you would buy the coffee beans, roast them and make the coffee from scratch in dedicated coffee houses, some of which date back to the 15th century in the Middle East.

The industrial economy

The industrial economy is an industrial-based economy where manufacturers make standardised products in high quantities. This is coffee advertised and delivered to the mass-market pre-roasted, grounded, packaged and ready for use at home.

The service economy

The service economy works around on-demand, customised service. A good example would be the rampant rise in the takeaway coffee culture, where you pay for a service such as, in this example, convenience.

The experience economy

The experience economy is an experience-based economy where it's about creating outstanding personal experiences. As a knowledgeable coffee drinker, I'm no longer interested or satisfied with a commoditised bland product or service. I want the experience and brand to reflect who I am and what I'm willing to pay for that. An example could be gourmet coffee places where the coffee is roasted and ground in front of your eyes and the brewing is almost a molecular science.

As an example, Starbucks revamped in 2014 some of their outlets in the United States to better reflect the community, local corner store experience that launched the brand to success rather than the uniform, commoditised experience you're being met with in most markets. Starbucks realised there was too high a price to pay for lowering costs and offering convenience because what people really wanted was a community-led, local experience. This is also a testament to why most people buy coffee: it's a social ritual.

From sensational experiences to transforming people

Gilmore and Pine argued that we're in the experience economy and that the most prevalent reason for buying is to conform to one's self-image. You seek out like-minded brands following the dictum: I like that, I am like that. You're the sort of guy who values your family's safety and well-being, so you drive a Volvo. Or you might be the adventurous, the sky-is-the-limit type of guy working around the clock, so you grab a Red Bull. It's a reason to buy above affordability or quality; it's about how it reflects on you as a buyer: is this really who I am?

An example used in their book tells the story of Disney and how the brand successfully transformed its animated film success on the screen into a tightly choreographed three-dimensional story-driven experience where audiences where transformed into participants. From Disneyland to its high street stores, every little touch point is designed as if were it a scene in a movie.

We are no longer passive consumers of products but active participants. And if you've ever been to Disneyland, you would know from the price tag that people are willing to pay for those experiences. Interestingly enough, Pine and Gilmore don't stop at the experience economy. They believe that we're seeing a fifth economic system developing: the transformation economy.

Agrarian economy: Access to reliable supply (Availability)
Industrial economy: Cost (Affordability)
Service economy: Quality (Performance)
Experience economy: Conforming to self-image (Authenticity)

Transformation economy: A transformational advantage (Self-actualisation)

Whereas the experience economy was about creating sensations and memorable events, these don't last on a day-to-day level, and Pine & Gilmore argue that in the transformation economy it's about creating lasting change by transforming people and helping them become "*healthy, wealthy or wise.*" When you offer a transformational advantage, you're moving away from a commoditised or easily imitated market promise. It's about helping people. There is a permanent beneficial gain for people. Take the app Blinkist that turns leading professional books into 15-minute knowledge infusions to keep people on their toes or when Nike launched the Nike+ app in 2016, pushing runners to new heights, and called it a "new area of sports – the era of personalised performance." It's a difference people can feel.

In the transformation economy, Pine argues the primary buying criterion will be: edification. As an organisation, one should aspire to transform or change people towards a desired state of mind. This corresponds to the very top of Maslow's hierarchy of needs: self-actualisation. Maslow described this level as "*the desire to accomplish everything that one can, to become the most that one can be.*"[5] This emerging shift is very much aligned with the research I described in an earlier chapter from Sitra, where trendsetters increasingly are buying what was dubbed a "better me."

To stay with the coffee analogy, self-actualisation is exactly what the earlier mentioned example of the bicycle coffee chain Wheelys is offering. Wheelys turns people into the coffee maker to discover and express their love for coffee while running their own business. When you're in the transformation economy, the experience, product or service moves to the background and the organisation can charge for the demonstrated outcomes people achieve, like better health, finance, skills or even freedom. Wheelys is essentially selling freedom to passionate entrepreneurs, taking a transformational approach to its business.

What does personal growth cost?

I'll give you a personal example. A group of my friends and I was out for dinner and got to discuss the ongoing challenge today's parents have keeping their little darlings away from being glued to a digital screen 24/7. One of my friends described how his daughter had tried everything from tennis to swimming, but nothing kept her interest for long. Finally, she found something she really liked: ballet. The issue with ballet classes is that they come at a steep price, but my friend argued that he would welcome any opportunity to get her away from the screen and developing new interests. In other words, my friend was willing to pay a premium price for his daughter's transformation. You can probably think of similar examples.

Some companies deliver products where personal transformation is at the very business core, such as Headspace, the mindfulness app. Headspace offers a subscription-based service with unlimited access to mindfulness sessions from about $6 a month. It's good business: Headspace reports an annual revenue of over $50 million and is valued at around $250 million.[6]

Other companies position their products as part of a personal transformation, such as eyewear company District Vision. The company sells eyewear to runners but sees its offerings as part of a much bigger issue: "*mental wellbeing is the foundation of every form of physical exercise.*"[7] The brand helps runners couple performance and mindfulness, a position that sets them apart from other players in the running eyewear market and enables them to price their products at a premium.

Better product or better me?

The role of brands is changing away from the transactional relationship where you as a consumer saw the brand as an extension and you could buy into that self-image: "*I like that, I am like that.*" Essentially, you bought an image, or a certain way people should perceive you. The classic movie *American Psycho*, portraying a wealthy New York City investment banking executive, Patrick Bateman (played by Christian Bale), sliding into a perverted, murderous world describes in meticulous detail the nineties obsession with buying an image: *"he turns around and straightens his Versace tie ready to face whoever. Courtney opens the door and she's wearing a Krizia cream silk blouse, a Krizia rust tweet skirt and silk-satin d'Orsay pumps from Manolo Blahnik."*[8]

It's a powerful picture of the time, but today it's not enough for an organisation to deliver on people's *"identity"* or *"who they are,"* but they'll increasingly have to enable people's desire for acting to make things better from self-growth, better relationships, taking care of themselves to taking care of our community or planet. Organisation should not just reflect who we are but enable us to become better.

A couple of years back, I joined a cross-fit gym in Copenhagen; I believed it could supercharge my fitness level. Guess I bought into the marketing hype that was touted as the exercise the actors from the film *300* went through. If you haven't seen the movie, it's like a Greek war myth meeting Magic Mike. Those barely clad Greek warriors were seriously pumped. I attended the classes a couple of times and admittedly they were tough, but what turned me away was that for the other cross-fitters, this was simply not about a quick fix. It felt more like I had entered a religious sect or was part of an ancient Greek ritual. One time, the whole class had to do 100 push-ups as a punishment because I quit in the middle of a "let's-smack-a-car-tire-with-a-sledgehammer-exercise."

I'd thought this was yet another fitness subscription I passively could buy into, but no. The brand – the community – demanded more of me. In this case, I wanted the muscles, not the whole transformation.

What truly motivates us

There are other incentives for moving from product to experiences to transformation. When looking at what truly motivates us, you might be in for a surprise. Traditional economic understanding promotes the idea that rewards or monetary gain drives motivation, and hence one rewards top performers. We're brought up with the idea that if we do well in school, we'll get an A, or if we put extra effort into work, we might get a bonus or a raise. This is what's called extrinsic motivation, which refers to behaviour that is driven by external rewards such as money, fame, grades and praise.

But what truly motivates us goes against the classic stick-and-carrot approach. When it's your own choice to do something, you're more motivated than when somebody tells you do to something or you're paid to do it. This is an intrinsic motivation because you are self-motivated. It's when one simply enjoys an activity or sees it as an opportunity to explore, learn or realise a potential as opposed to extrinsic motivation, which are external factors such as, for example, status. You probably recognise this motivation from yourself. When you decide to do something, even if it's somehow a tedious task like painting the walls white in your apartment, it brings a sense of fulfilment or accomplishment at the end versus if being something you are told to do. Or maybe you recognise this from the workplace? There is nothing more demotivating than a boss behaving like a dictator, giving you little to no say over your workday. Why should this be different when it comes to your organisation's relationship with people? How much of a say do people really have?

When people feel in control and are self-determined, they are more motivated and fulfilled. Studies within social sciences and psychology have been looking to uncover that connection. One such study[9] was conducted in 1985 by Theresa Amabile, a professor at Harvard Business School, among 72 creative writers at Brandeis and Boston University who were tasked with writing poetry. The group was divided into three and given various motives for solving the assignment. The first group was given a number of extrinsic reasons for writing from impressing teachers (status) and cash rewards to getting into graduate school. The second group was given intrinsic reasons for writing, such as the joy of writing, playing with words and an opportunity for self-expression and reflection. The last group was given no brief. The results underscore how we like to be in control over our own lives. The students given extrinsic reasons for writing such as personal gain saw the quality of their writing drop significantly compared to the two other groups. This study and other similar studies in, for example, a work environment clearly indicates that when it comes to mental tasks, complex problem solving, critical or creative thinking, extrinsic rewards have a negative effect on results; we are motivated by selfish reasons. We are not walking piggybanks hungry for coins; we have interests, passions and beliefs driving us – things we want to achieve.

Self-determination and how we stay motivated

Professors Edward L. Deci and Richard M. Ryan have, throughout their careers in psychology, argued for the connection between self-actualisation and motivation. In their Self-Determination Theory[10] the two professors break away from the causality-based view on motivation: "*I do this, because I expect this in return.*" They argue instead that we are in fact: self-determined – or call it self-motivated. For example, I like wave surfing, and while I'm not the best surfer, just being out there on the ocean on my board makes my day. I don't get paid to surf, but I do it because I like to do it. Or take volunteering for example. How can it be that people who already work long hours and get paid to do so still take precious time out of their calendars to clean plastic off a beach?

We actually do surf, volunteer and even pull those extra hours at the office because we do like it; it's in our own interest – we live out our dreams, passions or aspirations through those activities. But imagine if somebody told you to surf or to volunteer. Suddenly that feeling of freedom and self-exploration disappears. What you love suddenly turns into a task. Self-determination, our own ability to determine the outcome, is important for motivation. Who would have guessed that people would value a product like a Billy bookcase higher simply because they assembled it, as the IKEA Effect proved?

We all strive to be independent agents in our life, in control of our own behaviour and setting our own goals. This universal factor is key to explaining how we are intrinsically self-motivated and do things because we want to do them. Unless you are self-motivated and taking control of the change, you rarely succeed, which anyone who's ever tried to quit smoking can tell you. Your doctors can tell you to pack it in, your wife and kids can try to motivate you, ads on the packaging can scare you to quit, but, at the end of the day, you need to make that conscious decision yourself.

A real change story about family

I kept inviting my 80-year-old grandmother to visit me in Copenhagen, but she always declined, because she didn't want to feel as a burden. Admittedly her legs, eyes and ears don't work that well any more. I kept insisting because I wanted her to overcome the challenge. My grandmother trained each day for several months to get as fit as possible and took the challenge to fly by herself. We had some slow connecting time only with each other, navigating through space and time, comparing past and present. But the best thing is that she wanted to visit me next spring for the Sakura Fest. She doesn't count herself as a burden anymore. YAS!![11]

– *Greta Valvonytė, Space and Sustainability Enthusiast*

Motivating people to change

In a Scandinavian Airlines magazine from February 2019. I read about travel trends and came across the story of Camilla Elden, a 30-year-old social media influencer from Oslo in Norway. Like many others in her generation, she felt the Internet and social media had taken over her life, and she decided to go on a three-day digital detox sailing trip in Northern Norway. On the trip she realised how great it was to disconnect from the digital world, and when she came back, she established a rule not to use her phone an hour before going to bed. It's a small change, but one by which the cruise is helping transform Camilla from "*who she is*" to "*who she wants to become.*" That's a transformation worth paying for.

The magazine shared other stories about how travel changes people as part of Scandinavian Airlines' efforts to convey a story about the bigger role the airline plays in people's lives. As part of a study into travel trends in Scandinavia, the airline discovered that a majority of their customers believed travelling gave them more knowledge, new ideas and a more global mindset. In late 2018, Scandinavian launched a campaign called "Arrivals," where you witness a documentary-style portrayal of the arrival hall in an airport and how people arrive changed from their travels by having discovered new love to new ideas to becoming more mature. Scandinavian Airlines's claim that travel changes us is borne out of the research, and it's a position that sets them apart from their competitors in the industry typically talking about price, services or destination. Going forward, it'll be exciting to see whether they expand this approach across the marketing mix, such as to services or new products, and whether they'll be able to convey this story in an even more compelling way.

Give people the remote control

Enabling individuals to take control has not been the traditional modus operandi in marketing, business or for that sake in leadership, which is typically hierarchical, centralised and carefully choreographed. There's probably nothing as angst-provoking as to let go of that power and control. After all, if you're a marketer, the million- or billion-dollar brand value is your responsibility. Or maybe, if you're the content creator tasked with the storytelling, how can you possibly let loose and trust an online community dominated by trolls? We've all seen what happens when you free the trolls, right? It's actually one of my pastime activities – looking for online trolls – when I need time out from writing. I pick a random political story at any major news network and read the comments. I don't know if I should laugh or cry. If you are ever in doubt whether people want to invest time in things they care about, then just scroll down and look at the comments. Okay, undeniably most of the time I laugh.

You probably don't think about how your organisation tries to dominate the relationship. Think for a minute about the power companies convey. How they dominate almost every medium from TV and digital to our cityscape with their brands and messages. Or how they want to take control over the customer experience.

I remember to this day when I went to open my first savings account as a kid. My mum made sure I had nice clothes on, shirt stuck into the pants, wearing those odd old man leather shoes, the curls wet and carefully combed down. Arriving at the bank didn't make me feel less at odds. Banks always have these high ceilings where, as soon as you enter, you feel insignificant. An architect friend told me this is a common design feature of most corporate HQs – they're designed to make you feel unimportant and insecure as you arrive. Designed to exhort power. That day, that's exactly how I felt.

I went to the cashier and, after going through all the hoops, the checks and balances, the paperwork, signing documents, I deposited the money, and by then I felt like the bank was doing me a favour of letting me deposit my money rather than me being a valued customer. Is this really how a customer experience should be? Before I left the bank, I was given a small booklet. As I got outside, I started to cry. My mum and dad, embarrassed by the onlookers, tried to comfort me, but nothing helped. My dad lost patience and angrily asked, "*What's wrong?*" And I told them I was crying because I thought I paid all my savings for that little booklet. I didn't realise that the booklet was simply my account statement. I felt utterly powerless.

It's really not a surprise that banks rank at the top of the charts for the most hated industries by Millennials.[12] Or think about phone companies or gym memberships with all their contractual bindings and legal blurbs in small writing that, you know, is going to screw you over. Again, it is all designed to say, "*We the company are the big guys, you're the little guy.*" In my early advertising career, I worked for a Danish challenger gym brand called Fitness World, which went up against the major players in the market with a simple preposition: one fixed membership fee, no binding, no small prints. In a matter of three years, it became the market leader thanks to a transparent, no bullshit approach.

Relive your last retail experience. I observe on a daily basis how brands treat me like just another one in line or as a number rather than as a beloved customer or individual. The other day, I was at a high-end bakery that charges up to double the amount of other bakeries in the neighbourhood for bread and cakes, yet still I have to pull a number and wait in line. It might seem like an insignificant detail, but it does reveal how I'm perceived or valued as a customer: just another number or "*Hey, Thomas, how are you? The usual?*"

That tree-hut building joy

The motivational effects of having a say or being in control have thoroughly been studied in terms of performance and satisfaction. While traditional advertising offers little to no interaction, digital opens up unlimited possibilities to interact with people or maybe even get them to take part in a campaign or parts of a campaign.

One study[13] I want to share is by Christoph Fuchs, Emanuela Prandelli and Martin Schreier called "The Psychological Effects of Empowerment Strategies on Consumers' Product Demand." The study looks at what happens when a company makes people democratically decide what products to launch. The study was carried out on 264 undergraduate students from four parallel classes at a European university. The students were given different design options for T-shirts similar to the online designer community Theadless.com (if you know that site?). Afterwards, the students were asked to democratically choose which T-shirts should be produced. The results of the empirical test showed that the students who could select the products to be marketed showed a stronger demand for that exact product. The students simply developed a stronger psychological ownership of the T-shirts that they themselves had a say in producing. This is different from the IKEA effect, where the participants had no say in shaping the product, but the increased valuation came down to the fact that the participants themselves were crafting and building.

Either way, both studies demonstrate that, when you've invested time, love, work or opinions in something, you care more about it. I guess we all know that feeling whether it's at work doing a project or at home when building a tree hut for the children.

Time to act!

For an organisation or leader this is an opportunity to build a different relationship with people, from being an evangelist trying to impose your way of thinking to someone who helps people achieve their goals or discover new sides of themselves. I keep reiterating this point. Sorry, organisations: when you know you're powerless or defenceless, it becomes even more pathetic or ridiculous to insist on your power. You might remember the film *Monty Python's Holy Grail* (1975)? In one scene, King Arthur played by Graham Chapman is riding towards the Holy Grail, and the Black Knight played by John Cleese suddenly blocks his journey. A bloody but quick sword battle ensues, leaving the in-his-own-opinion "invincible" Black Knight without any limbs and clearly defeated. King Arthur leaves behind the limb-less Black Knight, but the Knight is not ready to give up and shouts: "*Running away, eh? You yellow bastards! Come back here and take what's coming to ya! I'll bite your legs off!"*[14] So, unless you want to subscribe to the reality of the fable, "*If you never give up, you can't possibly lose,*" it's time to act.

Everybody is on a search for meaning. For most people, it might not yet be discovered or clearly stated; it could be a flimsy idea, it could be set in stone. But for anyone to ever believe that our fellow friends, colleagues and family members don't have a goal in their lives, or aspirations or dreams, is a degrading misconception. It's more likely that you might not understand or empathise with his or her life-goal-in-progress. You never want to underestimate people's aspirations. And there are many triggers behind motivation, from extrinsic like those most marketing has played on, such as status or acceptance, to intrinsic like our curiosity to learn or develop, but no matter the trigger or the motivation, there is an untapped potential for organisations and leaders in motivating people to reach those personal goals.

The result can be felt rather than being a marketing sales pitch or a lofty corporate purpose statement. Twitter user @ClaireMarkhamFH wrote in the beginning of 2019 about the reading app Blinkist: "*Excited about today's #Blinkist by Stephen Hawking. Roll on lunchtime.*" The excited Twitter user couldn't wait to learn, thanks to Blinkist. This is heaven for any organisation wanting to make a meaningful difference in people's lives.

Key takeaways

1   There is a gap between people's formulated intent to buy from purposeful organisations and their actions.

2   Stakeholders are becoming an organisation's licence to operate, but most organisations get lost in their corporate purpose rather than enabling people to realise their own goals, aspirations and dreams.

3   The market is shifting from an experience economy where it's about value alignment with people to a transformation economy where it's about making people's lives better across body and mind.

4   When looking to motivate people, self-determination beats sticks and carrots.

5   When you give people a greater say or more control, they value your product or services more.

Questions to ask yourself

1   Do you feel an increased pressure for interaction from your stakeholders?

2   Do your product or service ultimately transform people's lives?

3   Are you experiencing a different demand from people towards personal transformation, such as better health, finance or skills?

4   Does your organisation use rewards to drive motivation internally or externally?

5   Do your products or services offer any possibility for people to interact?

3

4   The Arrow towards a better you

I think Precious Plastic give people some guidelines to contribute their small part. I think that's often the thing that's missing in the puzzle – we too often think that we can't do anything about big problems, that we are too small. We need to show that even a small piece of the puzzle makes an impact.[1]

– Dave Hakkens, Designer and Founder, Precious Plastic & Phonebloks

Take a look at the (wo)man in the mirror

"*We buy things we don't need with money we don't have to impress people we don't like.*" You can learn a lot from toilet writings. Although admittedly after the mobile phone, it does seem that the time for contemplation has gone down the drain. In an age where everything and everyone are screaming for our attention, those quiet minutes are becoming rarer, and so are snappy comebacks – even in the toilet: "*We vandalise things that aren't ours with quotes we didn't write to impress people taking a shit.*"

It's a human condition to reflect on our lives, to think about what we could be, what we could achieve, who we could become. These are all aspirations waiting to come alive, and it's where I see huge untapped potential for organisations.

I believe enabling people to take charge of their own lives and passions is what can be the bridge from intent to action and ultimately drive not only business growth, but also human or planetary betterment. For an organisation, there's no greater role to play than to help someone become who they want to be. And it doesn't have to be life transforming, but maybe it's just a small life hack, a little helping hand. If you want to lose weight, the help might simply be a smaller can of soda packing fewer calories, or it might be a brand like Apple helping you keep an eye on your goal of exercising more with the simple and visual help of their iPhone health app tracking your daily physical activity.

Think about your friends. They each play a valuable role in your life. One might always be there for fun times and partying, and another one is the listener, but what makes your best friend? Isn't it the one who's always there for you through good and bad times making you feel special, making you feel like you can? Why wouldn't that be the same when it comes to the organisations you're letting into your life? It used to be that brands would tell people what they wanted or needed, preying on insecurities. But today, as an organisation, you can strive for more and become that best friend or that coach pushing people further, making them believe in their own ability to bring about change.

A never-ending quest to find yourself

We are on a constant quest for our better selves, and that quest is reflected in the end chapter of our lives where in some cultures, it's customary to have a final moment of reflection to say what you could have done differently. We do things because they develop us, because we explore another side of ourselves. Let me give you an example.

I had a contract to write a book before this one. It was an easy book for me to write, as it was a version 2.0 of my previous book. But halfway through the book, I felt demotivated and bored with the topic, and I realised I was writing the book because people expected me to write it since I hadn't published anything since 2012. I didn't do it for my own sake; extrinsic versus intrinsic motivation. With this book, I had to be on my toes to understand and share a tough and exciting topic. And thank you to all the people who helped me out; I couldn't have done it without you! This book I write not because I'm driven by monetary gain (writing a book is closer to economic suicide), but because I want to. I feel the book wants to get out, it's alive and kicking. The book is part of my own personal development.

From my years in the agency world, I've seen art directors and copywriters burn the candle at both ends, and it definitely wasn't for the money or the client; it was because they like what they're doing and because advertising for them is a passion. That's the thing, we're driven and motivated by different passions, which seen from the outside can be difficult to understand.

People are no longer simply buying marketing messages or a company's good-willed approach; they're looking for a personal transformation. Anyone can sell them things, stories or identity, but very few organisations can help people achieve their goals. That's brand heaven as it's moving the relationship from transactional to transformational, helping people be more, do more, see more, experience more!

With statements like "*You're the beauty editor*," "*Democratic beauty*" and "*Your voice fuels Glossier*," the 33-year-old founder of challenger beauty company Emily Weiss has created a fast-growing direct-to-consumer cult company.[2] What began as a blog, Into The Gloss, when Emily worked at *Vogue* developed into an anti-establishment rallying cry to its customers: people should have a say in shaping the beauty narrative and its products. Glossier is keeping a friend-like dialogue with its following and has even launched a fast-growing ambassador program Glossier Girls, which formerly consisted of unpaid brand evangelists.[3] Glossier is giving people the say over what beauty means to them – they feel like a beauty editor – and the story seems to resonate as Glossier is expanding across markets and recently got another investment of $52 million.[4]

From your mission to my life

The navel-gazing focus on the corporate purpose, "*the why*," can end up blinding you to what truly matters: what you can help people become.

Take Apple and their encouragement: "*Think different.*" I buy who Apple makes me capable of becoming: a more creative Thomas. And they've succeeded so well that even five-year-olds can, with ease, make their own video edits on an iPhone, something that just years earlier would have required a professional editor and a hundred-thousand-dollar editing suite. Women and girls buy into Glossier's empowering message that they are the ones who should dictate beauty, not some beauty editor. And travellers connect with Scandinavian's message that travel broadens their horizon and changes them. Every organisation can claim to have a big role to play in your life as their burning "why," but it really comes down to one thing: if you can't see or feel the outcome, it's simply just another broken promise or patronising corporate purpose.

For a leader or an organisation, there is no higher accomplishment than to help realise somebody's dreams or aspirations: that should be the bullseye. A better boyfriend? A mindful runner? A better vegan chef? Or maybe all three? If your "why" as an organisation doesn't answer the "who" you can help people become, you'll end up being a screaming idealist. Apple can be the most creative and innovative company in the world, but without enabling me to "*Think different*," it's fruitless. This changes the very relationship by putting me, the customer, in the driver's seat with a single-minded goal to transform my life. As people are their own biggest barrier to change, it's really a no-brainer. If we want to create a better life for people, better societies, a better planet, we need to give people the ability to become actors in creating that better life!

When an organisation begins to focus on a societal purpose bigger than itself like making transportation electric, rather than people-transforming, such as a conscious traveller, it loses sight of people and the foothold that ultimately drives the business forward. The profit is dependent on the customer relationship; if not, the corporate purpose quickly becomes a two-headed purpose monster where profit and purpose aren't aligned. When the organisation's purpose – or as I prefer to call it, "promise" – is ultimately to enable people, it'll always be focused on growing its customers, which inevitably will grow the business. What seems more meaningful to people: your organisation's purpose or people's own dreams and passion?

How LEGO avoided bankruptcy

It can be brutal to forget who you are in business to serve – a lesson the Danish toymaker LEGO learned the hard way. The family-owned company was close to bankruptcy in 2004 after years of failed marketing and product investments typically centred on Hollywood blockbusters.[5] Essentially, they forgot who they were in business for and what role they played in people's lives. The company name reflects the essence and purpose of the company as it's made up of combining two Danish words: *leg*, which means "play," and *godt*, which means "well." Together it's "play well."

LEGO is one of the world's best loved brands with a stunning 94 bricks for every person on this planet. Initially the company began with producing wooden toys but moved into the well known LEGO bricks in the late 1950s. As you might know – and as a Dane I grew up with them – all bricks work together, opening up endless possibilities for the imagination to build one's own designs.

After the strategic detour, LEGO went back to its core and a launched a new credo: "*Inspiring and developing the builders of tomorrow.*" It was a transformative credo to parents and children alike. The parents were happy to give the bricks to their children to boost their creativity, to develop their skills. I set up a call with David Hall, who's senior director at LEGO, to better understand how LEGO views its purpose and how it's activated. David explained how he himself was attracted to the purpose initially when joining LEGO and how anchored it is in the organisation: "*People come to work here because they believe in what we do at LEGO and everyone is very bought into that purpose, it doesn't need to be written on a wall anywhere.*"[6]

LEGO early on acknowledged through research that there was a difference between their normal customers and their core customers, who knew the product almost better than LEGO. At their builder events, the "*super builders*" are feted like rock stars, and often LEGO would step back and invite the press to talk directly to the super builders so as to get the authentic, non-corporate stories out there.

And those stories garnered attention. One example is when super builders in 2011 built a 12-meter-tall Christmas tree, made of 600,000 bricks, placed in the concourse of London's St Pancras International railway station. That's hard to ignore. The super builders are supported and supervised by LEGO but are encouraged to do their own thing. In North America alone, there are 126 so-called super builders, and a whopping 31,000 members worldwide. Some of those super builders even turn out their own supported LEGO products carrying a "*Certified Professional*" logo. For example, a line of sets released in 2014 to mark the 30th anniversary of the *Ghostbusters* movie was entirely designed by super fan Brent Waller. LEGO turns their super fans into the very creators of the marketing and even the products. "*We look to our consumers so as to be in their shoes, and we take decisions from there,*" explains David. "*Is this something a seven-year old would engage with?*"

A key element of the strategy was to make the brand part of customers' own transformation and for them to embrace their creative urge. According to David, it's always about the physical bricks as a starting point for the creative journey, even when venturing into digital, for example with the augmented reality app Playgrounds, where the customers can see their brick creations come alive with animations, interactive moments and even games. David also notes the importance of respecting customers' privacy and digital lives: "*While digital is very important to the future of the business at LEGO, there are some opportunities that we turn down based on our values. We are always very mindful of children's safety and well-being when considering what to go after.*"

Core credo

Enabling LEGO's customers to play has been "*one of our big successes,*" explains David. "*Even if we have really creative people working for us, it's inspiring to see the creativity from our fans.*" LEGO IDEAS is one such example. It's a crowd-sourcing platform where customers can submit ideas, and if 10,000 other fans like it, LEGO might develop it into an official product. David admits with a chuckle that he's bought quite a few of those customer-created sets himself. LEGO also connects its customers with one another through the LEGO Life app, where they can share their creations and meet like-minded kids.

LEGO offers an impressive number of touch points, from LEGOLAND theme parks to in-store experiences and a TV show where their customers can feel like an integral part of the story and become advocates for the brand. The LEGO movie was a pinnacle in this new strategy released in 2014; the computer-animated feature film became a box office success grossing over $250 million in the United States alone and has since been followed by *LEGO Batman, Ninjago* and a second LEGO movie in 2019.[7] In the development of the first LEGO film, fans were given briefs to create 60-second videos for usage in the actual movie. Only one final winner was supposed to win the honour of going into the movie, but in the end more than four fans' ideas made it. Again, the LEGO customers had a big say.

But it's also important not to overstep certain lines or to dictate what their young customers should think, David explains:

> *It's not that we don't want to involve ourselves in big societal issues, but we really want to protect our consumers. Our research shows that parents don't want their kids to grow up too fast, so we need to give the kids freedom to be kids. Unless it's something the kids really care about, like for example the environment, where they want us to take action.*

As a response to the environmental challenge, LEGO has pledged to create bricks that are not made from fossil fuel – as plastic historically has been – but is working towards finding sustainable substitutes by 2030. In 2018, LEGO began using plant-based plastic sourced from sugarcane in one collection.

David also mentions the LEGO Foundation as very active in expanding the power of play across the world. He shared a story about a heart-warming video from a refugee camp by the Mediterranean Sea and how it ultimately proves the creative power of the simple brick. In the video, a girl in the camp is given all these multicoloured bricks, but at first, she doesn't know what to do with them. When she suddenly realises, she can connect the bricks, the magic happens, and she begins playing and making towers, houses and other creations.

Stimulating creativity runs like a red thread through the organisation: "*We never really talk about profit first,*" says David. "*And the family owning LEGO will never talk about earnings first either, they're very down-to-earth and approachable. We're here to serve our consumers – to inspire and develop the builders of tomorrow.*" In the conversation with David, I can, throughout the call, sense an authenticity and clear direction that's guiding LEGO in its decisions across products and marketing from what they do to what they do not do, and it all begins with putting their customers' creativity and well-being first. It's a truly transformative promise.

The LEGO story demonstrates what happens when a brand forgets who it should be there for and how then, through a reignited effort, focuses on transforming its customers – it achieves a spectacular turnaround. Today LEGO keeps inspiring and sparking creativity among children and grown-ups alike.

We have to change the way we show leadership

Leaders and organisations don't hold any power; they don't exist simply because of a burning why but because they matter to someone. We as people give them power, we give them meaning by our participation.

Organisations, like leaders rely on that interrelationship, and when organisations, like leaders, forget who they are there for, they lose relevance. Most organisations didn't become irrelevant because they forgot their why but because they forgot who they were there for. You have to ask different questions if you as an organisation want to enable people's personal transformation and move them from intention to action. Life is one long continuous journey towards realising ourselves, and as an organisation one valuable contribution is to show people the way.

Let me introduce a new tool, the Arrow, which focuses your efforts on who you can enable people to become. In shaping the Arrow, I was inspired by coaching and psychotherapy methodologies, and I kept reverting to those techniques to make sure I had a razor-sharp focus on moving people towards their dreams and aspirations. By using the Arrow with leaders, organisations and brands around the world, I noticed one interesting thing each and every time: the marketing people or the leadership in the room realised they had "*forgotten their customers,*" "*the role they played in people's lives* or to "*create a meaningful relationship.*" They were selling what made the brand special in the market, not what could make people special. They were selling a predefined identity or vision instead of a personal transformation.

The Arrow

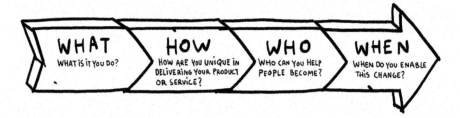

WHAT product do you sell or service do you deliver?
This is the product you sell or the service you deliver, such as running shoes.

HOW are you unique in delivering your product or service?
This is what makes your offering stand out, such as convenience.

WHO can you help people become?
This is the personal transformation you enable, such as a mindful runner.

WHEN do you enable this change?
This is your call to arms: a specific time of day, a situation, a life-phase or a state of mind.

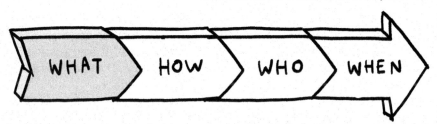

WHAT product do you sell or service do you deliver?

WHAT you sell obviously shouldn't give you too much of a headache. It's the product you make or the service you deliver; for example, for Volvo it would be its cars, trucks and buses. The WHAT is not necessarily set in stone as you might change your product or its delivery, like Apple suddenly pivoting into music with the iPod.

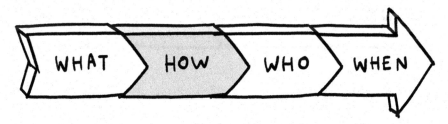

HOW are you unique in delivering your product or service?

HOW are your products or services unique? How do they stand out from your competitors'? How are you unique in delivering them to people? For the American chocolate company Kind Snacks, it's a snack made with "*premium, better-for-you ingredients that are kind to your body without sacrificing quality or flavour.*"

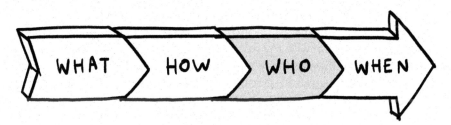

WHO can you help people become?

The WHO question moves the product or service to the background as it's the personal transformation people essentially buy. You don't buy the running shoes from Nike, you buy who you can become: a superior runner. Nike's mission reads: "*To bring inspiration and innovation to every athlete* in the world.*" And the asterisk is not be missed as it reads: "*If you have a body, you are an athlete.*" Their mission is for everyone despite proficiency level or qualifications. For Nike it's about the very essence of moving you from inaction to action.

As an organisation, you're selling the transformative outcome people potentially are achieving: better health, finance, skills and the list goes on. It's your potential as an organisation to stand out in the market by owning a transformative role in people's lives. You're taking people up to dance on the very top of Maslow's Pyramid – that's not a bad place to take anyone.

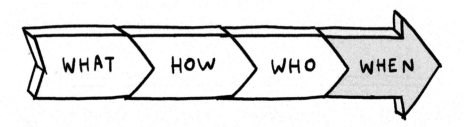

WHEN do you enable this change?

People's best intentions or biggest dreams are not enough if they don't turn them into action. WHEN? is your call to arms: a specific time of day, a situation, a life phase or a state of mind. This is where it gets really interesting. When organisations can get us to live more in balance with ourselves, get us to achieve our goals, we experience the difference. It's a realised outcome that's difficult for any competitor to compete with.

When the hygiene pad brand Always can make a young girl use "*Like a girl*" as a statement of power or defiance instead of an insult, that's magical. Always is changing a state of mind. When District Vision gets me to run with my mind and body as a whole, I can feel the improved result. There is no higher accomplishment from an organisation as you're moving from people's hearts and down into their hands: changing behaviours for the better, changing people for the better. For an organisation or leader, it's really about pushing people towards that desired state and instilling them with the confidence needed. When is not a simply deadline, it's an attitude, it's a constant drive towards change.

A health insurance company that makes you healthier

Remember how many people in The Good Life report that aspired towards good health? As the saying goes, you don't go to the doctor to get medicine, you go to the doctor to get the cure. If you're a health insurance company, what transformation do you want to own? Remember the Arrow's WHO question! WHO can you help people become? Yes, healthier. In 1992, Adrian Gore founded Discovery with that one simple idea: a health insurance to make people healthier. The South African start-up grew into a global player and now operates in 19 countries, serving some 18 million people.[8] Not only did they have a transformative promise to *"incentivise people to be healthier, and enhance and protect their lives,"* but they also answered the WHEN question by delivering the services, innovations and marketing efforts to make it happen, turning intent into action across the customer journey, from gyms to supermarkets.

Through what they call the Vitality program, their customers receive discounts or are rewarded for the right behaviour like going to the gym or buying healthier food. Independent research has established that Discovery's Vitality business model has lowered morbidity and mortality rates. Discovery brilliantly aligns profit and purpose: the results show that Vitality members generate up to 30% lower hospitalisation costs and live from 13 to 21 years longer than the rest of the insured population (up to 41 years longer than comparable uninsured populations).[9] That's no small accomplishment.

A substantial behaviour change study[10] on physical activity examining more than 400,000 people in the United Kingdom, the United States and South Africa went even further. The study investigated whether the incentives with the Vitality program and Apple Watch are associated with enhanced levels of physical activity among Vitality members. The results were clear and showed an increase in activity of 4.8 extra days per month regardless of location, health status, age or gender, which Vitality estimates translates into two extra years of life. Discovery estimates that within a year, participants would additionally achieve numerous benefits, such as improvements in blood pressure, cholesterol and cardiorespiratory fitness, as well as lowered health care costs.

The Arrow focuses your efforts on the transformation (WHO) – and on the outcome (WHEN). Discovery's mission was focused on incentivising its customers to be healthier, so the company's ingenuity, capabilities, products and services go into realising what we know from research is a top priority for people: to become healthier. It's the company North Star and it's paying off for company and customer.

A real change story about friendship

On our way to Vesuvius with my girlfriend we got lost, but a couple of Italians stopped in their car in the middle of the street and asked if we needed any help. We explained we wanted to camp on Vesuvius, but they laughed and thought we were crazy facing the low temperature and wild animals. Instead they invited us home to spend a night at their terrace with a view to Vesuvius. They ordered Neapolitan pizzas, baked donuts, invited the rest of their family, parents, and cousins, just so we could feel like home. Just before we went to sleep, they kissed and hugged us as well. None of them were speaking English, and we talked mainly in signs and laughs. We couldn't believe that some complete strangers could create this sense of belonging in such an unconditional way.[11]

– Sarunas Kazlauskas, Photographer

The Arrow is moving people

Nobody, besides people themselves, can turn their aspirations and dreams into reality. You can teach them, give them the tools, you can hold their hand, but by the end of the day, it's up to them. Transforming people is about aiming for the very top of Maslow's hierarchy of needs; it's about understanding WHO you can help people become but also about realising, as Deci and Ryan advised us, that self-determination is critical: people should be in charge. This is a simple, universal truth; the more you put people in charge over their own lives, the happier and more fulfilled they are. As in any other relationship, you stay around those who make you the best you can be. As previously described, we're inherently self-motivated, and leaders and organisations need to serve as that fertile ground for self-growth. It's a shift from an inside-out approach – *"This is what we can do for you"* – to a transformational approach – *"This is who we can help you become."* That's where the Arrow helps you as a leader or an organisation to focus your efforts and truly move people.

The WHO

The WHO relates to your role as an individual at any given moment, how you see yourself and how you want to be seen by others. A WHO can be something to hide behind as a social armour; "*I'm a business woman*" feels powerful to some women, whereas "*I'm a housewife*" may not. WHO can relate to many different sides of people's lives, from how they eat "*health conscious,*" "*vegan*" or "*traditional*" to an attitude toward life like "*optimistic,*" "*charitable*" or "*kind.*"

Who are you? Who do you want to be? It's one of the most central questions in psychology, philosophy, coaching as well as in marketing. Typically, it's been a commercial battle where brands are selling an identity or a predefined image like I described earlier in the scene from *American Psycho*, where Courtney seems more like a walking billboard than a person with heart and soul: "*Courtney opens the door and she's wearing a Krizia cream silk blouse, a Krizia rust tweet skirt and silk-satin d'Orsay pumps from Manolo Blahnik.*"[12]

WHO people are and want to be are pivotal to your success. Just take the question, "*What do you do?*" It's one of those questions you'll inevitably encounter either at a social function, on a first date or delivered in an interrogating way by a mother-in-law-to-be. Our work has been a key defining WHO in how we view ourselves and how we want others to view us.

I worked on the advertising account for an unemployment fund, and it was clear from the focus groups that the stress of having no job to define you in society was taking a big toll, as a bank manager was, in his own eyes and words, demoted to the male version of a stereotypical housewife. The WHO is pivotal to our self-worth and how we want others to view us and an opportunity to play a bigger role in our lives. As an organisation, you are forced to take a transformative look at the WHO people are today – and the WHO you can enable them to become.

WHO can be seen as an ideal or something people want to become: a certain character or a certain character trait. The positioning of a brand and the building of a character has in that sense much in common. It's what defines you as a company or an individual, and it's a continuous battle about being true to values and beliefs. The focus by most organisations have simply been wrong because they focused too much on their own transformation, their WHY, rather than enabling people and helping them discover their WHO.

In terms of semantics, both "*character*" and "*branding*" ultimately originate from similar roots; creating a distinctive mark with a hot iron or tool. The word "*branding*"[13] comes from my forefathers' language, Old Norse, a North Germanic language from the 9th to the 13th centuries, and it's derived from the word *brandr* or "*to burn,*" which around the 18th century meant the practice of stamping livestock or items with a hot iron to show ownership. Interestingly enough, the word "*char acter*"[14] comes from Greek *kharaktēr*, "*a stamping tool,*" which later, when passing into French, was translated into a "*token, feature, or trait*" in the early 16th century.

It's this dialogue or reciprocity between brand and people that's interesting. Discovery is viewed as a good health company as its customers are becoming healthier. Brand and character are shaping each other, strengthening each other. Your brand's essence is ultimately derived from the role you play in people's lives. The same can be said about your leadership or how your organisation create meaning.

A kinder you, a kinder company

Daniel Lubetzky, the son of a Holocaust survivor and a Mexican Jew, has through his career advocated for peace and coexistence and through a combination of for-profit and philanthropy made ventures facilitating better coexistence between neighbours striving in the Middle East. In 2004, Daniel founded the US snack and granola bar company Kind Snacks to take a holistic view of health and to encourage people to "*do the kind thing for your body, your taste buds & your world.*"[15] That's Kind Snacks' WHO, spreading kindness be it between neighbouring countries at war, two kids fighting in the sandbox or strangers in a cramped metro.

I called Daniel[16] on a poor connection out of Cape Town and heard how the mission resonated: "*It gave people a lot more meaning. It really became a movement and we took it from being a company with a transactional thing to a community, a movement of all of us together trying to inspire kindness.*"

Across its marketing activities, Kind urges its customers to live up to the mantra of kindness, the WHEN. Kind has, for example, produced videos showcasing Americans' random acts of kindness from volunteers leaving jugs of water across the US–Mexico border for immigrants and refugees to a firefighter and Iraq War veteran who volunteers at a kids' camp for burn victims.

In Daniel's view, kindness doesn't have to be about the big things in life; it's a mindset. It's not always easy to choose kindness, and Daniel shares a personal story of how he was late to an important meeting, simply because he wanted to help an elderly person from one platform to the next in the New York Subway. Anyone who's been in the rundown

New York subway knows that's not a simple task. The community, as Daniel calls Kind's customers, are motivated to take a holistic view of their health from what they eat to how they treat others: "*It became much more meaningful once we started doing things where we invited the community to be agents of change with us. Then, it made all the difference.*"

Kind has a transformative belief about how kindness can change you and me, and Daniel sees it as a journey for all of us:

> *We've tried a number of things and one of my favourites is the monthly big KIND challenge, where our community is triggered to do small kind acts. Today, we have upwards of half a million people in our database that pledged to join with a range of actions. Some of them buy KIND products, but some of them engage with different projects like the Empatico platform that connects students globally and fosters empathy.*

It's a narrative that also resonates internally as kindness is a human condition. Each year they do a survey and 80%–97% of Kind's team members say that they "*felt kinder in their daily lives both at home and at work.*" When you as an organisation make people kinder, healthier, sportier, they can feel the difference, and that reflects on the brand or your organisation. Your customers become living proof of your brand – and even your employees can feel a transformative outcome.

The WHEN

"*My 12-year-old told her Dad and brother they could run #LikeAGirl if they ran a little faster. How to protect this attitude?*" Lindsey Mead wrote this on Twitter @lemead about her young daughter self-confidently teasing her brother and father.

This tweet is just one of many being a testament to how Always has succeeded creating a dialogue and has given a new meaning to the phrase #LikeAGirl with its video achieving more than 85 million global views on YouTube from more than 150 countries. In a study conducted after the campaign (December 2014), almost 70% of women and 60% of men claimed that "*The video changed my perception of the phrase 'like a girl'.*"[17] But more importantly, it has helped build confidence in girls. The campaign encourages them, changes them. The company's mission statement reads: "*Always empowers women to live life with-out limits through trusted feminine care products and confidence and puberty education.*" There is no doubt about who Always is in business to serve. Always is focused on transformation: empowering women.

It's time to evolve purpose to serve people. Most organisations treat the biggest issues of our time from equality and poverty to climate change as a new trend, as if showing care is simply the "*new black.*" Just as every brand in the 1990s was all about lifestyle, brands today are firmly about the social and environmental issues bandwagon like bees around a honey pot. (And yes, those diminishing bee populations are seriously a cause we should worry about.) No doubt, sustainability is a must for any organisation, but from a brand perspective care can be faked, while a tangible outcome for people can't.

When is a state of mind, a moment, a situation . . . ?

The Arrow is focused on creating transformative leadership helping people achieve their goals, whatever they might be, and the latter part of the Arrow asks: WHEN can you enable that change? Is it today? Every day? Each hour? Try to be as specific as possible. Is it at a phase in life? When people have kids? When they turn from child to teenager? Or is it simply an attitude like Nike's rallying "*Just do it.*" Always found its enabling WHEN in empowering, educating and giving confidence to women. In the Like a Girl campaign, Always is there to help young women grow up and challenge the societal stereotypes of women. The period Always is targeting is the exact moment these young women are building their brand preferences, and Always is there to move them from consideration to purchase. It truly matters when you enable peo-ple and give them the confidence to succeed, like the often cited quote by Dalai Lama: "*If you think you are too small to make a differ-ence, try sleeping with a mosquito.*"

Time vampires

When looking at transforming people, it's worthwhile putting their choices into perspective. Let's take your life as an example again. It's often when you lose focus on what truly matters to you that you become disenfranchised. So many things in an average day, from fam-ily time to studies and homework, can steal your attention. For the most part, advertising is one of those time bandits as well. But advertising is also an opportunity for organisations to bring back focus on what mat-ters. There's a difference between what you think you spend your time on and what you really spend your time on. That's why in coaching, one of the first things the coach does is to go through your day and compare your priorities with your personal goals.

When Apple in 2018 launched Screen Time, it suddenly enabled its iPhone users to see how they use their iPhone and for how long. It would break down the usage of every app and show you how much time you spend, and it would show you facts like daily usage and weekly usage. This is the first step to change. Personally, I was shocked at the time I spend on my phone and on what activities. My average was around four hours a day, and a substantial part was on social media. I felt bad about it and was incentivised to change. I didn't want to be that person glued to an iPhone 24/7 – that's not how I see myself or want others to see me. For more and more people, coping with the intrusiveness of technology is getting harder, so much so that people are paying for a digital detox. The Intercontinental Montreal offers a Digital Detox hotel package where the guests surrender their digital devices upon check-in, and the rest of the stay is about pampering and well-being. The guests are paying extra for a small transformative digital detox moment – and at $499, the moment doesn't come cheap. For you as an organisation, it's looking for those moments where you can bring people's choices into perspective, where they are the most open for change.

Anchor your mission in people

There is a winning position for organisations in the intersection between WHO people are – and WHO they want to become. Aren't we all on a daily basis battling to do the kind thing, be just a pinch more climate friendly or for once move from saying no to a plastic bag at the supermarket to actually really doing something about rampant plastic pollution? For an organisation, it's really about understanding that people are not buying the product or service but ultimately the promised transformation. As a customer, I buy into the deeper connection to kindness that Kind Snacks invokes in me.

Don't look inside the organisation to find the why you matter to people, but rather look to people to see how you as an organisation can matter to them. If you want to fix the broken relationship, the answer lies in the relationship. Very few organisations can answer the question, "*Who can you help me become?*" When making life better for people is the driving force behind your efforts, people can feel the difference; there's a concrete outcome, and you drive the whole organisation towards fulfilling that promise. You become hyper-transformation-focused; at every contact point in the organisation, it's about saying: "*I'm there for you.*" Just like Discovery has successfully accomplished. It's a goal that's truly bigger than yourself as an organisation and, for me, the truest purpose. Purpose is not an eternal burning flame that inspires everyone around your organisation. It's something people will have to find for themselves. All you can do is give them some dry wood, matches and good advice and hope for the best.

As in in any relationship, when you forget each other, when you don't spend enough time together, when you don't listen to each other, when you don't support each other or when one plus one doesn't make three anymore, you put the relationship at risk. You can have a shared passion or mission with someone that makes you good friends, colleagues or kindred spirits, but if somebody empowers you and makes you see or experience a better version of yourself, that's a companion. Maybe even a companion for life? Think about your own life partner, girlfriend or boyfriend. Do you feel that he or she makes you feel better, worth more, capable of more? (If that's a no, I take no responsibility.) As a leader or an organisation, you should always aim to be in the transformation business asking yourself the pivotal question: WHO can you help people become?

Key takeaways

1   As the market shifts towards a democratic, empowered, prosocial marketplace, we don't buy what you make or why you make it but WHO you can make me become.

2   The Arrow unlocks business value by putting people in the driver's seat and aligning their goals with the organisation's goals.

3   The Arrow asks, "WHAT, HOW, WHO and WHEN" to bridge the gap between intent and action, ultimately leading to fulfilled individuals and realised sales.

4   With the Arrow, products or service move to the background, and organisations can ultimately charge for the outcomes people achieve like better health, finance or skills.

5   As an organisation always ask WHEN; WHY is passive.

Questions to ask yourself

1   Are people living or acting on your purpose?

2   Does your company's mission convert into better lives and increased sales?

3   What meaningful role do you play in people's lives?

4   How does your offering change people's lives?

5   When do you enable this change?

5 The transformative promise

We believe we only exist because our customers exist and we are here because of our tribe and if they didn't care for us, we would not be here.[1]

– Marcello Leone, CEO, RYU

MARCELLO
LEONE

If you're portraying yourself as an angel, you'll fall like a can of soup

Back in 2009, I started rallying for purpose as a must for organisations: simply focusing on profit was not enough to have a meaningful presence in the market. Today purpose has become mainstream, and organisations trying to outcry each other in their societal efforts seem only to garner more cynicism from people. Although people are aspiring towards living better lives, they simply don't seem to be viewing most organisations as their knight in shining armour coming to the rescue.

Overall trust in brands is, to say the least, troubled – something I touched on before but a crucial point. The "Enabling The Good Life" study[2] from Sustainable Brands show a dire picture: 80% of customers globally say that they want to buy from companies that they believe are doing a good job in the world, but at the same time, those same respondents feel confident that only 6% of the companies they do business with are actually good. Ouch! Other surveys show a similar strained relationship between brands and people, such as Edelman's research[3] from 2019, where 56% of global respondents agree that brands are using a stance on social issues as a marketing ploy, and 53% believe that brands are less than truthful when talking about their impact on society. When people value brands that do good but so few people trust they are actually doing so, the very motive of these companies is at stake. The often cited Havas's global Meaningful Brands survey drives home the point. The survey has been going on since 2008 and in 2018 showed that 77% of global consumers don't care whether the majority of brands are around tomorrow or not.

Corporate purpose often ends up being a slogan on the CEO's coffee mug rather than a guiding principle from boardroom to factory floor. Under Armour CEO Kevin Plank received fierce criticism after, in an interview with CNBC in February 2017, he touted President Trump's achievements: "*To have such a pro-business president is something that's a real asset for this country.*"[4] Players sponsored by Under Armour, celebrities like actor Dwayne "*The Rock*" Johnson and customers were far from happy with Kevin's statement, as the supportive words for a divisive figure such as Trump didn't align with the brand's embracement of diversity and equality. Purpose and profit were clashing, and Kevin's statement shed an inauthentic or even false light on Under Armour's diversity stance as portrayed in its advertising and through sponsorships.

An example from the other end of the scale is Starbucks CEO Howard Schultz, who put personal political views before shareholders when he challenged a number of policies such as immigration promoted by President Trump in a letter to employees. The reaction from Trump supporters was swift: they rallied for a boycott using the #boycottStarbucks, which quickly became a top trending hashtag on Twitter. Howard, in this instance, put purpose before profit or values before short-term revenue. That said he might not really have risked that much as his target group loved him for defending the inherent Starbuck's values.

Or take another example of a brand balancing purpose and profit. When Nike in 2018 celebrated 30 years with its tagline "*Just do it,*" they featured a controversial NFL player, Colin Kaepernick, in a TV spot and a print ad with a cunning caption: "*Believe in something. Even if it means sacrificing everything. Just Do It.*" The sacrifice in question referred to Kaepernick's kneeling protests before NFL games against police brutality that landed him on the bench. The ads sparked protests and on social media people shared their anger by burning their Nike apparel but ultimately the campaign gained more praise, and, according to an interview with Nike CEO Mark Parker, resulted in "*record engagement with the brand.*"[5] Nike sales surged 31% in the days after the Kaepernick ad was unveiled, and the stock was performing well above the previous year. For Nike, it might have been a calculated risk, as they knew the majority of their customers would appreciate Nike's standing up for its beliefs.

Starbucks and Nike are classic examples of purpose in practice, but let's be honest: most brands are *not* iconic brands like Nike or Starbucks. And as a brand you should never run the risk of pretending to be. Iconic brands prove time and time again that they can bend or even break the usual playbook for brands. Just take Martin as an example: the CEO of a sporting goods store in Colorado, he stood up for his belief that nobody should disrespect the American flag: not Kaepernick, not Nike. As a consequence, Martin stopped selling Nike products. The result? The store went bankrupt. Martin explained to Fox News:

> I didn't give in to big Nike and big dollars. I didn't give in. I did it my way. That part of the military respect that's in me just cannot be sacrificed or compromised, as I believe Brandon Marshall and Colin Kaepernick both did. I don't like losing a business over it, but I rather be able to live with myself.[6]

Martin didn't have the iconic brand status, and his belief cost him the business.

Should purpose be a positioning battle between the organisations that care the most? Sacrifice the most? What are the business implications? Who cares most about the ocean plastic challenge? Adidas plugging its ocean sneakers in collaboration with Parley for the Oceans? Carlsberg waving goodbye to the six-pack ring? The supermarket down on the corner? The start-up? Who?

The hero trap

For more than a decade I've touted the business case for corporate purpose, but today I question my own convictions. More often than not, purpose ends up as what I call a "*hero trap.*" If you asked a psychologist to evaluate most brand purposes, I guess the diagnosis would be somewhere between megalomania or delusion. The whole purpose-space has moved from being a trust-building commercial exercise to a blind crusade with each brand trying to outdo the other's efforts. In the developed world where more and more companies are embracing more sustainable business practices, adhering to the United Nation's Sustainable Development Goals and crying their world-bettering commitments from every rooftop, it shouldn't be a surprise that people are turning increasingly sceptical. Saying no to straws! Committing to wind energy! Minimising food waste! The space is over-communicated, and purpose is losing its meaning as it's become what "*great, long-lasting taste*" was to chewing gums in the eighties: tacky advertising lingo. As a consequence, it's increasingly difficult to claim or own a purpose positioning.

Every brand is on the purpose bandwagon, but one should never confuse becoming a more sustainable company, which is a must, with using every opportunity as a brand to shout: "*We care!*" I see newly advertised commitments from companies every day for 2025, 2030 and even 2050. It's not enough: people (especially the young) want to see change now, not tomorrow, as is evident from movements like #MeToo, Climate Extinction or Greta Thunberg's School Strike for Climate. Think about any other troubled relationship. Let's say you've been unfaithful, do you think your wife or husband would be head over heels if you simply committed to being more and more faithful by 2030? Remember, people have a choice, and if you can't deliver today, people will choose differently – and there are lots of exciting new eco- and social businesses with less of a negative impact. An organisation's commitments can set people in motion, but ultimately it's about people's commitments.

You can barely buy anything without it being labelled hipster handmade, community-improving, no this-or-that and lots of this good stuff. The problem is that most brands are going head-on into the hero trap. If you as a brand try to take the number one spot on the world bettering podium, that makes for a very long way to fall. We've all read about the mishaps, the collisions and obituaries. And more will come. Sorry to say, no matter how perfect you are – everyone has a weakness. For Superman, it's kryptonite; for Wolverine, it's the Muramasa Blade; for The Flash, it's running too fast. For organisations, it's their brand that is the Achilles heel. Volkswagen was touted as the world's most sustainable automotive group in the Dow Jones Sustainability Index[7] multiple times only to see itself go through a public outcry because it was cheating with its cars' emissions. Chipotle, an American chain of fast-casual restaurants, has for years advocated its sustainable and healthy eating practices only to face scandals around the inhumane treatment of its pigs, bad labour practices among its tomato farmers and foodborne illness scandals across its restaurants. The result is loss of trust, shaken stock value and the potential loss of sales. It's challenging to put on that hero cape.

We're asking the wrong question

If you ask an organisation to sit down on a bench and philosophise about its larger role in this world beyond profit, its big WHY, it is no wonder we see so many grandstanding, out-of-this-world bettering purposes. This is how organisations have always communicated in the mass-marketing world: "*We make the greatest tasting chewing gum*" and now also in the purpose space: "*We as a brand want to fix climate change, rid the oceans of plastic, solve world hunger!*" Please listen carefully to those commitments: We, we, we. It sounds megalomaniacal! If one of your friends said that, you would most likely shake your head and wish him or her good luck or do your best to suppress a giggle. Sorry to say this, but there might not be a hidden superman-power-purpose-position anywhere in that toilet roll company; they may just sell toilet rolls. Try to do the same exercise in your own life. Why do you do what you do? What's your purpose? Do some pondering. If you emerge as a new world-saving messiah, then good on you, but most likely, you'll have a couple of things you want to improve in your life – things like being a slightly better husband, remembering to curse less, saying no to plastic bags more often or pursuing passions like finding more time to play the guitar or finally getting fit.

That's probably it. We're asking the wrong question. How many people do you really know that have a burning purpose? Frankly speaking, very few of us are the Ghandis, Nelson Mandelas, Greta Thunbergs or Leonardo DiCaprios of this world. It's no different for organisations. Truly purposeful organisations are the exceptions for the rule, and trying to aspire towards that exemption is a dangerous path. If you haven't found your organisation's purpose yet, it's most likely because you don't have a one.

Obviously, organisations should play a bigger role than just selling, but that role doesn't have to be found within the organisation but rather from the lives it's serving. And there are a hell of a lot of reasons your organisation – or yourself for that sake – can play a truly meaningful role in people's everyday lives. Not everyone is born with a burning purpose, but everyone has the potential to lead others towards their goals, aspirations or a sense of meaning in life.

Instead of painting your brand as the hero, there's a new leadership emerging where the organisation takes the backseat and makes people the heroes. There is really no other choice as people have the upper hand anyway. Great leaders make us better, motivate us, grow us. At the end of the day, organisations and people are alike and face the same daily choices between values and wallet, between time and convenience. If you can be the leader or organisation that listens to people, that helps people achieve their goals, you're not overpromising. Think about the brands that have played a transformative role in your life. The relationship is different, right? I'm thankful to Nike for pushing me towards an active lifestyle. I'm grateful that Aarstiderne taught me how to cook more plant based. What's your list like?

Organisations should avoid being the self-absorbed activists or the howling missionaries but rather aim to be coaches or helpers, to be there for you and me. It's about Me with a capital "M," My values, My goals – not some crusade that ends with the organisation as the winner.

Can profit and purpose coexist?

How you view the world matters, and it's easy to fall into the trap of taking our current view for granted or simply trusting earlier held beliefs. Up to the 16th century, the Earth was the centre of the universe, and this view was enforced by the Church, which saw the geocentric model as borne out by religious scriptures. If God had created the universe, he would for sure have put the world at the centre, the thinking went. Nicolaus Copernicus and Galileo Galilei were curious astronomers whose observations simply didn't fit the geocentric model; they challenged the popularly held belief and instead placed the sun at the centre of our solar system. The church didn't accept people going up against its teachings and placed Galileo under lifetime house arrest. Who's the centre of your organisation's worldview? Your organisation? Or your customer? Your employees?

People are really not in doubt why most organisations exist: to make money. As the previously mentioned Deloitte study[8] among Millennials and Gen Zs stated, nearly 66% say companies have no ambition beyond wanting to make money (up from 50% the year before). Organisations should be genuinely people-centric, life-centric, or they'll risk losing their relevance.

WHO focuses on the role you can play in people's lives enabling their beliefs and dreams, whereas WHY focuses on your organisation's beliefs and dreams. You tell me, which sounds more beneficial for people? That's why I want to reframe purpose and craft a new North Star for organisations called a *"transformative promise"* – a commitment to people that your organisation is there for them! I see the transformative promise as a much needed evolution of corporate purpose towards truly serving and enabling people. After all, people want to be in charge of their own life and happiness.

The market pressure on purpose to evolve is clear from *"We care about this"* or *"This is why we do what we do"* to enabling people to become agents of change. It's a move from a transactional relationship – *"believe in us as a company to bring about change"* – to a transformational relationship – *"believe in your own ability to bring about change."* The organisational-centric view on purpose is without doubt a leftover from earlier decades of mass-marketing and mass-production where brands were king. It's an increasingly dangerous strategy in a people-powered marketplace, where I'm not buying what you make but striving towards a *"better me."*

From functional benefit to transformational benefit

Societal, planetary or personal betterment, I believe, begins with an individual behaving differently. As positioning has moved from functional benefits (the faster car), to emotional benefits (the most masculine car), to societal benefits (the most environmentally friendly car), we're now moving to the very top of Maslow's pyramid to a transformational benefit, unlocking self-actualisation (a more conscious traveller). The idea about a differentiating position has been the cornerstone of branding since Rosser Reeves and the USP (Unique selling preposition), but as products and services were becoming more and more generic, the sustainability space has become a welcome opportunity in the last couple of years to differentiate one product or service on its environmental and societal performance, from a more fuel-efficient car to one that's battery powered. That societal difference is complex to measure and difficult to decipher or for that matter to believe. It's not getting easier as more and more companies speak up, and, admittedly, most people are too busy or convenience seeking to take the needed time to review any potential metrics. The transformational benefit reshapes the branding landscape and focuses efforts on the tangible outcome that people can feel organisations play in their lives, such as making them healthier or wiser. There's proof behind this, like RYU's customers feeling that the brand is pushing them towards realising their gym goals.

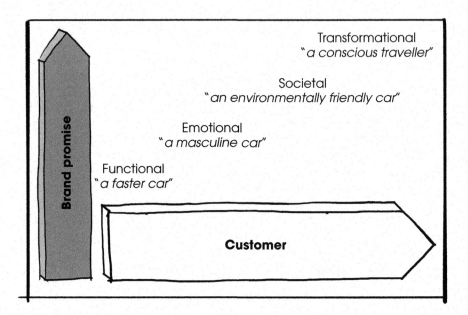

Let me give you an example of the shift towards a transformative promise. Take rental car company Avis's famed strapline, "*We try harder,*" which in the sixties did differentiate the company from its competition and eventually led to the brand conquering the market leader position. Today, Avis has shifted focus in the United States with the promise, "*It's your space,*" offering the busy business traveller peace of mind, a place to relax or work. In an interview with *AdAge*, the global chief marketing officer, Jeannine Haas, explained the change: "*Consumer-centric brands must always evolve in order to keep pace with ever-changing customer needs and preferences.*" The new tagline, Haas said, is "*reflective of Avis' ongoing mission to be a customer-led, service-driven company, and presents the brand in terms of the customer experience and the advantages inherent in renting from Avis.*"[9] It's an important shift for Avis because the most important factor for any organisation in today's marketplace is to wake up in the morning to enable its customers.

Looking at mission and vision statements (or for that matter, purpose statements) of hundreds of organisations, it's astonishing to realise how very few organisations actually put people's lives, their transformation or their personal well-being first. As people are expecting and demanding more from organisations and these organisations are playing a game of catchup by shouting, "*We care*," and trying to deliver wider societal benefits, the approach is gradually losing its relevance and differentiating power in the marketplace. For the most part, these organisations head into the hero trap, doing the chest-bumping behaviour we've come to expect from brands. All people are asking of organisations is that they care about our lives. Like really care. And in that competition, the stories and actions that are centred around my life and enabling me to live a better life without doubt eclipse a value crusade by a brand.

The recipe for a better life

Brand and people are ultimately shaping each other, strengthening each other. Your brand's essence is ultimately derived from the role you play in people's lives. Nowhere is this truer than with the previously mentioned Danish organic meal subscription service, Aarstiderne (which means "*Seasons*" in my mother tongue Danish), which delivers a food box with the recipes and the organic produce needed to cook one or more meals. Aarstiderne was founded almost 20 years ago by Søren Ejlersen and Thomas Hartung. I met with Søren[10] over a cup of organic coffee at their farm north of Copenhagen, overlooking the fields. He shared his vision for the company and its customers.

Before Aarstiderne, Søren was a chef with many successful restaurant businesses behind him but always had a passion for organic produce and farming techniques. On the Danish food scene, he was one of the early ones to adopt more plant-based recipes in his restaurants. Talking to him, I could feel the passion; something he thinks is a big part of the success behind Aarstiderne is "*that passion is contagious.*" At one point during our conversation, he jumps up to fetch a jar of a rediscovered variety of small, black chickpeas to show some of the experiments they're doing in bringing more variety to their customers. But he was very clear that, for him, Aarstiderne began with a moment of self-enlightenment, something he thinks is pivotal for Aarstiderne's success.

At the time, he'd taken over a restaurant in a rural area of Denmark, which brought him even closer to the produce, the earth and biodynamic farming techniques, something he wanted to expand to more people. What began as one community farm, where the nearby inhabitants would participate in planting and at harvest time receive the fresh produce, quickly evolved into Aarstiderne. He joined forces with Thomas, who was a farmer by trade and who was also experimenting with a community farm.

Today, Aarstiderne is a thriving business with close to $110 million in turnover and 40,000 weekly subscribers. Denmark is a small country with around 6 million inhabitants, so that's no mean feat. But for Søren it's important that Aarstiderne never preach or brag about all the things they're doing. It's about being at eye-height, conversational and giving people a chance for themselves to discover the joy of the connection with the land and the produce. This self-discovery is reflected in the company's pay-off, which reads "*Earth connection.*" When people have their hands in the earth harvesting beetroot and they see their hands get coloured red, something happens – something almost spiritual, Søren explains.

It was clear through the stories Søren shared that community was important and that they try to engage their customers as much as possible, from what should be in the meal boxes to what the company should concentrate on next. Besides traditional advertising, Aarstiderne is focused on one-to-one through events or social media. There is no doubt that Aarstiderne's customers can feel the difference, "*the earth connection*" – and I'm one of them. Through their meal boxes and the accompanying recipes, I've learned to become better at cooking vegetarian and have learned many new food cultures and produce I didn't even know existed before – like those small, black chickpeas. Aarstiderne plays a transformational role in people's lives.

From purpose to promise

I've always enjoyed and respected the US director Martin Scorsese's storytelling skills (behind films like *Goodfellas*, *The Aviator*, *Gangs of New York* and *The Departed*). One of the insights behind his success across generations is simple: "*When I'm making a film, I'm the audience,*" [11] says Scorsese. For the director, it's all about putting himself in his audiences' shoes to create strong, emotional narratives.

The end result, the delivery point of the Arrow process, is what I call a transformative promise: it's a steadfast focus and a rallying cry as an organisation to enable better living for people. It's what people can expect from you, it's how you help them transform or get what they need. It's an organisational mission that matters because it's ultimately about fulfilling people's goals, dreams and ambitions. Whereas most corporate purposes focus on the organisation's goals, dreams and ambitions.

The transformative promise forces you as an organisation to put people's needs first with a single-minded focus to make them happen.

It's your promise to people, your organisation's raison d'être; this is why you exist, this is your mission, this is what should get you up in the morning.

If your brand's transformative promise is focused on motivating people to face their challenges and overcome obstacles, I argue that the chance of their crossing the purpose gap and buying your product will be higher. The promise should answer all four steps along the Arrow: WHAT, HOW, WHO and WHEN.

Let's use Discovery as an example. Discovery sells health insurances (WHAT) and are always by my side (HOW), as I want to be healthy and live a long life (WHO) and they are always there to incentivise me towards a healthier life and protect me from accidents (WHEN). Discovery's transformative promise, then, is "*to incentivise people to be healthier, and enhance and protect their lives.*"[12]

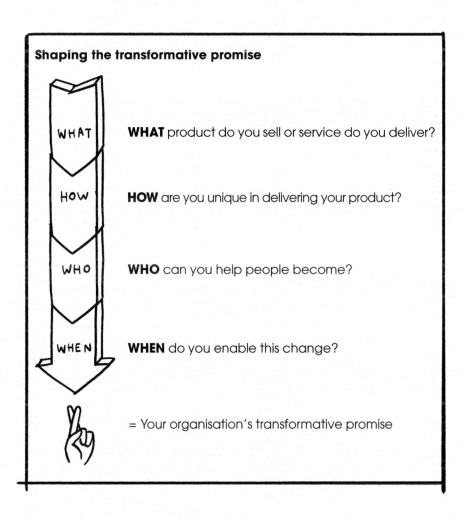

Shaping the transformative promise

WHAT   **WHAT** product do you sell or service do you deliver?

HOW   **HOW** are you unique in delivering your product?

WHO   **WHO** can you help people become?

WHEN   **WHEN** do you enable this change?

= Your organisation's transformative promise

I see the transformative promise as an important and much needed distinction between those organisations that have an internal purpose focus – "*This is what we do*" – and those that serve people's passions – "*WHO can we help people become?*"

Moreover, a promise is a declaration that one will do something or that a particular outcome will happen. It's goal-focused, it's people-focused. It's the difference between Discovery's vision "*to incentivise people to be healthier, and enhance and protect their lives*" and a thought-up example of an internally focused purpose from Company B: "*We want to make the communities we operate in healthy and safe.*" Discovery acknowledges people's pivotal role in succeeding and knows action is key by using the wording "*to incentivise.*" Whereas Company B places itself as the agent of change and without addressing WHEN that change might or might not happen, the company simply risks becoming too self-centred and too broad, forgetting who they're in business for. Your eyes should be on people's transformation, or you'll risk being self-consumed by your own corporate purpose.

Def.: transformative promise

A transformative promise is a commitment towards a positive change that you enable in people's lives.

Keep it simple, promise!

I've also chosen to call it a promise instead of a purpose to avoid grand-standing and the mistake organisations make of elevating purpose to a fourth guiding principal besides vision, mission and values. A purpose that's not integrated into the vision and mission becomes anything but mission critical and operational but ends up like a towering and shaky house of cards. How many people in your organisation can remember your vision, mission and 5–10 values? And now some organisations want to introduce a purpose into the mix! Aspiring to a bigger role in people's lives than simply being transactional should be part of both the mission and vision because creating change is both a daily fight (what the mission deals with) and a fight to turn your big aspiration into reality (vision).

Be the helper people need in their lives

In storytelling, when the protagonist is faced with his or her biggest challenge, which seems insurmountable, there's always somebody there to push the story forward. This person is called "*the helper*" or "*the guardian*," like when Obi-Wan in Star Wars Episode IV *A New Hope* helps Luke discover the Force and gives him a needed tool – his dad's old lightsaber. Only then can Luke continue on his quest to save the galaxy and rescue Princess Leia.

The storyline from the Hollywood blockbuster is really no different from how organisations like Nike or Red Bull push people further towards realising their goals. The story about Luke is also a story about becoming and finding his true self in the Force. That's Luke's WHO, moving from an orphaned pilot to a Jedi warrior fighting evil in the Galaxy. As an organisation, you need to become that helper.

The chocolate company Kind has taken up this approach with success and is on a mission to "*make the world a littler kinder,*"[13] which they believe is only done one act at a time. And their focus is to push people to be kinder because, as they say on their website, "*Nice is something you say, whereas Kind is something you do. Nice is passive, but Kind is active.*"[13] Through a foundation, they celebrate people who make a difference in their communities, but they also encourage people to do small kind gestures daily like, "*Write and mail a letter to an old friend,*" "*Donate lightly used clothes to a local shelter*" or "*Offer someone your seat on public transport.*" As a Kind customer, you are given "*the force*" of kindness through its bars, its challenges and its enabling marketing activities.

The inner coach

Your organisation is *not* the hero; your products or services are *not* the hero; you have to focus on supporting people to become heroes and turn their aspirations into reality. This is exactly where you want your organisation to be. Take, for example, a 47-year-old male CEO of a medical company who values knowledge but in his day-to-day job doesn't feel smart enough compared to his peers and doesn't feel he has time enough to catch up. He's realised there's something that's important to him, knowledge, and his inner critical voice is probably telling him: You're dumb, you're not knowledgeable enough. It's a tension between, "*Am I satisfied with the status quo?*" and "*What am I prepared to do?*" There is an opportunity as an organisation to enable the transformation and change the inner critique to an inner coach that enables him to become wiser and free from old patterns or self-critique.

One company to answer the CEO's call is the app Blinkist. Friends Sebastian Klein, Niklas Jansen, Holger Seim and Tobias Balling found it hard to combine working with learning after leaving university. In 2012, they launched Blinkist, which offers best-selling non-fiction books in just 15 minutes – "*blinks*" that can be consumed in audio or video formats. Blinkist encourages learning with messages like "*Fit reading into your life,*" "*Excel in your career*" or "*Discover life-changing ideas.*" The mission behind Blinkist is "*to inspire people to keep learning.*"[14] And, yes, I know, for traditional book lovers, books can't be compacted into a 15-minute "*blink,*" but for lots of other people, Blinkist truly plays an important role in their lives.

The transformative promise is motivating people to change; the end result is a fulfilled individual. I'm not buying the Kind Snacks granola bar, I'm buying a kinder me, a transformation. The busy CEO isn't buying the 15-minute "*blink*" but a knowledgeable him. When you're promoting a positive trigger, a "*need,*" like being a better dad, instead of a "*want,*" like drinking alcohol and partying, you're enabling people to live a more fulfilled life. As an organisation, that's not a bad promise to make come true for people!

A real change story about mindfulness

All my life I used to lie, whenever I felt that the truth would arouse any negative feelings, so I polished reality around me well. What my 11-year-old daughter taught me is to tell the truth, whatever it is, because actually, nothing terrible happens. I love to perceive the world as it is by simply saying the truth, now I feel calm and enjoy life's uncertainty.[15]

– Sarah Lindgren, Journalist

Your new North Star

It's not easy to get purpose right when one side of the organisation talks about its world bettering commitments, while another side talks about short-term financial results and profit. Maybe it's not so strange that companies tend to end up managing purpose like a two-headed monster because companies are essentially a group of people coming together underneath a shared mission – and as people, we are ourselves a two-headed purpose monster. Think about it. How often have you had something you believed in like organic farming, but then the organic chicken is sold out and the regular one is on sale? Oh yes, habits, convenience and price often beat values in people and in companies.

It's essentially a value gap between what people aspire towards and their will or ability to realise it. Within an organisation, the gap between profit and purpose is the same battle: ideals versus market reality, values versus sales. The transformative promise is an organisation's pledge to help people overcome personal battles and move from intent to action. When people succeed thanks to the organisation's offerings, inevitably the organisation is rewarded at the cash register, and purpose and profit become aligned. The transformative promise is goal oriented.

Changes in lifestyle change lives

Take Jukka Peltola, the CEO and co-founder of Goodio, a fast-growing Finnish chocolate company. I met Jukka[16] back in 2018 when visiting Helsinki for a conference, and we sat down at the brand's first café in central Helsinki overlooking the harbour while I was munching on some seriously nice vegan Goodio ice-cream and chatting about what sparked the concept. Jukka was horrified by a sickening food system with bad ingredients and de facto social inequality. He set out to create chocolate that's truly good for you (and for those who make it). It is handcrafted, high-quality, vegan chocolate with foraged Nordic ingredients like Sea Buckthorn, with beautiful packaging and a taste like nothing I've honestly ever had before (read: real chocolate with no added sugar). A brand like Goodio doesn't need glossy purpose statements or extensive CSR reports to show they care. The love for what they do comes naturally, and their business plays a meaningful role in people's lives. Goodio is on a mission to "*deliver healthier plant-based eating habits*" through the power of chocolate.

And that power is considerable, as Jukka passionately explained:

> *Food of the gods is the actual translation of its scientific name* Theobroma cacao, *which was named by the Swedish botanist Carl Linnaeus in 1753. In Mayan, Olmec and Aztec cultures cacao had very precious, if not even sacred status, and it was a privilege only for the royals, acclaimed warriors and the wealthy.*

Today, that elevated status has been lost. Says Jukka:

> *The glorious history and value of cacao is now a vague memory suppressed by a capitalist market economy. The highly competitive mass-market quantity over quality-based operation model has led into many issues with vast negative impacts like deforestation, extreme poverty and child labour, among many others. My belief is that there could be something better in between these two extremities.*

Jukka's own life was changed by raw cacao. He explained how a couple of years before he'd been through a difficult period where he wasn't feeling well, he was always demotivated and lacked energy. He quit traditional dairy products and adopted a new vegan diet and lifestyle:

> *Due to my changes in diet I experienced some sort of awakening. My energy levels peaked, my mind fog was gone, I was able to focus, I started feeling feelings again, empathy started rising, I found meaning again. Due to these extraordinary results for myself, I wanted to help others too. Goodio is one of my vehicles to help others and drive positive change.*

When Goodio gets people to discover the pleasure of eating more plant based, the company is ultimately growing their own market. In other words, the push to realise people's goals will potentially lead to more chocolate sold. Goodio is a growing business case, and Jukka's next stop for the company is the US market.

The transformative promise is your organisation's competitive edge, when every brand has a why and screams, "*We care,*" the final judgement is in its delivery. Or in other words, when a hundred princes are fighting for the same princess, it's ultimately the prince that slays the dragon and frees the princess who gets the kingdom. Full stop. The transformative promise becomes a competition among organisations to deliver transformation. As the healthy food category is getting increasingly cluttered, it's the brand that not just enables me to once buy healthier food but keeps me on track towards a healthy lifestyle and ultimately a healthy me who wins. People don't buy the vegan, low-sugar chocolate but the personal transformation towards a healthier life (the WHO).

If a transformative promise isn't transforming, fix it

The stringent focus on enabling people keeps your promise relevant. In the late 18th century, photography was far from the click of a button: it involved water, chemicals and metal plates to capture an image. In 1880, George Eastman founded Kodak with a simple but bold mission: *to make photography as simple as using a pencil.*[17] This was undoubtedly an inspiring vision, as George was taking on the frustration of most photographers at the time. The vision also offers a timeless relevance, because photography and photographic editing are ever evolving and becoming more simplified. As digitalisation changed photography forever, the company forgot to live its purpose and constantly strive to make photography easier and instead stuck with old habits and earlier practices. It's a testament to what happens if one forgets the needs of one's customers.

When you as an organisation have a transformative promise, it forces you to keep a steady eye on the outcome. Do people experience photography as easy? Does your company's promise still hold truth, or are there easier ways to do photography than we currently offer? The transformative promise focuses an organisation's efforts and puts everyone working in the organisation, from managers to people sweeping the floor, in the customers' shoes.

Examples of transformative promises

Oatly:	Make it easy for people to turn what they eat and drink into personal moments of healthy joy without recklessly taxing the planet's resources in the process
Kind Snacks:	Do the kind thing for your body, your taste buds and your world
Pearson:	Help people make progress in their lives through learning
Apple:	Think different
Lego:	Inspire and develop the builders of tomorrow
RYU:	We're here to help you achieve more than your gym goals, RYU is here for your life goals
Blinkist:	Inspire people to keep learning

Serving your customers doesn't mean ignoring your stakeholders

The transformative promise doesn't ignore the wider social or environmental impacts but puts them into perspective by viewing them through customers' lens. It's a hygiene factor to be a responsible organisation. A healthy planet supports healthy people, the same way an unhealthy planet leads to unhealthy people or even casualties. We're already witnessing the rising consequences of climate change, pollution and resource scarcity on people's lives and well-being.

Let me give you an example. When Discovery promises "*to incentivise people to be healthier and enhance and protect their lives,*" one has to scrutinise the whole organisation and its impact. If Discovery was in climate change denial and didn't support a transition to a renewable and carbon-friendly future, it would ultimately harm people's health as we've witnessed from wildfires, landslides and other extreme weather phenomena.

The transformative promise forces you as an organisation to focus on the broader impact – directly or indirectly – through the eyes of your customers. Yes, Red Bull can "*give wings*" to daredevils on the ski slopes, but if Red Bull is ignoring climate change, they're ruining their daredevils' beloved playground.

The transformative promise works as a guiding principle to focus the company's overall commercial and sustainable efforts where those add (or erode) value to people's lives.

How to shape the promise

Obviously, when you work your way through the Arrow and answer the WHAT, HOW, WHO and WHEN questions, you'll end up with a focused promise to people. But to assist you, I've created these five recommendations as reminders or pointers towards a transformative promise, which needs to be people-centric, transformative, specific, active and operational.

1 People-centric

Is the promise focused on an obstacle or benefit for people?

Most organisations focus on their capabilities rather than on people's needs. It's a common mistake to take an organisation-first approach. Make sure your promise is focused on people. It's the difference between Avis's "*We try harder*" and their new enabling promise "*It's your space.*"

2 Transformative

Does the promise focus on a personal change or transformation?

In many corporate purposes, there is a tendency to focus on the societal or planetary benefit, and it's never translated into a concrete transformation or personal outcome. Make sure you focus on a personal transformation. Take the Swedish oat milk brand Oatly. They focus on people's transformation towards a climate-friendlier diet, and the outcome evidently will be an environmental benefit.

3 Specific

Does the promise focus on a specific challenge or opportunity?

Many companies don't focus enough on the specific personal obstacle or opportunity but use general terms like "better," "sustainable," "improving lives" and similar, which becomes too broad for an organisation to steer by. Choose your words carefully. Take the professional networking platform LinkedIn; they are very clear about what transformative role they want to play in people's lives: "*To connect the world's professionals to make them more productive and successful.*" If you can't measure the specific outcome, it's probably not specific enough.

4 Active

Is the promise an active encouragement?

It's helpful to think of the promise as an imperative. You want to encourage a change. Take a look at some of the transformative promises and the words they use like "*incentivise,*" "*inspire*" or "*lead.*" If you're not asking people to transform, why should they?

5 Operational

How is the promise enabling people across the organisation?

This is not a narrative that needs to be part of the transformative promise, but it's an important reminder to make sure you can anchor and deliver the promise across your organisation, products and/or services. Look at how Discovery has been able to deliver on "*incentivising healthier lives*" or Nike on "*inspiring athletes*" across the business and with a range of products and services, where people clearly can feel the outcome.

How to shape a transformative promise

1 People-centric

Is the promise focused on an obstacle or benefit for people?

2 Transformative

Does the promise focus on a personal change or transformation?

3 Specific

Does the promise focus on a specific challenge or opportunity?

4 Active

Is the promise an active encouragement?

5 Operational

How is the promise enabling people across the organisation?

Make my WHO your WHY as a brand!

As an organisation, when your reason to exist, when your transformative promise, when your organisations capabilities, products and services go into helping people to achieve their goals, then you're constantly pushing people towards a "*better me.*" With such focused organisational efforts, I'll argue there's a higher chance I act, and those actions convert into sales at the cash register. If the Force and story about Luke from *Star Wars* is not convincing you, I hope Goodio, Aarstiderne, Blinkist or many of the other organisations with a transformative promise will. Instead of asking why you exist as an organisation, always ask who you can truly exist for.

Purpose shouldn't be a crusade to show what an organisation cares the most about or sacrifices the most for, like a Nike Colin Kaepernick commercial gone nuclear: "*Believe in something, even if it means sacrificing everything.*" Instead, I believe an organisation should trust fellow citizens, human beings, colleagues, mothers and fishers to bring about change – more like a version of the Tom Cruise scene from the nineties movie *Jerry Maguire:* "*I am out here for you. You don't know what it's like to be ME out here for YOU. It is an up-and-down, pride-swallowing siege that I will never fully tell you about, ok? Help me . . . help you. Help me, help you.*"[18]

Key takeaways

1   There's a market pressure on purpose to evolve from a societal benefit to a tangible outcome for people – a transformative promise.

2   The transformative promise is a new competitive edge, and it's "the positive change an organisation enables in people's lives."

3   The transformative promise motivates people and raises the chances of bridging the gap between intent and action, between purchasing intent and sales.

4   The stringent focus on personal transformation keeps the promise relevant and engaging for the whole organisation.

5   When shaping your transformative promise, make sure it lives up to the following five criteria: people-centric, transformative, specific, active and operational.

Questions to ask yourself

1   Does your organisation offer a transformational or societal benefit?

2   Do you experience a gap between purpose and profit in your organisation?

3   How can people feel your purpose come alive?

4   How much focus do you have as an organisation on the betterment of people's lives?

5   Is your current purpose people-centric, transformative, specific, active and operational?

6 The WHO void

If not you, who?

We don't preach or shout up about what we do, instead people have to go on a journey of self-discovery. They'll have to find the magic for themselves.[1]

– Søren Ejlersen, Co-founder, Aarstiderne

SØREN EILERSEN

A real friend brings the best out in you

Most societies typically celebrate and honour those who stand up against fears, limitations, biases, personal ghosts or those who dare to reach for what they dream about. The homeless alcoholic turned into a community leader running a non-profit or a sailor returning from an around-the-world trip like Thor Heyerdahl's *Kon-Tiki* expedition. I did it. I succeeded. I overcame my own fear and I won. It's a journey from your "*old you*" to a "*new and wiser you.*" That's where you want to position yourself as an organisation, coupling yourself to people's transformation, to people's becoming. The brand and market potential are there in enabling people to move from aspiration to realisation. And isn't that in fact what great leadership is about? We look to those leaders who walk beside us and help us climb that mountain.

In a time when products and services are essentially generic, brands and leaders are not. Your transformative promise should ultimately be to differentiate and enable individuals to achieve their goals. What you as an organisation should aspire towards is that position between what your products and services can enable, standing out from your competitors' positioning and WHO people want to become. I call this a WHO void.

It's an unused or underdeveloped position – a void – where you can play a transformative difference in people's lives. Potentially it's a blue ocean that goes against conventional positioning, competition or category thinking and opens up new possibilities. In the world of branding, Red Bull owns that the-sky-is-no-limit role in people's lives, pushing them further and elevating a caffeine-enriched drink to a transformative positioning. It's a distinctive WHO void; no other energy drink – or no other brand for that matter – has been able to compete with it.

Def.: WHO void

A differentiating position in the market where you can play a transformative role in people's lives.

For an organisation, it's really about taking a hard look at where it's possible to make a transformative difference in people's lives. For banks, it seems like there is much work to be done, as most go down the financial empowerment route. And, yes, it's true that banks provide funds the same way a car gets you from A to B, but it's hardly an ownable and value-adding position. The Brazilian bank Bradesco wanted to explore a different positioning by launching a new bank called Next targeted towards young people. Compared to the traditional bank, Next is a mobile-only bank that empowers Millennials and fits into their lifestyle. The bank is tailored to each individual's financial life and gives them insight into how they can spend and save wisely to achieve short- and long-term ambitions. It's an enabler and helps young people achieve their goals rather than being a dad figure always there to point fingers like most banks. Next found its WHO void in giving their young customers freedom and control over their money.

The results show that Next understood its customers, clocking up more than 1.3 million downloads by the time of writing, growing active clients at more than 40% per month and delivering more than 1.7 million transactions in March 2018 with 70% month-on-month growth.[2] Young people value that freedom.

This is the secret behind the transformative organisation's success in the marketplace – they focus on driving people towards transformation, and the products/services are the tools. The organisation becomes a welcome agent of change in people's lives.

WHO void: towards a blue ocean

The answer to your company's success isn't necessarily found in the lab or by one of your truck drivers' ingenious ideas to pack more goods into a load but by looking at people's lives as a positioning canvas. Where can you matter? What can you make people achieve? Where can your products and services play a meaningful role in transforming people's lives?

If done right, you unlock business value by putting people in the driver's seat and aligning their goals with the organisation's goals. In the case of Discovery, the more people live healthy lives, the less payouts. Or take Nike, pushing you towards becoming an athlete in life, which inevitably translates into more equipment (or services) needed for your sport endeavours. Branding is essentially about creating a distinctive position in people's minds, and transformative organisations enforce that brand by always playing a meaningful role in people's lives – not just in their corporate minds.

Think about the majority of reality TV gluing millions to the screen every day. It's essentially a story of transformation, from *Survivor*, where it's about facing your own limitations, to *The Biggest Loser*, where it's about overweight contestants battling to lose weight. Or take the TV program called *The Luxury Trap*, where ordinary people with bad or irresponsible finances are helped by two financial experts to save their personal economy. When your organisation plays a similar part in people's lives and can own that position, you can potentially charge for the outcomes people achieve, like better health, finance or skills.

Look again at the example of Next banking. Most banks simply talk about financial empowerment, but Next took it a step further and offered their young customers the freedom, most young people are yearning for. That's a strong WHO void to conquer as a bank. It pays to use the WHO void as a positioning canvas: look at your competitors' position, look at your products or services, look at WHO people want to become – and you'll potentially find your WHO void. The idea that somehow an organisation has to dominate our world, have a strong opinion or shape our world in its own image, that's an old view. An organisation should first and foremost play a meaningful role in our lives.

The WHO void

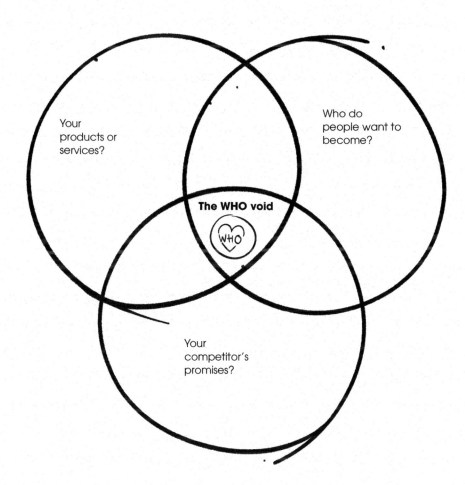

An insight is the key to people's hearts

The advertising legend Bill Bernbach was, throughout his career, fascinated by studying human nature, and his view adds a timeless perspective to the value of finding a real insight into our minds and motives: *"Nothing is so powerful as an insight into human nature . . . what compulsions drive a man, what instincts dominate his action. . . . If you know these things about a man you can touch him at the core of his being."*[3] An insight is never bland and always makes you feel spoken to like it was the whisper between two lovers or a candid conversation between two long-time friends. I define an insight as an understanding of people's fundamental needs and wants. It's the key to why people do what they do and believe what they believe. To find an insight, you have to behave like a psychologist trying to understand the underlying reasons for actions. What you want to stay away from is confusing an insight with an observation, a cliché or a stereotype, which unfortunately a lot of advertising plays cheaply on. An observation or a stereotype would be *"women want to look pretty,"* whereas an insight into women's self-awareness would be something like how society has put an expiry date on women's beauty. Asian beauty brand SK-II challenges that notion, and with their transformative call *"Change destiny,"* they urge women to go up against societal conventions and live their lives without limitations.

It's all about self-actualisation. One of SK-II's campaigns, #INeverExpire, was launched in 2017 with a commercial called *"The Expiry Date,"* an emotional two-and-a-half-minute narrative that tells the story of a girl growing up but with a visible expiry date printed on her arm set at 30 years and the pressure and prejudice she's facing. She eventually overcomes with the uplifting message: *"You are more than your age. Don't let others put an expiry date on you."* The film had more than 100 million global views across all platforms and sparked a Pan-Asian discussion around age-related pressures on women. In 2018, the SK-II brand grew more than 10%,[4] showing that the be-the-girl-you-want-to-be message connected with the target group. SK-II had found a WHO void they could own. As most other beauty brands convey messages of eternal youth, SK-II goes up against these stereotypes and empower women to find pride in themselves.

Organisations should look to activate this untouched potential where people would like to be better, situations they wished they were better at tackling, or maybe social situations where they feel at odds with themselves. When measuring the relationship between organisations and people, it's not just about brand love, intimacy or an identity-building exercise, but there's a developing interdependence as the organisation enables people. You have probably noticed this interdependence from cases like District Vision, Aarstiderne and Precious Plastic, where the community and organisation are cross-pollinating each other with ideas, insights and enthusiasm. When talking to the people behind these organisations, it was clear they viewed leadership differently: it wasn't the typical missionary, a single-minded value quest, the macho-this-way-forward leadership we historically have seen from organisations, but an empathetic, listening, empowering leadership that's all about growing people and people growing the organisation.

The People Transformation Canvas

We all have something we want to see changed, improved or even removed from our lives. What we seek to improve is often connected to what we view as a good life: as The Good Life survey, shows, there's a pivot away from status and money towards simpler living, better health and better connections with friends. Do you relate to this in your own life?

There are as many challenges and personal struggles as there are people in the world, so for the purpose of overview, I've reduced the complexity down to a framework of 12 overall triggers for personal transformation. These can work not only as an inspiration for you as an organisation to help transform and enable people but, equally impor-tantly, as a way to position your organisation against your competition or to discover new untapped market potential, for example, how LEGO is fuelling their customers' self-development and creativity through play (**Personal development**) whereas most other toys go for **Friends** or **Passion, fun and excitement**.

The most iconic brands are often built on a strong human insight, like LEGO's, that taps into our inherent human ability to play. An insight is like a looking glass into your thoughts and feelings, a voice formulating an unmet need or an indistinct feeling. Throughout my advertising career, I have always worked hard to unlock insights like these as they are the emotional building blocks of a strong and lasting brand platform.

The Movember movement's grow-a-beard-challenge might have started as a jest among friends, who wanted a more light-hearted approach to a disease killing millions of men every year, but the approach touched on a fundamental insight: men don't feel comfort-able talking about diseases or visiting the doctor as it might be per-ceived as unmanly. The three Australians turned the insight on its head and converted the unmanly into a fun, manly exercise of showcasing one's facial hair, and a campaign that spoke and made men laugh across cultures was born. Today, Movember is a global annual event encouraging men to grow a moustache during the month of Novem-ber to raise awareness of men's health issues, such as prostate cancer and testicular cancer. The founding principle of the organisation is of course all centred around men's health and stopping men from dying too young, which from a positioning stand-point is a hard one to own. Instead Movember wanted to play a more invigorating and enjoyable role in people's lives, building around **Passion, fun and excitement**. In less than ten years, Movember has become one of the world's Top 100 non-profits according to NGO Advisor, in large part thanks to its distinc-tive offering and position.[5]

In the fast-paced world of marketing, we often forget the most basic element: playing a meaningful role in people's lives. If done right, it's not a gimmick, a short-lived mass-marketing message or an activation, but a relentless drive towards growing people. It's an outcome people can feel, which will inevitably lead to a transformation, a change in their lives. Let's take a look at the 12 triggers and how they can serve as an inspiration to create relevance.

The People Transformation Canvas

Home: Providing people with a safe and secure environment for themselves and significant others.

Example: Lifestyle brand, KonMari, is on a mission towards simpler living: Tidy your space, transform your life.

Romance: Enhancing the ability of people to find love and discover new meaningful connections.

Example: Dating platform Bumble challenges female users to make the first move, basically eliminating the bro-culture of other dating platforms.

Family: Nurturing deeper connections with family members.

Example: The upscale hotel Wyndham offers a digital detox program, called Reconnected, addressing the vital need for quality family time over screen time.

Friends: Improving friendships and connections and giving a sense of belonging.

Example: Kind Snacks says: "Do the kind thing for your body, your taste buds & your world."

Mindfulness: Unlocking the possibility for people to discover a new, deeper meaning of altruism, self-esteem, forgiveness, ethics, dignity and respect.

Example: The app Calm is on a mission to make people happier and healthier through mindfulness.

Work: Adding to people's professional development.

Example: LinkedIn says: "To connect the world's professionals to make them more productive and successful."

Finances: Providing people with the skills and resources to feel economically secure.

Example: Next bank enables young people to achieve their financial goals no matter what they are.

Health: Improving people's physical health and well-being.

Example: Discovery incentivises people to become healthier.

Personal development: Making people understand their motivations and fears and helping them realise their goals.

Example: RYU says, "We're here to help you achieve more than your gym goals, RYU is here for your life goals."

Passion, fun and excitement: Helping people explore new horizons, new experiences and follow their passions.

Example: Red Bull's relentless focus on "giving wings" to daredevils.

Societal contribution: Providing people with a possibility to contribute to something greater than themselves and to experience community care and service.

Example: Precious Plastic's fight against plastic pollution.

Emotional well-being: Giving people increased confidence, security, vitality and emotional well-being.

Example: Always is committed to empowering young girls and women around the world.

Throughout the book, you have come across text boxes with real life stories about change, about challenges overcome, about getting on the other side of a crisis from individuals like Rich Faber who, despite coming from a lower-middle class family, found the guts to change majors or Greta Valvonytė's captivating story of giving her grandmother the confidence to travel. These stories are either shared on question-and-answer community sites like Quora.com or shared with me personally per e-mail. Each one of these stories have moved me and should serve as a steadfast reminder to you that, despite being in an organisation big or small, despite having a busy day every day or despite the complexities of the marketing space, it's about *real* people. Use these stories to be curious and understand the small and big changes we all go through in life. These testimonials are all marked with one of the 12 transformational triggers from the canvas and its icon from **Family** to **Finances** to add perspective and for you to explore where an organisation can really make a transformative difference in someone's life. In a transparent market, there is no space for bullshitting, but living offers plenty of challenges and opportunities that require real leadership and a willingness to answer the one question: WHO can you help people become?

Unsurprisingly, motivating people pays off at the cash register

When you as an organisation dare to play a meaningful role and help people cope with life's challenges, stronger bonds are forged. According to a 2015 piece of research, "The New Science of Customer Emotions"[6] by Scott Magids, Alan Zorfas and Daniel Leemon, brands that provide emotional motivators like *"Enjoy a sense of well-being"* (feel that life measures up to expectations and that balance has been achieved; seek a stress-free state without conflicts or threats) to *"Feel a sense of freedom"* (act independently, without obligations or restrictions) have a higher chance of enabling people to act on these motivations and consequently unlock sales.

The motivators identified in the research all touch on the People Transformation Canvas as these are the basis for any push towards self-actualisation.

"For example, the sense that a home furnishings store 'helps me be creative' inspires consumers to shop there more often" states the research. The authors explain how after a major bank introduced a credit card for Millennials that was designed to inspire emotional connection, use among the segment increased by 70%, and new account growth rose by 40%. The brands that can truly find the right WHO void to motivate people on their personal journey can potentially see a sales increase and bridge the gap between intent and action – and between a nice-sounding purpose and people acting on it.

Simply put, the brands that have the strongest, differentiating motivational pitch win at the cash register. The app Blinkist's clear focus on inspiring and motivating people to learn more has seen the start-up become one of the fastest growing in Europe, with over €30 million in funding and six million users.

Plus, a surprise find

But the research also discovers how the biggest potential for growth is surprisingly with the customers who already love your brand. How do you engage them more? Across categories and brands, the study concludes that, although there is a value increase in each customer segment when brands use the triggers to target customer behaviours, the highest potential is among a brand's most loyal customers, who are 52% more valuable, on average. The study also showed how it's important to target people with the right motivation: the research shows how the credit card designed with Millennials in mind threw up some surprising insights, such as that *"protect the environment"* and *"be the person I want to be"* were key motivators in the banking category for that age group. Typically, the banking sector would speak to motivations like a desire to *"feel secure"* or to *"succeed in life."* Essentially, the Millennials are buying not the product or service but what it enables them to become.

For an organisation, it's important to identify the right transformational triggers and avoid falling into the category's stereotypical promises but rather look for the real strong insight into people's lives. Or use the canvas as an inspiration to find your WHO void. Where can you stand out from competition and own a transformational role in people's lives?

From a brand building standpoint, there is more value in people feeling interdependence with a brand than simply liking it. As someone who loves cooking, Aarstiderne delivers value through its fresh, varied produce and recipes constantly pushing me to achieve my goals. There's an interdependence that would be tough to wave goodbye to.

Shaping a new North Star

Let me ask you a question. Is there anything you would like to change about yourself? Anything you would like to become better at? You don't have to get pen and paper out and start writing your list. Trust me, mine is long. Of course, we all have stuff we want to change from the smaller things in life like cutting down on time spent in front of the television to quitting those TV snacks to bigger challenges such as spending more time with our kids or finding a more meaningful career. And those battles continue throughout life.

Years ago, I did a series of interviews with people about their dreams as part of a project called "Project Dreams." And it was interesting to observe how younger people saw the world as a white canvas where everything was possible and ambitions were sky-high, from becoming a world-renowned fashion designer to visiting every country in the world. As the people I interviewed became older and had kids, their aspirations focused more on their professional careers, their material assets and the good health and well-being of their children. As people turned into grandparents, most of the aspirations were passed on as a baton to the younger generation – hoping for that grandson to make it into university or maybe one day become a doctor or lawyer. This is the lifelong opportunity for organisations to play a transformative role in people's lives – and it has to be enabling because at the end of the day, the only one who can make the change happen is people themselves. It's all about giving people a platform for their self-actualisation.

A real change story about work

This innate fear of failure is what kept me from tackling different business ideas that I had come up with. I was always so scared of pitching an idea or looking for investors because I was terrified of my prospects not working out. I also struggled a lot with finding the self-confidence to move past this initial stage and get the ball rolling. Overcoming these struggles is a fight I lead daily – I'm definitely not perfect, and there are still days when I feel a cloud of self-doubt come over me. Nonetheless, I'm a work in progress and it gets easier as the days go by. Nowadays, I'm not scared of failing and I'm even more confident in my ideas than I ever was. It took a long time, but I understand now that failure is, in some cases, a true necessity. Failure is, in my eyes, the best teacher out there.[7]

– Danny Morel, Founder of Intero Real State and CEO Inc 500, on Quora.com

District Vision: what happens when you put your mind to it

When Max Vallot and Tom Daly started District Vision, they discovered an opportunity in the market: make glasses for people to run in because normal sunglasses were too delicate or uncomfortable to run with and the other running sunglasses in the market were, well, too sporty and ugly. The glasses are sold at a premium compared to other running glasses, but for District Vision it's not about the product but about bringing people – or the community as District Vision calls them – on a transformational journey towards mindful running. It's about WHO their community can become.

I was curious about the thinking behind the concept and jumped on a call with the two founders, Max Vallot and Tom Daly,[5] who originate, respectively, from Germany and England but who now live in New York. They had earlier worked for fashion brands and felt a frustration with the way luxury brands were behaving and being marketed. What inspired them to create District Vision was really their own experiences coming from yoga and their own early experiments with mindful running and the community around it. Tom explains:

> *We felt because of the backgrounds that we came from, we're ulti-*
> *mately part of creating insecurity in people in order to sell products*
> *especially in the luxury end, so how can we flip that system on its*
> *head and ultimately serve a community through making people's*
> *lives better. It's not that we really thought about it – I wish we were*
> *that smart!*
>
> *We were hungry for new perspectives, feeding a curiosity out*
> *of our own experience, It's a community we became part of*
> *and that inspired us immensely, to put something out there and*
> *then hopefully we would be able to give something back to the*
> *community.*

It's obvious from the conversation that District Vision doesn't see itself as a missionary but rather as an equal, as a community member, and they keep coming back to how they feel a responsibility towards that community.

It's a notion that I picked up in other conversations with the likes of Wheelys, Dave Hakkens, RYU and Suop, who also saw themselves as being part of a community where dialogue is key. It's the community that's conversing, which I earlier mentioned as the power of the individual – many-to-many – a continuous dialogue.

"*If you talk about goals, it's really about people's transformational journey,*" continue Tom and Max.

> *Whether it's running for the first time, or running a 5k or 10K or mar-*
> *athon, or combining running and meditation for the first time or*
> *whatever they're doing, when they have undergone these jour-*
> *neys within the context of what we offer they have a different rela-*
> *tionship with the brand and they want to be part of what we do.*

This is not business-as-usual. There's a heartfelt curiosity towards what happens when mind and body are aligned. District Vision must be doing something right: from 2016–2017, they grew more than 300% and are present in more than 100 retailers and fashion stores around the United States. District Vision didn't, like other running glasses companies, position themselves on functionality or pure aesthetics but took a completely different approach. They aim to play a transformative role, one that's both touching on **Emotional well-being** and **Health.** District Vision takes each runner on a journey of discovery to experience the increased performance when mind and body works together. Without doubt, District Vision has found its WHO void and has created a position in the market that didn't exist before by truly understanding runners. For any competitor who want to maintain a premium price, District Vision has just made it harder by establishing a strong, distinct and valued brand. Going forward, District Vision can further explore how they can charge for this transformation across services, events, activations or by creating new transformative retail experiences. This is something Red Bull has been extremely successful at by expanding its promise of transformation across everything from global events to a growing media empire. It's less about the product, the red and blue cans, as the transformation moves centre stage. Eventually, it's readying these organisations for a post-consumerist world as they have more to offer than mere physical products.

A brand that gives you wings

Talking about Red Bull, they can barely be labelled as an energy drink company anymore because they have a relentless focus on giving people wings or, as their mission statement reads, "*To energise people when they need it.*" Red Bull is enabling people to tackle even the most extreme challenges and has created a successful media and event offering people love to engage with. Red Bull makes people tell their stories, travel the world, explore and push their own personal boundaries. Without doubt, Red Bull is a transformative brand, and its customers and employees feel part of the brand, live the brand, get transformed by the brand. People don't buy the red and blue cans, they buy the outcome: feeling energised to go further! They embrace that "*I can do*" attitude, and Red Bull is there to support people's bold endeavours, from building music studios for up-and-coming musicians to giving a world stage to obscure extreme sports, that were previously considered niche, like cliff diving. Within the multitude of Red Bull offerings, there's simply a braver you to be explored, enabled and transformed!

That said, a genuine transformative brand should always aim for a complete positive contribution whereas Red Bull has issues like the ingredients, the high-calorie content, the limited recycling and other environmental tolls, which ultimately might harm how people will view the brand as a true personal enabler going forward. The logic goes, "*Why would a brand that's out there to challenge me, make me better try to directly or indirectly harm me in other areas?*"

People don't buy the product, but the change they wish to see in their lives

The WHO void is a transformative position you can own and, as importantly, activate in people's lives. When looking to activate your transformative promise, it might be just under the tip of your nose. Take the camera maker Canon, whose following consists of professionals and happy amateurs alike with a passion for snapping great-looking photos. You probably have laughed at your local corner store's photographic skills on its menu or its web presence. Somehow, they succeed making the food or clothes look even more appalling than in real life. With limited resources, local business owners are hardly to blame for falling behind with their photography. Google's seemingly untouchable algorithms weren't helping the matter. In a campaign, Canon turned people into an army of the willing with the campaign slogan, "*Local business never looked so good.*"[8] Partnering with Google's Local Guides, Canon linked its photography users with local businesses, helping to highlight local business owners via photos alongside educational content featuring the photographers. Canon's Nordic following skyrocketed, while small businesses earned well deserved customers and Canon's users got their photos exposed to a greater audience. Canon gave their customers a platform to "*be like a professional photographer*" (the WHO). If your passion is photography, there's nothing better than seeing your photos come alive and being used (especially if you're an amateur). It has so far been a one-off campaign, but there might be more to explore and own for Canon whether it's **Work** or **Passion, fun and excitement.**

How an oat milk is really, really personal

Let me give you another example of an organisation that's found a meaningful role to play in people's lives. The Swedish company Oatly was founded back in the 1990s and is based on research from Lund University about turning oats into nutrient-rich milk. It's become a fast-growing alternative to milk across Scandinavia and it's quickly expanding into other markets. Oatly's transformative promise is to "*make it easy for people to turn what they eat and drink into personal moments of healthy joy without recklessly taxing the planet's resources in the process.*"

I had a video call with their global chief creative officer, John School-craft,[9] to better understand their journey. And John explained:

> We took away the marketing department and this might sound weird, but it's actually the greatest thing we've done. Because marketing departments are really poorly equipped to generate great work. They like to look at numbers on spreadsheets. When we removed the marketing department and replaced it with a creative department, we created a system where we could brief ourselves, do the work and then approve our own work which means there is technically nothing stopping us from creating something world-class every single time we write an ad, or design a shelf-wobbler, or work with farmers to create a more sustainable future. This is core to everything we do.

And you can definitely feel that Oatly has a different, tongue-in-cheek approach to their mission, brand and the world of marketing. One of their posters read: "*If we had hired a food stylist, a photographer and an ad agency, this poster would probably have been more successful.*"

John is very conscious about the role Oatly plays in people's lives and how the brand has to appear down-to-earth, honest and human at all contact points. In the beginning he even added his own e-mail and phone number for people to contact him, if they didn't like a product, and he wrote each one of them back, often adding a little poem. "*The whole idea of building a cult is that you interact with people in different, non-corporate ways.*" John explains: "*When Arla (the Swedish-Danish dairy giant) asked, 'What is your favourite breakfast?' in a Facebook competition, there were 900 responses stating Oatly oat milk. Once you give people a reason to be on your side, they can become super, super loyal.*" Oatly is nudging its customers to choose a planet-friendly, healthy alternative to milk – and with that a plant-based lifestyle, but by using fun rather than the scare tactics so often used in environmental or health campaigning.

> *If you ask me, are we a world-saving brand, I would probably say no because a brand cannot save the world by themselves. However every single litre of oat milk that is sold instead of a litre of cow's milk saves the planet 73% in greenhouse gas emissions. We might be looking to contribute to the planet in multiple ways, but the fact that the more we sell, the better off the planet is, is something very few companies can claim. . . . I'm saying look, we're just trying to inspire people, one person at a time, to make some personal changes on their own because we believe in collective change and the power of people making personal decisions that benefit not only themselves but other humans. If you use a company as a vehicle to contribute to society that must be more interesting in the long term than just a vehicle to ensure your shareholders have more profit in their books.*

Historically, Oatly has an innovative, patented formula behind its oat milk, but what drives the business is their belief in transforming people through healthy, climate-friendly moments of joy – something people across the world are increasingly more open to. And John makes sure to maintain the joyous approach, which also emanates from his laughter bursts throughout the call: "*We have a very specific kind of non-brandy way of looking at things that's more human. And sure, that undoubtedly has something to do with my own personal cynicism.*" The carefree, dialogue with people is working, and that might be the recipe: staying personal and giving people a hand to live more plant-based in a fun and humorous way! It's another example of an organisation embracing: **Passion, fun and excitement.**

From start-ups to multinationals, across categories, across countries, more and more examples are emerging of organisations embracing a transformative role, a new way of looking at leadership. Take a Washington hotel, Eaton Hotel, in the United States's political heartland. Eaton is fostering activism and social consciousness by featuring a co-working space, events, and speakers on topics ranging from climate change to race relations. The hotel facilities are not the usual list but include artist studios, a radio station and a 50-seater movie theatre that's screening movies on social good and human rights. That's definitely not your average hotel. Founder and President Katherine Lo explains the thinking in an interview to Fast Company: "*I feel like there is a zeitgeist happening among the younger generations. These hotels are going to get built anyway, so I thought 'why not take the framework of hotels and really reconfigure them and funnel them towards social change?'.*"[10] Eaton hotel has found an exciting WHO void to own nurturing the activist within their guests: **Societal contribution.** In the US capital where politics are part of the very fabric, one would have thought, that would be a no-brainer position to aspire towards for any hotel.

Great leaders never walk alone

If you put a strong focus on your brand and its mission, that's how people will perceive you – like a missionary, an egoist or an idealist. Think about your typical dinner party; you don't want to be seated next to the guy who keeps talking about himself and his accomplishments, no matter how world-saving they might be. It's no different in branding, communication or in leadership. It's not why you exist that makes people relate or love you; it's how you make them feel better or how you complete them. Great leaders never walk alone.

From activism, running glasses, hygiene pads, granola bars, cameras, running shoes and men's health to oat milk, people are willing to pay for the change they want to see in their lives. But beware of treating personal transformation as simply a campaign; people can smell it like a friend giving self-serving advice. It's a transformative promise, a steadfast positioning. According to Sustainable Brands' "The Good Life Report,"[11] 80% of people surveyed said they would be loyal to a brand that helps them live The Good Life, but most companies fail to do so. 65% say that products and services do not currently help them live The Good Life. There is tremendous potential in exploring the WHO void. And, yes, transformative organisations, I would argue, are better at motivating people, but it's not simply about sales. As detailed in previous chapters, there is little status in buying things; it's more about self-actualisation, and as a society, we'll have to adapt more sustainable practices. The material riches in the Western world aren't bringing happiness, or at least the happiness is short-lived, like opening a Christmas present. People are searching for creating that meaning themselves. For a leader or an organisation, there are unlimited possibilities in exploring how to help people on that journey towards a good life. Change is difficult, but you should aim to deliver the tools, the motivation, the recipe or whatever else helps people to get over the finish line. Real leadership is measured not in sales but on what you can make others achieve. The younger generations are demanding that organisations find solutions to overconsumption – a pressure that will only increase. The conversation will eventually shift from better products to a better you and me.

Unlocking transformation by putting yourself in people's shoes (or asking them!)

What goal do I want to achieve?
What do I really want?
What do I want to change?
What do I want my life to be about?
Who do I want to be, and what experiences do I want to create?
Am I giving my best where I have my best to give?
What do I want to do more of each day?
How can I make the most of the situation?
What can I be the best at in the world?
What would make life more wonderful for me?
What am I grateful for?
How did I make a difference today?
What are the thoughts and things that make me happy?
How can I leave this place more beautiful than I found it?
What is my truth about this issue?

There is a friend for your many sides

You probably recognise how your friends play different roles in your life and also bring out different sides in you. It's potentially the same with leaders or organisations. Sadly, most purposes I come across are rather industry generic, like a soap company fighting for hygiene, or a bank believing in financial empowerment. When you build your organisation's promise around the transformative outcome, you expand the possibilities, and can potentially create your own blue ocean and leave your competitors outcrying one another. From a branding perspective, it also makes sense to aspire towards playing the biggest possible role in people's lives as a greater interaction strengthens the brand's distinctiveness and affinity.

Look at people's lives and the competitive landscape, and see where there is a potential for transformation. It's not who people are, it's who they can become. As an organisation you're answering people's call – and there is a lot brands can help people achieve because life is a constant battle to become a better version of ourselves. You've seen that in the real stories shared by people throughout the book as well from the many organisations already playing their part.

I call the organisations who strike the right balance "*transformative organisations*" or "*transformative brands*" as they're setting a new agenda for leadership, a new agenda for personal and organisational growth. They ask people not to believe in them or their corporate why but to believe in their own ability to bring about change. As an organisation, you have to change the perspective from "*What you deliver*" as an organisation to how you enable people towards "*Who they can become.*" Transformative brands sow the seeds and deliver the platform (from products or services to whatever you as an organisation can think of) to enable people to create the needed change. As more and more organisations are on a journey to find their higher reason to exist and build relevance with people or communities, it's about delivering a tangible change and not cheap words. Who is it you can truly help people become?

This outcome will be felt and valued, like Nike helping me rediscover my motivation for running with NikePlus or Aarstiderne teaching me how to cook more plant-based. It's a move away from the last decades of mass-marketing and brand centricity – "*You get this*" – to enabling people with a promise saying, "*You can do this.*" Any organisation can sell stuff, but very few can help people achieve their goals, moving the relationship from transactional to transformational and enabling people to feel more, see more, do more, become more!

The transformative organisation connects people's hearts with the heads and hands, pushing them towards action: "*This is what we're doing for someone else.*" Everyone in the organisation can see how enabling people, in turn, drives sales and brand affinity. The organisation's North Star is action oriented towards driving people to self-actualisation. We are our own biggest enemies of change, so if any organisation wants to move people, it begins with the individual "you" as this quote assigned to the religious leader Hillel the Elder simply states: "*If not you, who? If not now, when?*"

Key takeaways

1   Most products and services are generic, asking WHO moves the organisation from low interest to high interest as it enables people to achieve their goals.

2   The WHO void is a transformative position you can own in people's lives.

3   The People Transformation Canvas identifies 12 triggers where an organisation can help transform and enable people, in areas ranging from their health to playing a bigger role in society.

4   Always deliver a tangible outcome: make people experience the transformation.

5   Brands prosper when they move people towards better, more meaningful lives.

Questions to ask yourself

1   Look at the competitive landscape. What transformative role can you play in people's lives?

2   Where do your organisation's products or services intersect with what people really need?

3   Personally, what brands matter most to you? Do they play a specific role in your life?

4   Do you gather insights and data on the role you play in people's lives?

5   Can you play an even greater role in people lives?

7 The business case

If not now, when?

People have taken back the power on food. They feel disconnected from the food they eat, and they are reconnecting, with or without us. Asking relentlessly where their food comes from, who are the people behind the brands, what are the values the companies behind the products hold dear. Food is politics. Each time we eat and drink, consciously or not, we are voting for the world, the society, the agriculture we want.[1]

– Valérie Hernando-Presse, Global Marketing Director, Danone

VALÉRIE
HERNANDO - PRESSE

Bridging the gap between intent and action

The Chinese artist and activist Ai Weiwei once said: "*Creativity is the power to act.*"[2] And I couldn't agree more, because without action everything is simply nice intentions, doodles on paper or unfulfilled ambitions. Think about it. Every New Year you might pledge to drink or smoke less, only to realise nothing has changed. You might plan for a great retirement, but you don't put enough money aside. You buy the gym membership to become fit, but it's the TV and time with friends that win time and time again. For your organisation, it's about helping people bridge that gap between intent and action.

Studies show us that people vote with their wallet for the organisations that they care about. In a research study from Edelman[3] from early 2017 across 14 countries and 14,000 people, 57% of those asked said they would buy or boycott a brand based on the brand's position on a social or political issue. That said, the underlying sales data reflects a different story, where people's aspiration towards buying better products aligned with their values across social and environmental factors, doesn't play out. There is a gap between formulated intent and action. According to The Good Life Report[4] 65% of people say they want to purchase from purposeful brands, but only 26% follow through and reward companies for their responsible practices by purchasing the products. That's a market potential of 39%, if an organisation can truly motivate people to follow through on aspirations or dreams.

The running shoes still stuck in the closet or the chips that seem to be eating themselves show that intent is not enough. Let's say you're in the supermarket and animal welfare is important to you, but next to the €9 animal welfare guaranteed sausage is a pack of discount sausages at €4. Your wife and kids – or friends – are in the cinema, so you don't have to defend your choice to them, and you put the discount sausages in the trolley, probably with an excuse like, *"The sausages are locally made, they probably treat the animals ok."* This gap is proven again and again in surveys.

One US study shows that there is a 46% gap between the intention to exercise and actually exercising, and nearly 80% of adults in the United States do not get the minimum weekly 150 minutes of moderate to vigorous exercise recommended by the World Health Organisation. The intent is there, but don't we all need a little push from behind? A helping hand? A word of encouragement?

When we do things that don't fit our value system, dissonance arises; and according to the psychologist behind the theory, Leon Festinger,[5] we'll try to limit the dissonance or the lack of balance of our belief and values with our action. The theory is used to explain why, for example, smokers, who know smoking kills, can still smoke. The smokers simply minimise the dissonance by distorting their value or belief system, saying things like, *"It doesn't happen to me."* Your actions have to correspond to your value system, so when you do something like purchase a brand, you'll have to defend that choice to yourself and your values. The Arrow focuses on driving people towards action, because if you as an organisation want to push people towards self-actualisation, neither aspirations nor values are enough. You have to get people out of their bad habits or remove the inner critical voice and push them towards change.

"I did it!"

Three powerful words we have all cried out when we accomplished a personal goal like a marathon or even when we finally crossed cleaning-up-the-attic off our to-do list: *"I did it!"* It's a feeling of accomplishment. Yet very few organisations remember to ask anything – besides buying – and if shouting *"buy, buy, buy"* is all you're doing as an organisation, no wonder you're treated like a sales guy rather than as a welcome friend. It pays to ask people to change in big and small ways, from your organisation's transformative *"Just-do-it"* promise to a campaign or activation level.

The Ariel Turn to 30° campaign, launched in 2006, was one of the first to promote washing clothes at 30° rather than the previous standard of 40° or even 60°. The message was simple, and people responded. According to an Ipsos MORI[6] survey from the UK, the number of people washing at 30° went from 2% in 2002 to 17% in 2007, and 85% of these people said they changed thanks to the campaign. Ariel gave people the "*I did it*" feeling and hopefully made them feel better about doing the laundry. People want organisations to help them live better lives.

Another example is when Nike in 2017 created Nike Unlimited: a full-sized LED running track that brings to life the saying, "*An athlete's greatest competition will always be himself.*" Individuals can race against an avatar of themselves, pacers, Nike athletes or record-breaking performances and will be given feedback. Again, Nike is pushing people towards realising their goals by asking when. It's even nailed into their credo: "*Just do it.*"

Purpose has to evolve. There was always this nagging feeling in the back of my head that there existed a disconnect between the corporate purpose and the people it was supposed to inspire. One question kept popping up in my head again and again: with all these great organisations espousing truly life-bettering goals, why is the needle not moving faster? What is holding progress back? You probably know the feeling of having forgotten your keys. Imagine that the keys are inside the house, but you're only looking outside the house for them. That's how I feel about purpose where most organisations look to a bigger role to play in society outside the organisation, while the answer to change lies within people.

Businesses want to be part of the solution to the social and environmental mess we're in. In 2019, 48% of CEOs[7] said they were implementing sustainability in their operations, from improving hygiene to expanding Internet access to environmental protection. Many organisations are rushing to jump on board the corporate purpose bandwagon, but very few organisations are turning their purpose towards truly enabling people to become more and to push them towards self-actualisation. It's the realisation, it's the fulfilment, it's the change, it's the transformation, it's that little powerful word called "WHEN" that matters.

Leaders and organisations might have an ambition about inspiring people to live better lives, but without asking that powerful word "WHEN," it's like a journey without a time schedule.

When I was a kid, my dad was teaching me how to bicycle. I practiced again and again, always with my dad by my side to keep the balance on the two-wheeled ride. And I still remember the first time I could cry, "*Dad, dad, dad, let go!*" and I rode the bicycle all by myself without his helping hand. That's when you as an organisation build a bridge over the gap between intent and action, between heart and hand. You create change, you don't just talk about it. As an organisation, you should be the supporting hand on the back. If you never ask when, change will stay wishful thinking.

From wishful thinking to when

How can you as an organisation motivate people to act on important issues in their lives? The action-focused approach dictated by the Arrow sets your organisation apart from your peers. It's no coincidence. As previously explained, the methodology is inspired by coaching, which is in itself a goal-oriented discipline. The Arrow is focused on enabling people to act on important issues in their lives. The stringent focus on change is the secret sauce behind the methodology rather than simply being a moon shot mantra on a boardroom plaque.

RYU, the Canadian sportswear brand, makes clothing it describes as "*technical, high-performance urban athletic apparel that is built around you, the individual,*" and it's ambitious on its customers' behalf: "*We're here to help you achieve more than your gym goals, RYU is here for your life goals.*" And RYU doesn't take its commitment lightly. In 2017, it launched a promotion giving people discounts on their apparel if they had realised their goals like lost weight or gained muscle mass over the previous year.

I immediately felt drawn to RYU's goal-oriented approach and got hold of CEO Marcello Leone[8] to better understand the business and its philosophy.

Marcello shared how he was born into the world of retail as an Italian immigrant whose parents started a shoe business that later became a big importer of high-end Italian fashion brands. After some restructuring of the family business, Marcello and his wife felt they had to do something different. Marcello had just turned 43. He had earlier invested some money in RYU, originally a martial arts brand, because he loved what RYU stood for: respect your universe.

"*We started a journey building a company, sticking to the principle of respect and building that culture based on everyone – our customers, their needs, their ability to feel being a part of a group, feeling safe, inclusive. Feeling that there are companies that care for humanity and what we stand for,*" Marcello explained. He and his wife decided to take full control of the company but maintain respect for its heritage. For Marcello it was also a very personal mission because, as an Italian immigrant kid, he always felt like an outsider and was bullied in school: "*We wanted to make a difference that speak to all individuals not just to one segregated group.*" This is an interesting inclusive stand in a time that's becoming increasingly divided and where more and more organisations adopt an activist approach rallying for their beliefs, which ends up being an exclusive movement. "*It's about respecting your choices, your journey, what you stand for. It is knowing at our core* that we are all human and that it's our differences that make us extraordinary," says Marcello.

In a highly competitive market, the brand's stringent focus on their customers' transformation is paying off. RYU grew to eight retail locations in 2018, saw nine consecutive quarters of growth and has expanded into the US market.[9] Marcello talks about "*meaningful retail*" and views its locations as experiential centres where people can get together, talk, use the in-store gyms and meet trainers who represent different disciplines. "*As we're successful in the journey, we strive to give back to our communities wherever we are,*" says Marcello. "*We wish to charge no one for that, for bringing people together, making an inclusive environment where people can connect and share, and be a part of something that they don't have to be supreme at in order to be recognised, to participate without charge because we just wanna do good and give back.*"

This is where RYU is different from other sports and wellness brands: it's open for everyone no matter their experience, background or goals. It's not about the athlete but about people as Marcello pinpoints:

> *Wouldn't it be a beautiful thing if we don't only celebrate one person or individual, one major athlete, but would look to develop an ethos or culture, a tribe based on human performance and thinking about each individual first? On that perspective RYU was born. You can't just flag about it, you have to live it and believe it.*

The role RYU plays in people's lives is really a differentiator their customers can feel from the service and products to in-store. RYU receives multiple e-mails daily from customers grateful for the goals they have achieved. As Marcello paraphrases: "'*I inspired myself to leave home, I lost 65 pounds, I changed my world, I am happy, and now I am getting married' – those are the celebrations that we speak to.*"

Marcello is in no doubt as to what's fuelling the brand's growth. It's the fact that RYU is there for people whatever their goals are: "*Our stand is that we do good for all, we are inclusive, we do not judge, we're here to help. Employees are not employees – they are partners. They love the brand. They're enrolled. It's their business. It's their goal to leave a mark. It's their ability to do more than simply be an employee.*" Marcello is excited about the journey going forward, but he also talks about humbleness and how it's important to daily earn the respect from the community: "*If you don't have an emotional connection, if you don't believe in it, if you're not a part of it, who cares? It's a beautiful thing to be able to build a business that serves personal performance in motion, in mind and in spirit.*"

When an organisation's skills and acumen go into enabling people to move from aspiration into action, better lives get unlocked and better business results follow. Sometimes we just need that little push, that little nudge in the right direction to make the wanted change come true from "*I can't do it*" to "*I can do it!*" It's an imperative, it's a rallying cry turning intention into actually motivating us to do something about it. Motivation is the basic drive for all of our actions. All of our behaviours, actions, thoughts, and beliefs are influenced by our inner drive to succeed, whether it's to realise ourselves through creativity or an incentive-based goal like relieving hunger or a need for love.

Own a share of people's daily lives

In the war for people's attention, it's important that, as an organisation, you have a meaningful role to play – and the clearer the better – from your transformative promise to your marketing activities. It might seem contrary to common business sense for Apple to show its iPhone users the time they spend on its devices as some might be heavy users, but by enabling this, users can better determine how the time spent corresponds with what they want – and how they need to change. Maybe they spend too much time on leisure like games and watching YouTube instead of work. Rather than jumping to the conclusion that spending time on my iPhone is bad, it might actually be what I spend my time doing on the iPhone that's less aligned with my personal goals. Apple is making people call the shot on what's important with the app Screen Time. Across any of your customers' day, a number of activities are stealing focus or needing more attention, and this is a moment to make a difference. P&G's laundry detergent brand Ariel uncovered that 70% of children in India believe household chores are women's work. Ariel encouraged men and their sons across the nation to "*Share the Load*" of washing. This was obviously a hugely controversial topic in a male-dominated country like India. The campaign created lots of conversations but ultimately also created a discussion around what women spend and should spend their time on. By the end of the day, don't we all need help with changing bad habits? Pinterest[10] shared in 2019 how "*sustainable living*" is the most searched term around sustainability (more than 69% since the year before), while searches for "*sustainable living for beginners*" is up 265% particularly among Millennials and Gen Z. These are people actually searching for help as they want to make small changes in their everyday lives, like getting rid of plastic or wasting less in their home and office.

Don't get lost in issues, focus on the role

I don't like to use the wording "*issues*" or "*causes.*" Too many organisations are paying lip service to the big challenges of our time. Statistics will tell you what people say they care about, but, if that is not translated into what people are trying to achieve (WHO), impact doesn't follow. It's better to use the WHO as it's linked to what people are aspiring towards or trying to accomplish. As an organisation, you translate an intangible issue like food waste into how it matters to people: being a good mother teaching her kids not to waste food. Focus on the goals and aspiration. See how you can give more time or focus to those activities during the day that matters for people or eliminate those activities that steal or limit time. The business idea behind Blinkist is essentially getting customers to focus more on learning whenever time allows (WHEN) and to become wiser (WHO) – and the non-fiction (WHAT) in 15-minutes formats (HOW) makes it easier for them. Think about how you can help people either by strengthening their focus on an activity, like Apple, or by removing obstacles, like Blinkist and Ariel.

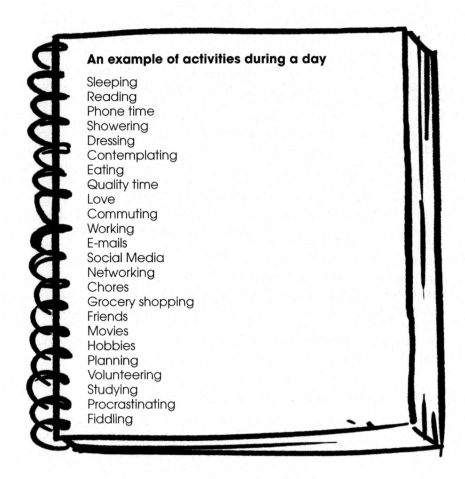

An example of activities during a day

Sleeping
Reading
Phone time
Showering
Dressing
Contemplating
Eating
Quality time
Love
Commuting
Working
E-mails
Social Media
Networking
Chores
Grocery shopping
Friends
Movies
Hobbies
Planning
Volunteering
Studying
Procrastinating
Fiddling

One of the organisations that have been successful at owning an important piece of their customers' day – their sleep – is South Korea-based furniture brand Cherish. In December 2016 they introduced a sleep consultation service in stores: Sleep D advises people on how they can improve the quality of their sleep through interior design and furnishings. That's a valuable position directly connected to the role the product potentially can play in people's lives.

Or take something as simple as hair that people can spend hours on in front of the mirror every morning (and every possible break). Unilever realised it was getting harder to cut through the noise with their broad portfolio of hair care products. From online search patterns, Unilever knew people had a great interest in hair, but rather than launching a product response to that interest, Unilever launched a YouTube channel called All Things Hair where they engaged vloggers (video bloggers) to create relevant advice. And people loved it. In just ten weeks, All Things Hair become the number one hair channel, amassing over 50 million views[11] – a testament to the fact that people wanted advice and help with their hair. The many influencers on the channel also gave Unilever much needed eye-height to its customers and a great showcase for all that Unilever can do with their hair products.

There are many possibilities during a day to transform people. Why not when they cook? One Swedish supermarket chain, ICA, saw interest from people in eating more climate friendly, so they launched climate-guided recipes with one, two or three leaves to indicate how environmentally friendly the recipes are, from ingredients' seasonality to carbon emissions. It's worth looking to own a share of people's lives.

The business of changing behaviours for the better

Changing behaviours is really one of the most difficult things to achieve. That's why it's so important to put a stringent focus on transformation, because it's the ultimate barrier to personal development and business success. Transformative organisations get this and unleash transformative innovations across the organisation, from marketing initiatives to product and services.

In 2017, Nike released On Demand: a one-on-one WhatsApp chat encouraging athletes to achieve their goals based on big data and experts' knowledge. The chat provides personalised nutrition advice, workout reminders and running routes, for example. The chat also helps athletes recommit to goals if their activity level drops. Over six weeks, Nike On Demand enabled 240 athletes to take their game to the next level, and the users embraced it: 83% would recommend Nike On Demand to a friend, and 81% would use the service again.[12] It pays to push people towards their goal; if you're selling apparel, active athletes are good for business.

Another small but powerful example is from the Unilever brand, Lifebuoy, that was founded on William Lever's goal to stop cholera in Victorian England in 1895 and today continues its commitment with a social mission to bring safety, security and health to one billion people through the active promotion of hand washing with soap. It's a very specific promise, making it easier to align the organisation with its efforts to achieve the audacious goal.

In India, Lifebuoy targeted a specific period, Kumbh Mela, a mass Hindu pilgrimage held every three years and attracting 100 million people. But it went even further and targeted a specific time of day, when the risk of bad sanitation and foodborne diseases was high: when people were eating. Lifebuoy partnered with more than 100 restaurants and cafés at the festival and placed soaps in the toilets. Every time the festival goers placed a food order, the first *roti* (traditional Indian flatbread) carried a heat stamped message "*Lifebuoy se haath dhoye kya?*" (Did you wash your hands with Lifebuoy?). A hard-to-ignore message delivered at the right time, and with more than 2.5 million branded rotis eaten, the impact was substantial.[13]

A real change story about finances

I feel like the queen of challenges, hahaha. . . . One of my most challenging was learning to live with no extra money when I kicked my husband out (he got his secretary pregnant). I went to the bank, but he beat me there and took our savings of $1400 out, leaving me nothing. I went on food stamps for a while to feed my son but climbed out of the hole. I got a master's degree and put all of my life challenges to use by counselling others. I never became dependent on anyone ever again and have conquered every mountain I've tried to climb. I tried to model to my two kids that even if you are down, you are never out.[14]

– *Barbara Meuleman, studied at California State University, Bakersfield, on Quora.com*

Because change is difficult, it's valuable

Change makes up the storyline of several Hollywood blockbusters like *When Harry Met Sally*, where Sally (played by Meg Ryan) tries to avoid turning into the cliché Harry (Billy Crystal) believes: "*men and women can't be friends without it leading to romance.*"[15] Through multiple chance encounters in their lives, Sally finally gives in to Harry in the final scene. It's helpful to deduct the complexity down to the individual level and try to walk in somebody else's shoes. Envision that person and then ask yourself, what stands in the way of moving from "*I want*" to "*I will*"? What keeps his or her goal from happening?

Unlocking action by putting yourself in people's shoes (or ask them!)

I want what by when?
Now what am I going to do about it?
How much time do I have?
How much time should I make for it?
Does my schedule reflect my priorities?
What can I do now to change this?
Is now the right time?
Is this the right forum?
What's holding me back?
Can anyone help me achieve what I want?

Digitalisation is opening up a host of new possibilities through apps, Internet of Things and gadgets as in the case with Apple's Screen Time. One of the companies that have embraced this opportunity is the health and well-being company Fitbit, which produces wearables that monitor your activity during a day. The company's transformative promise is: "*To empower and inspire you to live a healthier, more active life. We design products and experiences that fit seamlessly* into your life so you can achieve your health and fitness goals, what-ever they may be."[16] And there's plenty of people who want help with achieving their health and fitness goals. I'm one of them, and I'm not alone – Fitbit has grown in users from 6.7 million to 25.4 million since 2014.[16] Because change is so difficult, it's worth paying for. This is where transformative organisations have an edge as potentially they can charge for the outcomes people achieve, like becoming wiser, fitter or more skilled.

Technology allows you to quantify every action and reaction. Apps and smart devices give you the power, as an organisation, to measure people's very being, even as they sleep – and help them transform. Nike has launched NikePlus, Discovery has launched the Vitality App, and technology companies within their own rights are offering help for mind, body and soul from apps like Timeshifter, which helps you deal with jetlag. Sports giant Adidas has also ventured into the tech-enabling space with the launch of their All Day mobile app in 2017, designed to inspire and inform women, with daily content across four areas: movement, nutrition, rest and mindset. The app delivers exercise ideas and recipes, as well as offering performance tracking, with tips on how to optimise fitness and health, but also fea-tures regular challenges to engage and nudge women, plus workout playlists and yoga videos. We're just scratching the surface of how tech can help transform our lives for the better, and, for organisa-tions, it's a vital field to embrace. But never forget, ultimately change is about people, tech is simply a tool, no different from a yoga mat or pen and paper.

Turning people's motivation into marketing growth

As you've seen throughout this book, something truly interesting happens when an organisation becomes an enabler, a coach, a helper. We can discuss the challenge of digitalisation, lack of engagement or rising frustration with marketing today, but the diagnosis is clear. Growth in an open, pluralistic, transparent and pro-social market has to put people first. I was curious to better understand the correlation between organisations who motivate people to achieve small or big goals in their lives compared to the more traditional purpose approach, where the organisation pitches itself as the agent of change. It's the traditional purpose approach – "*Believe in us as an organisation to bring change*" ver-sus a transformative promise – "*Believe in your own ability to bring change.*" You've seen how one transformational organisation after the other has pushed people towards self-actualisation and, more importantly, action. My thesis is simple: if an organisation or leader motivates you, believes in you, energises you, there is a higher chance you'll follow through and act. Could a motivational and transformational pitch be the bridge across the intention–action gap? The missing piece in the puzzle?

Believe in people's ability to create change

Let me tell you a story about motivation from a social experiment I shot as a commercial years ago for a Danish unemployment fund Min A-kasse (roughly translated, "My unemployment fund"). Basically, you pay a monthly fee, and the fund provides insurance in case you become unemployed. All the competitors in the market talked about price or the quality of their service, but the client and I chose a different strategy: always stand by the unemployed. Losing a job is one of the most difficult periods in anybody's life, and on top of that, they face societal stigma. We set out to create a real, social experiment that would demonstrate what happens when you treat people with mistrust – as society does with the unemployed – although they're rightfully claiming their insurance payout. Or what happens when you treat people with trust. We enrolled two twins in the experiment, Anders and Jesper, without letting them know what was going to happen. First, we gave them an IQ test based on the Mensa guidelines. Then we asked the twins to come back the next week, when we would film a second IQ test, but this time an observer would watch them. What they didn't know was that we'd instructed the observer (a hired actor) to play, respectively, good cop and bad cop. Anders was treated with suspicion and mistrust from when he entered the room, and was subjected to remarks like, "*Didn't you bring your own pencil?*" "*Are you smart enough to answer that?*" or "*You're still not finished?*" Jesper was treated with smiles, support and encouraging words. In the end, the result was shocking. Anders' performance dropped 16% compared to the first test. It's part of a known psychological phenomenon called the Golem effect, in which lower expectations placed on individuals either by supervisors or the individual themselves lead to poorer performance. I think we all know that feeling from school, our family or the workplace. The campaign succeeded in sparking a conversation about how we treat the unemployed in society – and why we should treat people with trust, respect and encouragement rather than with mistrust and checks and balances. It's a cornerstone of my belief that, if you give people the ability to act, and if you trust them and encourage them, people blossom.

Transformative commercials versus traditional-purpose commercials

I wanted to explore the transformative approach further in an advertising or storytelling context. What's the effect of transformative commercials encouraging people to change for the better? We know there is this gap between intent and action: people say they want to buy from purposeful organisations and yet they most often don't. The earlier mentioned Good Life Report pinpointed that 39% didn't follow through on their goals or ambitions. That's a market potential of 39%, if you get it right as an organisation. Maybe all people need is that little push? Maybe they just want to feel understood and supported rather than listen to yet another organisation talking about its accomplishments and world bettering ambitions?

To test my thesis, I identified four commercials with a classic purpose approach ("*Believe in us as an organisation to bring change*") and four commercials with a transformative promise ("*Believe in your own ability to bring change*"). All the commercials are recent: five from 2018 and three from 2014–15.[17] Most of them were aired in the United States during the annual championship game of the National Football League, the Super Bowl, which is known as the most expensive commercial break in the world. In 2019, the television network, CBS, charged a record $5.25 million for just a 30-second spot.[18] It's going to be an important message for any organisation, if one is willing to spend so much money on the airtime. I thought this would be a great test bed.

Let me first explain a little more about the test parameters I was looking at while enrolling 299 participants in the test. Overall, I asked the participants to answer a number of questions and rate them from 1 to 7 (low to high score) across the parameters warmth (warm, friendly and likeable), competence (competent, capable and authentic) and motivation (relevant, energising and vigorous). Moreover, on a smaller sample basis, I looked at willingness to buy (WTB) and willingness to pay a premium (WTPP). If you do a quick search online, you can watch the commercials that I set out to test.

Transformative commercials

Always: "Like a Girl" (US, 2014, from Super Bowl)
Sport England: "This Girl Can" (UK, 2015)
Nike: "Dream Crazy" (US, 2018, from NFL season opener)
Land Rover: "Never Stop Discovering" (US, 2018)

Purposeful commercials

T-Mobile: "#Littleones" (US, 2018 from Super Bowl)
DB Export: "Brewtrolium" (New Zealand, 2015)
Hyundai: "Hope Detector" (US, 2018, from Super Bowl)
Budweiser: "Wind Never Felt Better" (US, 2018, from Super Bowl)

The Transformative commercials

Always: "Like a girl"

"Like a Girl" shows a fake casting-call where young women and men of different ages are asked to run or fight "*like a girl.*" The older boys and girls act out an insulting stereotype whereas the younger girls simply run and fight as hard as they can. The commercial encourages us to break free of stereotypes and redefine "*like a girl*" to mean just doing the very best you can.

Sport England: "This Girl Can"

"This Girl Can" shows women of all sizes, shapes and abilities participating in sport. We see the confident women's wiggling body parts, sweat and smiles, and lines are added throughout such as "*I jiggle therefore I am*" and "*I kick balls – deal with it.*" The commercial ends with "*This girl can*" hammering home the message that anyone can and should get active.

Nike: "Dream Crazy"

"Dream Crazy" shows a montage of people overcoming challenges and striving to become the best ever in their sport or becoming bigger than their sport. In the end it's revealed that American football quarterback, Colin Kaepernick, is the narrator with the words, "*Don't ask if your dreams are crazy, but if they're crazy enough.*"

Land Rover: "Never Stop Discovering"

"Never stop discovering" is a narrated montage showing a family going on an exploration of senses, smells and places like feeling the inside of a tree or running into a lake. The commercial ends with a shot of a Land Rover driving on a mountain road with the encouragement to "*Never stop discovering.*"

The purposeful commercials

T-Mobile: "#Littleones"

The 60-second commercial shows nine babies of different ethnicities as *Scandal* actress Kerry Washington delivers a message of openness: "*You come in with open minds that we are equal. Some people may see your differences and may be threatened by them, but you are unstoppable.*" The commercial ends with "*Change starts now. Are you with us? T-Mobile.*" Although the commercial uses the kind of motivational language and storytelling most commonly observed with transformative campaigns, I'll argue the focus is still on how T-Mobile celebrates diversity rather than an encouragement to you.

DB Export: "Brewtrolium"

"Brewtrolium" shows a world in peril from war and environmental challenges and shares how a brewery has made a biofuel from the yeast leftover after brewing DB Export and humorously tell people "*to drink DB Export to save the entire world.*"

Hyundai: "Hope Detector"

"Hope Detector" is a fictitious, live commercial showing Hyundai owners walking into a stadium through what appear to be regular security lines, but they're pulled aside to a room where they meet with cancer survivors through a screen thanking them for their donations to a non-profit because of their vehicle purchase.

Budweiser "Wind Never Felt Better"

"Wind Never Felt Better" shows a Dalmatian riding on the top of a wagon of Budweiser being hauled by Clydesdale horses through the California countryside, accompanied by Bob Dylan's "Blowin' in the Wind." In the background windmills are spinning. The text states that Budweiser is "*Now brewed with wind power.*"

The results

The test was done together with the University of Bari, Luca Petruzzellis, who's a professor of Marketing and Director of the BA and MS in Marketing, and his two team members: Valentina Mazzoli and Luigi Piper.[19]

I've been fortunate to work with Luca on a number of occasions and to teach at the university. 299 randomly selected individuals participated, with 56.1% women and 43.9% men between the ages of 17 and 68. Of the participants, 71.2% had a bachelor's degree or higher. Although the sample is small, it did show some interesting findings.

Transformative versus purposeful commercials

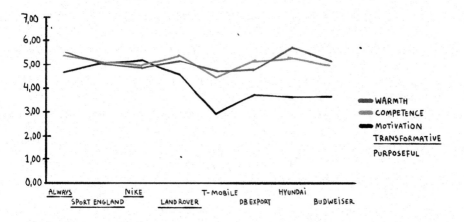

If you look at *warmth* (warm, friendly and likeable), which basically deals with how much our participants like the commercial and how they perceive the brand behind it after watching. All eight commercials do very well, with the lowest score of 4.7 for T-Mobile, rising to 5.74 for Hyundai. This is no big surprise as I would have expected these commercials to have been tested for likeability and similar factors before a massive marketing investment went into them. Before the test, I was nervous that the *competence* (competent, capable and authentic) parameter would take a dive when the brand took a transformative approach, but it didn't. So, although the brand is not talking about itself and its capabilities, people still trust the brand to be competent and authentic in its messaging. I guess you know this from other areas in your life. Take for example buying a new house, the real estate agent you're meeting with might not be the most competent just because he or she claims to be; you might value the agent's abilities higher based on how well your needs are met or understood. Across the eight commercials, the *competence* score goes from the lowest being T-Mobile at 4.43 up to 5.4 for Land Rover. Again, all fairly high scores across the board.

Making people feel energised

The variation happens when you look at *motivation*. The participants were faced with questions covering how motivated and energetic (active, energetic, vigorous and the like) they feel, but more importantly how they might behave after watching the ad, from their *willingness to buy* (WTB) to their *willingness to pay a premium price* (WPPP). Obviously, these are questions asked in a test setting and don't reflect actual behaviour, but the participants own sentiment or judgement at the time. Still, when it comes to *motivation*, this is where the transformative commercials really stick out. The lowest transformative commerical score is 4.61 for Land Rover, and the highest is Nike's at 5.17. Then the dramatic drop happens with 0.86 point down to the highest-rated purposeful commercial DB Export with 3.75, whereas the lowest-rated purposeful commercial T-Mobile gets a score of only 2.9. If you look at the graph, you can see the four transformative commercials like a plateau around a score of 5 falling down to a plateau of the purposeful campaigns around a score of 3.7. The test shows that the transformative commercials' focus on motivating people to change pays off. The average score is 4.2, and the transformative commercials' average hovers around 4.88, whereas the purposeful commercials' average comes in at 3.49, which is a 1.39 average difference or 29.5%. Think about the potential when people are 29.5% more motivated to act on your messaging when you are taking a transformative approach?

Translating people's motivation into buying

When we look at people's willingness to part with their money, *willingness to buy* (WTB) and a bigger share of their money *willingness to pay a premium price* (WPPP), the results are not as outspoken, but still worth a closer look. In the following you'll only observe the four commercials that showed a significant enough result: Always and Land Rover versus Hyundai and T-Mobile.

Willingness to buy

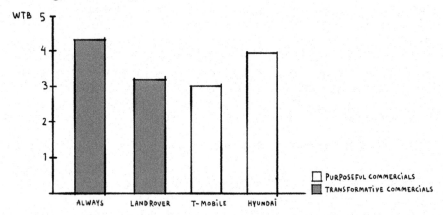

When you look at the *willingness to buy* (WTB) scores, the difference between the two approaches is not as visible. At the top it's Always (4.41) and Hyundai (4.02) with a drop down to Land Rover (3.29) and

T-Mobile (3.16). This time the transformative Land Rover commercial didn't make its mark, with a score below average, whereas Always performed really well.

Willingness to pay a premium price

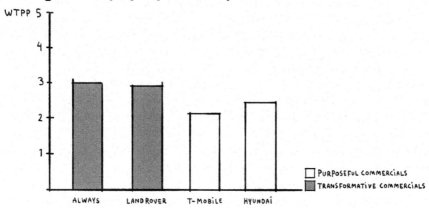

When you look at the *willingness to pay a premium price* (WPPP), you see that the transformative commercials jump again, although at lower levels around a plateau at 3 with Always (3.04), Land Rover (3.00) and, half a point further down, Hyundai (2.51) and T-Mobile (2.14). All in all, the results of the test with a sample of 299 individuals demonstrate that transformative commercials make people feel more motivated on average +29.5%, and indicate, although at lower levels, that people are on average +29,6% more *willing to pay a premium price* (WPPP). The transformative Always commercial is the overall test winner and does show a clear correlation among motivation, *willingness to buy* and *willingness to pay a premium*. As I've reiterated earlier, I believe that the organisations that are good at motivating people to change behaviours or mindsets inevitably will also be better at translating this into sales as long as the service or product is clearly part of the transformative journey. If you're a hardcore explorer type and Land Rover motivates you to get out there and discover, Land Rover's positioning should appeal to you, and consequently you should feel more inclined to buy the car.

From what people say to what a brain scan reveals

I wanted to dive deeper into the difference between the two approaches: purposeful versus transformative. Professor Petruzzellis and I applied a brain scanner, an electroencephalography (EEG), to better monitor emotional responses. We selected two transformative commercials for further testing, Always and Land Rover, and two purposeful, T-Mobile and Hyundai. The experiment was carried out at the Neurology Unit of the Vito Fazzi Hospital in Lecce, Italy, under the supervision of a neurologist. Ten participants were invited for the test: three men and seven women, aged between 21 and 45 and from four different countries (six Italians, two Norwegians, one Russian and one American). All of them master English proficiently, but obviously culture plays a role. The activity of the brain was measured by the Micromed EEG Brain Quick with 16 electrodes positioned in the frontal, prefrontal, parietal and temporal areas. When comparing the brain's electrical impulses from the right prefrontal and left prefrontal regions, it's possible to distinguish the positive emotional states such as joy or happiness from the negative ones such as fear or sadness. The results were laid out on a scale from positive, through neutral to negative and measured 0%–100%.

EEG brain scan

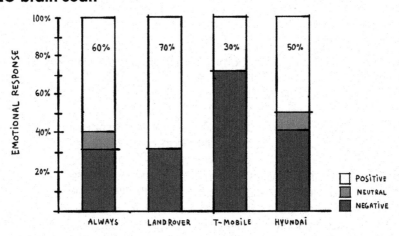

The brain's response is obviously a more direct and unfiltered way of telling how a specific individual feels about watching commercials. In the earlier test where people were asked about *warmth*, the results were more equal across the board, but it's interesting to see from the brain scan how the transformative commercials evoked a stronger response. Land Rover and Always, respectively, scored 70% and 60% positive responses, whereas Hyundai and T-Mobile scored 50% and 30%. Clearly, lots of factors are at play in judging the outcome of a brain scan from the positive influence of the music, style of editing, tone of voice, specific actors, story line and so on, and in the earlier test using questionnaires, there was no similar jump in *warmth*, only in *motivation*. Could it be that the transformative commercials' positive belief in people and framing around empowerment leave a positive brain footprint? I guess, you know that heart-warming feeling, when someone believes in you, right? Nonetheless, the two transformative commercials do leave the participants with a more positive emotional outcome.

It's interesting to look at this test when we're talking about campaigns' effectiveness at motivating people to act or buy. I've been a vocal advocate for how purposeful commercials outperformed traditional commercials at the cash register as people were looking for more authentic products with a higher meaning. But I'll have to update my view. As more and more organisations talk about the bigger societal role they're playing in the world and as sustainability is becoming increasingly mainstream, the effectiveness or differentiation in that societal messaging is weakened. The focus has to shift away from the self-important purpose message to one of a transformative promise ("*Believe in your own ability to bring change.*") You can see how the transformative commercials have outperformed the traditional purpose commercials and made people feel energised to take change into their own hands and to be positive! People want organisations to play a part but only on people's terms. The mass-marketing, mass-branding approach where brand is king has to give away to a people-first approach with a stringent focus on individual change! This is when the change can be felt in one's own mind and body – rather than being just a slogan or catchy campaign line. This is not simply about the messaging but about the totality of the organisation's behaviour and mindset; else people will quickly call you out. If you beat the drum to motivate people to live healthier but your products are directly or indirectly unhealthy, your messaging will still ring hollow.

Believe in people, and they'll believe in themselves

Unless you as an organisation focus and plan your efforts, and your entire brand for that matter, on enabling people's transformation, you can't be surprised if their intentions don't convert to sales. My experience is that most organisations find it difficult to identify that insight or create that stringent focus: I often hear as an excuse, "*Our brand appeals to everyone.*" I would argue you can truly touch everyone only if you begin with someone because the danger is that, when you try to appeal to everyone, you appeal to no one.

Starbucks has from the very beginning pledged "*to change the community one cup of coffee at a time,*" but wouldn't it be stronger if Starbucks tried to change you one cup of coffee at a time? It's not semantics; think about the creativity that would unlock. How could that one cup of coffee or that one visit to the outlet be one of personal transformation? You have to look for that simple, strong human insight. Disney inspires us through magic moments. Lifebuoy enables you to live a healthier life. When you as an organisation or leader are on a mission to transform people's lives at every step, your resources, thinking and activity bring you closer to enabling people and ultimately changing behaviours and driving sales. Take the mindful running company District Vision: their transformative promise is to get more runners to become mindful. Part of the customer journey is to join classes, get inspired in the store, which eventually leads to buying District's products, which leads to profit. District Vision has a strong growth case to suggest so. It's a win–win for company and people.

People's expectations are getting higher every day. Reports, certificates and glossy marketing campaigns won't cut it any more. This is not a race for transparency, it's not a race to being better, but a race to make a meaningful difference in people's lives. The idea of a consumer defined only by buying is giving way to a new role where it's all about better living or self-actualisation. From having worked on behaviour change campaigns targeting alcoholics, I know that the only thing they need is someone who believes in them. Someone who believes that they can change, when they often have given up hope themselves. It's worth helping people help themselves. Your organisation is no greater than what you can make people achieve. As the cases and tests show, the rewards are plentiful for both organisation and people.

Key takeaways

1   Bridging the gap between intent and action is a pivotal step towards self-actualisation and ultimately as an organisation towards realising your mission and unlocking sales.

2   Without asking that powerful word "WHEN," your mission becomes like a journey without a time schedule.

3   Look at people's daily lives, and see where you can play or own a transformative role.

4   Don't get lost in issues or causes, but always focus on the WHO.

5   You can only touch everyone if you begin with someone, because the danger is that when you try to appeal to everyone, you appeal to no one.

Questions to ask yourself

1   Is your mission directly connected to a transformative outcome in people's lives?

2   Do you have a step-by-step plan for changing your customers' behaviours?

3   Do you measure the progress and the impact?

4   Can other industries, organisations or technologies help with your customer's transformation?

5   Are your marketing activities today focused on sales or customer transformation?

8   Pass the steering wheel

If you are being the most helpful, most nutritionally rich and most delicious product then you have the license to do more to make society better and to do it in a way that's not self-righteous.[1]

– *Daniel Lubetzky, Founder and Executive Chairman, Kind Snacks*

DANIEL
LUBETZKY

Make people grow, and they'll grow your marketing

At preschool I made this little grey elephant out of clay in class, and I was very proud of the result and engraved my initials on it. I felt it was my little piece of art, my grey clay elephant, and it had been so much fun to make. That coming Christmas I gave it to my parents – frankly speaking, adding to a pile of other useless creations from woodwork to drawings. The grey clay elephant is a good analogy of how important it is for our individual development to feel we are realising ourselves as we transition from being kids to adults and to feel that kick of shaping things, opinions or our lives. It's the IKEA effect mentioned earlier, and it's part of our DNA in the form of Maslow's self-actualisation. Think about your job and how you feel when you're being dictated an assignment by your boss or a client. There's probably nothing that can make you feel more disenfranchised, right?

It's important that you change the way you look at value. Typically, value is created by making products or services that are marketed at people. It's a product-centric view, ignoring people's urge for creation, ambition and self-realisation. There is little to no room for play, no space for little clay elephants!

Today, it's not about selling but about satisfying people's urge for painting, shouting, dancing or however else they want to realise themselves. As more and more marketers are complaining about the lack of engagement online and declining engagement numbers, one has to ask whether it's simply because the marketing industry in itself is to blame for not offering enough possibilities for engagement. The diagnosis is clear: marketers are stuck in a mass-marketing mindset. So how can you give people a part to play across the marketing mix through their personal transformation?

Expressing yourself through the marketing mix

I spend my fair share of days stuck in a plane seat, travelling the world and spreading the goodvertising mission. Even writing this very sentence on board a Lufthansa flight on my way to Bogotá. Often, I rent my space out on Airbnb, which actually does demand time and attention to detail as the guests evaluate my effort on a five-star scale and even write meticulous reviews of their stay at my place. I guess I always liked the hospitality part of giving people that extra special feeling of being welcome, from leaving a customised guidebook or a good bottle of wine with a little welcome note. I invest my time, but I also do it for my own pleasure – I like the hospitality part!

Your most loyal customers can be like me, willing to play, to invest their time, to give a hand or essentially to deliver the whole shebang. But do you let them? In 2014, notoriously busy art directors and other graphic aficionados voluntarily spent thousands of hours to engage with an intricate murder mystery created by graphic software giant Adobe where the mystery could be solved only by using the full suite of Adobe's graphic tools. The art directors loved it: they learned something, and their graphic skills were challenged. More than 22,000 people downloaded the game, and people valued Adobe for the effort, as demonstrated by positive brand sentiment rising from 15% to 76%.[2]

For the art directors, it was their little grey clay elephant.

Turn people's passion and creativity into engagement

When your transformative promise is clear, the marketing mix is an open box that's ready for play, and people are increasingly expecting a bigger say – if not the whole control. Don't forget you're most likely dealing with digital natives (or you are one yourself) who are used to controlling everything with the click of a button. It's time to open up your marketing for creativity, passion and self-expression – and people will engage.

At one end of the spectrum, it's simply giving me as a customer the power to tailor any experience or product with the ease of the click of a button, removing any barriers and making everything customisable to fit my needs and wants. And it makes business sense: as the co-creation T-shirt experiment at universities showed, co-creators, in this case the students, were willing to pay more. McKinsey did a study[3] on ten co-creation projects and the biggest motivational factors were intrinsic;

that is, we do it for our own self-expression or self-actualisation. The largest percentage of participants (28%) was driven by curiosity and a desire to learn, followed closely by entertainment and social play (26%), and an interest in building skills (26%). Only some 20% were driven by extrinsic reasons like recognition and rewards.

The tip of the pink-or-whatever-colour-you-like iceberg

In Japan, KitKat[4] already offers more than 300 different variants of their famed chocolate waffle snack, from all pink to a Hello Kitty version, and you would think there would be one for everyone's liking. Still, in 2018 they opened up a dedicated store in Osaka where people could create their own. Like a Willy Wonka factory, people can choose from six different chocolate bases and more than nine different toppings and watch their personal KitKat take shape as it's exposed to nothing less than liquid nitrogen. Prices vary from $6 to $9 a piece, yet despite that rather steep price tag, customers are queuing up. It can't possibly be the need for new variants that drives people to the store but the simple fact that they get to co-create. There's an inherent value in that.

Take another example. The fast-food restaurant concept 4 Food caters to the creativity of people and makes them create their own local, healthy meal, but it's social as well. I can share my cooking creations with friends or the community and make it to a leader board. The website will also help recommend food based on my health and dietary profile and offer customised discounted coupons based on those preferences. Nobody wants to be treated like "*a mass*" or "*target group*" anymore but wants to feel like someone who has a say. Without doubt, customisation is on the rise and we've just seen the tip of that iceberg – pink, blue or whatever other colour you want it to be.

One thing is opening up for co-creation, but why not open up your marketing for people to play and use as a means to their self-actualisation? Think of it as a white canvas, a clay elephant drawing board. As millennials expect to be able to express themselves across the digital and physical world, and digital nomads and side-hustle projects are being idolised, it's an effective way as an organisation to truly turn people into the creators – not simply the co-creators. The activity can be challenging as long as people feel it's contributing to their story, who they are or who they want to be. It's the IKEA effect gone wild, making demands of people and triggering their sense of accomplishment. In a cluttered market space, enabling people to turn marketing activities into one of discovery, creation and self-development is a strong point of differentiation – a potential to activate your WHO void and make your transformative promise come alive!

But it's not only in the affluent world where it makes sense to turn people into creators: with jobs needed in many parts of the world, micro-franchises can scale up the reach and empower people and communities better than a traditional employer/employee model. In South Africa, the National Youth Development Agency is tackling youth unemployment by launching Buddibox, a retail home delivery service across local townships. The deliveries are done by young people each looking after around 200 households and delivering everything from groceries to toiletries. The young people taking part in the program feel like proud business owners or entrepreneurs, and that's a different feeling from being a "*delivery boy or girl*" doing delivery for just the cash.

Or why not teach people how to help themselves? This was the insight behind Litter of Light, a fast-growing non-profit which, among other projects, teaches people in impoverished communities to light up their homes with readily available materials: for example, a used plastic bottle filled with bleach that magnifies the power of the sun and lights up dark spaces. Litter of light has according to their website facilitated "*more than 350,000 bottle lights in more than 15 countries and taught green skills to empower grassroots entrepreneurs at every stop.*"[5] Again, you give people dignified roles to play rather than treating them as helpless or as a submissive target group.

From mass to individualisation

How people perceive products and services in the marketplace is changing. The industrialised mass-market model is giving way to human creativity, passion and ingenuity. People are willing to pay a higher price and prefer the extra care being put into it – or the possibility to shape or create. I've been drinking my fair share of gin and tonics and witnessed how gins like Bombay or Tanqueray quickly lost ground to those of smaller, locally crafted gin makers foraging their ingredients from the nearby flora. The same is happening with what used to be the preferred tonic water that no one would question: Schweppes Tonic Water. Today the brand is losing market share to the same incumbent local, small-badge tonic water makers, where the tonic can cost one a fortune.

It seems that no organisation goes unchallenged in this hyper-local, pro-social, creative marketplace honouring personalised craft over standardised big brands. Every aspect of business seems to be democratised, and there's an unprecedented pressure on organisations to respond to people's chant: everything you can do as an organisation, we as people can do better.

The legacy trust built into these big global power institutions is no longer enough to wow people into buying a product: the smaller players can more easily make people feel valued across the board, from customer service to the product itself being small-batch bread with local ingredients hand-baked just around the corner from where you live, compared to an industrialised, bland brick of bread.

Why should young people look to big business as a deliverer of premium goods or, even more hypocritically, as a world saviour? In their lifetime, their only experience with big business has been one of standardised goods produced often with high social and/or environmental costs, in contrast to the post-war generation, which saw business as bringing prosperity and higher living standards (read: TVs, fridges, cars and the like) into every home.

Generation Z (born from the mid-1990s to the early 2000s) is the first one to be able to work, do business or love on their terms (not to ignore the controversies around some of these digital platforms), and that "*first*" is not to be overlooked!

One individual, many roles

I never really liked the word "*consumer,*" and I do think the word in itself is disrespectful towards people and their ability to reflect, but it's a cunning description of how most organisations have been seeing and treating people (and how some organisations still see them) and is symbolic of the earlier decades of marketing tactics. Still to this day, most organisations are stuck in a self-centred role where the relationship is the one-sided: "*We can offer this,*" "*We are good at this.*"

But there are many other roles for people to play than being a consumer. Most people today are shifting among multiple roles within a couple of minutes, such as a co-producer of content when, for example, doing a Facebook update; as a co-promoter when taking part in a Nike running eco-system and urging their friends to join; or as a co-innovator when they contribute to a company's research and development like Tesla inviting its customers to take part in open town hall meetings or Starbucks asking its users for ideas for new food or beverages with My Starbucks Idea.

But the big change is happening as people's contribution is becoming the value add. The gig economy moving from niche to mainstream is evidenced by the exponential growth of Airbnb, Uber and other similar people-powered platforms. These platforms are stealing market shares across industries in Europe, up to 20%–50% across industries, according to a PWC report for the European Commission in 2016.[6]

Just look at how many of these platforms have become market leaders in their industries: Uber in the taxi industry, Airbnb in the hotel industry and so on. People aren't sitting idle and waiting for companies to open up and give them a say, as the growing communities of hackers, makers and creators show. Fast-growing communities gather off- or online to voluntarily play with the whole marketing spectrum like IKEA customers adapting furniture to their needs and hacking IKEA's products and showcasing the results on a dedicated website, ikeahackers.net.[7] At the time of writing, more than 5,000 hacks were available. If you don't open up for people to have a say, they'll have a say anyway.

A real change story about health

Decided to get into competitive kickboxing around 10 years ago now. Going from largely inactive and unworried about nutrition to monitoring body fat and eating egg white omelettes. I am no longer that intense about it, but it marked a permanent lifestyle change that I haven't lost; discipline in physical fitness, body consciousness, nutrition. The decision more about self-esteem and the effects of it trickling over into other areas of my life than other factors. The result is that I'm a better person and make better decisions in all aspects of life.[8]

– *RochelleH, on Reddit.com*

People are realising themselves through brands

The change in mindset away from the mass-marketing model is a founding thought behind more and more companies. The anti-establishment cosmetic company Glossier gives people a say in defining beauty and their products, but it also turns its loyal customers into influencers, spreading the democratised beauty ideals. Suop, the collaborative Spanish phone company, is going even further and enabling its customers, which it calls "*collaborators,*" across three areas: marketing, customer service and product innovation. Suop has built a platform that measures the level of engagement at which each collaborator is contributing, and they're being rewarded in real time with points or discounts. There are many ways to collaborate for Suop's customers: they can create and share content, help other users in customer support, actively participate in a customer forum or send proposals to improve Suop. Business models like these are enabling people across the marketing mix and putting pressure on business- or marketing-as-usual. They don't offer a ready-made product or brand-centric purpose but do encourage people to realise themselves through the brand. Marketing used to be about economic power, about pushing advertising, conquering shelf-space, aggressive pricing, but evidently a shift is happening away from transaction towards reciprocity where the organisation's network or social capital can matter more than classic brute marketing force. Organisations like Glossier, Suop and Kind grew through a community of people, who cared about those brands and felt the brands cared about them.

From targets to people of flesh and blood

As I urged, your organisation should put enabling people's dreams and ambitions as your North Star, and so should your marketing. People are increasingly moving from being passive recipients to co-creators of every aspect of marketing and to creators themselves. I see this power exchange between "*What you can do*" as an organisation and "*What you can enable me to do*" as a customer playing out as a strong emerging force in the marketplace, where an organisation should aim for that hotspot where people's means are resources that become part of the marketing mix and create a ripple effect. Think about the people hacking the IKEA furniture; they're not getting paid to do be hackers, but they do it because they care. It makes them tick. In marketing, it goes a long way if your organisation can stand behind people's passion and dreams and unlock their capabilities and resources. I call this "*transformability.*"

Def.: transformability
The ability to enable people to leverage their passions, means and capabilities as a resource in the marketing mix, from product to promotion.

This reflects the previously mentioned shift from the power of the organisation to the power of the individual. This transfer of control stands in stark contrast to most organisations' current "*We do*" mindset; we make the greatest products that we deliver in the best possible way because we do the coolest promotion where we dictate the best price in the marketplace. A lot is dependent on your organisation's ability to adopt a new paradigm – transformability – if you are to shift people from being passive targets to agents in the marketing mix.

The further an organisation moves from a centralised model and enables its customers or stakeholders, the more it's freeing up resources and enabling others to act and leverage value on its behalf from product to promotion. This opens up a treasure chest of unlimited interactions in a spider web of many-to-many mimicking the digital landscape rather than being stuck in the old one-to-many marketplace where the organisation is the barrier for growth. Take the previously mentioned Starbucks Idea, where Starbucks has unleashed people's creativity by asking them to come up with product ideas. Over a five-year period, Starbucks have seen over 150,000 ideas submitted[9] and roughly 300 implemented. It's a two-way street because the organisation is not the only one to grow; people grow too. You are not being marketed to, dictated to or shouted at, but you gain something, you learn something, or you're a part of something. Your engagement as a customer in the marketing activity potentially transforms you.

Your organisation holds no power in itself but is legitimised by your stakeholders, and eventually the very organisation's growth rest in your stakehol'der's hands. I have pointed out the need to look at our most basic human traits and to put people in charge of their own self-actualisation. If we look at time spent on services and products or, for that matter, on campaigns that offer a possibility to take part in and that can become a part of people's personal transformation, the numbers are there, demonstrating that when you open up and touch people's personal development goals as triggers, engagement follows.

Uncover transformability

What am I doing today that people could be doing?
What internal resources am I lacking that my customers could leverage?
I'm lacking resources, but could any of my stakeholders have the means to provide them?
How can I turn people into co-creators or creators?
Can I give people increased control?
Could people take over any processes?
How can I make people customise the service experience?
How can I make people express themselves through changing or upgrading products or services?
How can I make people more engaged across the marketing mix?

Taking a backseat for change

Meet Dave Hakkens again. You remember the Dutch designer who created the open-source project Phonebloks that turned into a viral hit, right?

After trying to tackle the problem of obsolescence in phones and the waste stream, he tackled another waste problem he felt passionate about: plastic waste. He set up Precious Plastic with a simple and enabling mission: "*Let people in every corner of the world know they can start their own local plastic workshop.*"[10] His open-source plan was simple. As an initial step, he developed a do-it-yourself machine to recycle plastic on the spot and turn it into, for example, toys, but more importantly he's encouraging people to create and share the blueprints for their DIY plastic recycling machines, so that all these great DIY machines can spread to every corner of the world.

I had a Skype call with David,[11] and it was clear he didn't see his role as a leader but more as a facilitator:

> It's really just being a group of people trying to get along, listening to each other. You sort of try to understand what's needed in the world from people that want to contribute. And they're all very smart and they have a lot of knowledge. So, it's just a matter of listening. I like to see it more as I am just a part of it.

For David, solving the problem is bigger than he is, and it's really about making what's normally reserved for the industry available to as many as possible and to give everyone a chance to find what's in it for them in joining the project – their WHO. Again, in David's words:

> In the beginning, people wanted to join the project because of the environment. And because they wanted to educate others. Now, they see that they can run a business. Some use fab labs and stuff, others just love to push the limits of the machines, create amendments for the machines and work with printing and stuff. So, it's a very diverse group of people, that is sort of playing around with it.

Precious Plastic opens up for people to engage and for themselves to discover their own meaning, fun and excitement in participating.

Across the world, Precious Plastic has given people a platform where they can become makers themselves and do their part in solving the plastic problem, whatever their motivation is. It's alive and kicking community with hundreds of machines being built around the world, showcasing how plastic waste can be repurposed into beautiful objects like furniture in Odessa, souvenirs for tourists in Sri Lanka, and colourful bowls in Bratislava that have even been showcased to Slovakia's president. David shares the beauty and advantage of this open-source approach:

> *I think the upside of open source is that the knowledge is distributed. You can't really kill the project anymore, it's sort of a common good. It's not a single company working on it with engineers in-house, but really people all over the world, people contributing to it.*

Unleashing people's urge to create or express themselves can potentially reach and touch people globally.

Business to business or business to human?

This is not only about a transformation of the business to a consumer market, but the same principles count in the business-to-business market. After all, it's about people. I never really like the term "*business to business*" but prefer using "*business to human.*"

A supplier or a business partner also has dreams and aspirations that you as an organisation can enable. If you are a global logistics provider like DHL, you want to empower your customers to make their logistics as smooth as possible. DHL understands the importance of innovation being customer focused. And they have for years been bringing customers and DHL service partners together in innovation centres for workshops to share best practices and co-create value, which have sparked innovative projects like Parcelcopter, an agile and cost-efficient drone delivery project, or Smart glasses, an augmented reality project set to improve inventory and warehouse picking efficiency by 25%.[12]

It's really a matter of organisational mindset and of truly daring to enable people – no matter the business. If you are in charge of logistics, you want structure and to stay on top of the day. If DHL can deliver that, then well . . . your day just got better. The possibilities across the marketing mix are limitless if you can enable people to play a part and give them that feeling of accomplishment that I got from the grey clay elephant.

The Wheel of Transformability

People can and should play an active and flourishing part across the whole marketing mix. So I have redrawn and expanded the well known 4P model of the marketing mix from "*Product,*" "*Placement,*" "*Price*" and "*Promotion.*" I call this model the Wheel of Transformability, and it describes how an organisation can give people more control as one moves outwards across the four axes. The model is meant to inspire you as an organisation to look for opportunities to enable people even further – and drive new growth through transforming their lives.

The four axes from "*We do,*" "*We engage,*" "*We collaborate*" to "*You do*" show the intermediate steps of how the control is transferred from the organisation to individuals, not only enabling them but, more importantly from an organisational standpoint, also turning their efforts and means into an asset in the marketing mix. It's also about what people view as meaningful, fun or exciting. When (almost) everyone (in the affluent Western world) can buy the latest iPhone or designer handbag, flaunting your status through buying loses its meaning. Instead, time and effort become a valuable differentiator for people where they can showcase to the world that they're smarter, healthier or more skilled. This speaks to the fifth and underlying force in the marketing mix, the bullseye of the model: The transformative promise. It's marked by two crossed fingers symbolising the promise you are making to people to enable a transformation in their lives. It's easy to call out the organisations that enable people across some of the 5Ts (transformative price, transformative product, transformative placement, transformative promotion, transformative promise) but that do not live it wholeheartedly. Behaviour and attitude distinguish Nike's enabling "*Just do it*" from Coca-Cola's self-centred product cry, "*Taste the feeling.*"

At the end of the day, transformative organisations are built on a simple premise: the more you put people in charge over their own lives, the happier and more fulfilled they are.

The Wheel of Transformability

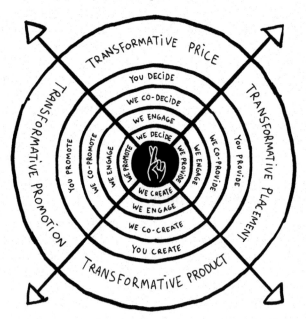

Each of the 5Ts represents an opportunity to enable an organisation's stakeholders, and each of them individually or in combination offers a growth potential for people and organisation: transformability.

The transformability steps

We do

When you as an organisation deliver a complete effort.

We engage

When you as an organisation engage your stakeholders but decide on the complete effort.

We collaborate

When you offer your stakeholders to co-create or customise the effort.

You do

When you enable your stakeholders to create the effort.

Turning a whole country into part of your marketing efforts

Trust in institutions, businesses, governments, media have been on a downward spiral in recent years, according to Edelman's Trust Barometer 2019:[13] NGOs (57%), business (56%), government (48%) and media (47%). We'd rather trust those we are close to: our friends, our neighbours and even strangers online come out as more trustworthy in surveys. You simply win trust by making people do the talking.

In a tourism campaign for Sweden in 2016,[14] they didn't turn to glossy brochures, fake testimonials done by smiling actors or a call centre to sell the best Sweden had to offer but to those who would know best what to say: the Swedes themselves. As a global first, Sweden introduced its own phone number that people from all over the world could call, and everyone who lived in Sweden had the opportunity to answer. The phone worked like any other phone, but it would just connect to an average preselected Swede. The campaign wasn't just about selling Sweden but also celebrating a cornerstone in Sweden's democracy: its free speech and the fact that censorship was abolished 250 years ago. More than 197,000 calls were made, totalling over a year's worth of talk time. And the campaign's open-minded message got people to call from 190 countries, with 25,000 Swedes answering the phone – including Prime Minister Stefan Löfven.[15]

Everyone has something to say if you touch their passions and give them a chance to voice up. Your customers, stakeholders or, in this case, citizens are your best and most trustworthy ambassadors. When an organisation dares to turn people into active (co-)creators in the marketing mix, people grow, and the organisation grows. Self-serving organisations stuck in mass-marketing gear will lose out as people are looking to realise themselves or challenge themselves across the marketing mix. If organisations want to play a meaningful role going forward, they'll have to serve as the workshops or platforms for people's creativity, skills and ambitions. Your marketing mix has to open up for people's urge for self-actualisation – even if you sometimes feel it's adding to a pile of useless creations as my parents probably felt about my grey clay elephant. It's not about you as an organisation, it's about people, it's about me.

Key takeaways

1   People are increasingly looking for meaning and participation across the marketing mix from promotion to product.

2   As the mass-marketing model is dead, turn people's passion and creativity into engagement.

3   The Wheel of Transformability describes how an organisation can enable people to leverage their passions, means and capabilities as a resource in the marketing mix, from product to promotion.

4   Across the market forces, the Wheel of Transformability describes four steps from "We do," "We engage," "We collaborate" to "I do," where the organisation increasingly is turning people into creators of the effort.

5   When an organisation dares to turn people into active participants in the marketing mix, people grow, and the organisation grows.

Questions to ask yourself

1   How important do you see customer-centricity to the success of your business?

2   Do you find people are more or less engaged today?

3   What are you doing today that people could be doing?

4   Are there any processes or efforts across the marketing mix that you, with advantage, can make people do?

5   Where do you see people's passions or resources possibly adding the most value to your marketing efforts?

9 The five transformative market forces

> You've got to be integrated in where life happens, where people pass time talking about having babies, the downfall of our political systems, what they are going to do on their holiday . . . just being as accessible as possible in as many ways as possible. It's like being a McDonald's. I know this sounds like WHAT? Really?? McDonald's? But if you want to create real change, I mean real systemic change, you eventually have to dare to step into the mainstream.[1]
>
> *– John Schoolcraft, Global Chief Creative Officer, Oatly*

JOHN
SCHOOLCRAFT

From "*We do*" to "*You do*"

"*I got a bit obsessed with #preciousplastic so my friends and I built a plastic shredder. Still works!*" writes @harkinworld on Twitter in 2018. The Tweet is a testament to the power of giving a go to people across the marketing mix as Dave Hakkens did with the project Precious Plastic. Engagement is not something you get; it's something you earn. The Wheel of Transformability showcases the benefit of turning people into passionate creators across your marketing efforts. Step-by-step moving away from the classic mass-marketing approach with the brand shouting "*We do*" to enabling people to say with @harkinworld-like satisfaction "*I do.*" Discover how you can turn on people's passions, means and resources across the marketing mix: transformative price, transformative product, transformative placement, transformative promotion, all centred around the model's axis, the transformative promise.

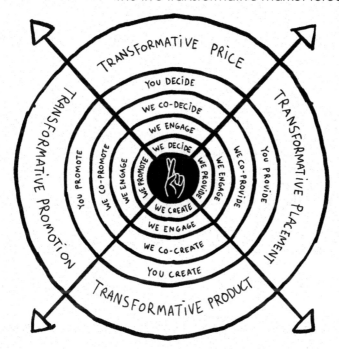

Transformative product: a dream in the making

Oh dear grey, clay elephant. . . . When you help shape or create something, it simply matters more to you. I've renovated two turn-of-the-20th-century Copenhagen apartments and invested sweat and tears, and although admittedly not everything is completely straight and polished, I'll always treasure the result. Scholars C. K. Prahalad and Venkat Ramaswamy,[2] who popularised the term "*co-creation,*" demonstrated in 2004 how an organisation can gain knowledge, higher profitability and superior brand value and loyalty by making customers part of the product or service creation, which is the "*We co-create*" step. But nothing gives people a higher sense of accomplishment than the possibility to live out their dreams and passions. When people are turned into creators or producers, they are no longer just tailoring that handcrafted coffee with the Barista, but brewing the coffee themselves as part of their self-development. You are not asking people in a survey what they think of a new product or what they potentially would like; you're asking them to shape it, which in return builds loyalty and increases demand. Take Wheelys as an example. It gave people a possibility to define their work life on their terms, from the love of coffee to putting food on the table for their families: from aspiring towards being a knowledgeable barista to a responsible mum or dad.

People are looking for human wealth

Today most industries are challenged by people's increasing access and ability to produce and manufacture, from craft beers to communication services. There's no exclusivity, and developments are pushing us towards what economic theorist Jeremy Rifkin calls a "*zero marginal cost society*,"[3] where we all can produce and manufacture at marginal costs. This puts unprecedented pressure on organisations but also unveils new opportunities for those who can think in terms of turning people into creators or service providers rather than simply pushing products and services. Nowhere is this clearer than in the digital space, where peer-to-peer platforms are increasingly taking over their traditional counterparts.

This decentralisation also challenges the very concept of quality. Unilever's Ben & Jerry's ice cream have without doubt been perceived as a high-end mouth-watering ice cream craved by a generation of children, teens and grown-ups alike, but today when most cities offer local fresh ice-cream makers down on the corner, Ben & Jerry's seems like a rather bland and industrialised product. The customer focus and superiority of Ben & Jerry's, the beating heart of the founders Ben and Jerry, seem far away today compared to your local ice cream maker where you are on a first-name basis and easily can suggest an ice cream made out of oranges picked in the rooftop garden next door. At your small, local, ice cream maker, it's about dialogue and passion, not about taglines, processes, customer support or e-mails. The same is happening across industries; so, rather than trying to work against it, how can you as an organisation turn people's goals, dreams and aspirations into a reality by making them the self-realising creators, makers or shapers?

Transformative product

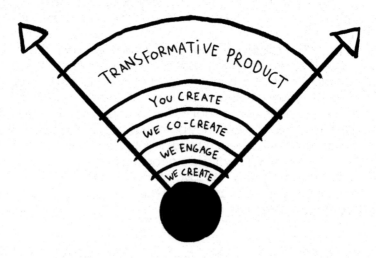

We create

This is the traditional product and service model, where the organisation is responsible for the manufacturing, production or service, and people's interaction are limited to research input, focus groups or the like. An example could be Coca-Cola when launching a new taste such as Vanilla Coke, which the company was very tight-lipped about. Coca-Cola did their research and consumer insights and determined there was a viable market for a new product line with vanilla flavour.

We engage

With its existing services, products or developed product concepts, the organisation does some engagement or outreach to people, such as asking them which one of five ice creams should be this summer's new flavour? In 1997, brewing giant Carlsberg asked people to vote for which of six specially brewed beers – Carls Special, Master Brew, Old Bond, Red X, Ottilia and Stout – should go into production and be the winner of a so-called beer election. The winner ended up being an alcohol-heavy beer called Master Brew, but because of the massive support for the beer election, Carlsberg also decided to go ahead with Carls Special. The engagement paid off. Both beers to this day form part of Carlsberg's portfolio, and the beer election was repeated in 2003 and 2011.

"*We engage*" covers giving options, doing outreach, asking questions or engaging people. At the end of 2016, Brian Chesky, the CEO of Airbnb, asked his followers on Twitter: "*If @Airbnb could launch anything in 2017, what would it be?*" The response was overwhelming with more than 2,000 suggestions, and Chesky continues his open outreach efforts on social media. Too many organisations simply forget to ask people what they want, think or feel. After all, people want to feel valued and like to have something important to contribute, it's up to you to give them the possibility.

We co-create

In the early 2000s, co-creation was a big marketing fad, and many organisations launched customisation stores, pop-up shops or websites to deliver a co-creation experience to people. With much appreciation, I'll borrow the definition of co-creation coined by Prahalad and Ramaswamy: "*Co-creation is a management initiative, or form of economic strategy, that brings different parties together (for instance, a company and a group of customers), in order to jointly produce a mutually valued outcome.*"[2]

Like the earlier example of KitKat, Rittersport, the German chocolate maker famous for their quadratic chocolate bars in a plethora of different variants, also went for a co-creation strategy. In 2017, I visited one of their stores in Berlin where people could design their very own chocolate bar from an extensive choice of ingredients and witness the whole process of its making. In front of my eyes, the quadratic chocolate bar moved from being less industrialised and more about passion and craft. And I even got curious about trying new flavours and combinations. Online they offer a similar experience, *Sortenkreation* ("chocolate creation"), where people can generate new ideas for products, choosing ingredients and creating a design for others to like, comment and share. One doesn't get the chocolate in the end, though, but there are valuable insights for Rittersport to harvest, and a playful experience for people, who feel cherished and listened to.

Another example comes from the other side of the planet: Australia. Tahlo is the opposite of mass-market, they are a made-to-order fashion brand where people customise the pieces to suit their taste and needs, choosing from a number of options from materials to shapes. Tahlo is against the wasteful practices of the fashion business and believe that if people get better quality clothing done by trusted makers with fair working conditions, it's a step in the right direction. Co-creation can be applied as valuable input in the innovation phase or downstream as a way to offer a more personalised, valuable experience.

You create

Nothing beats the sense of accomplishment when you're the maker or creator rather than just a cog in the wheel.

Wikimedia, the foundation behind Wikipedia, has inspired millions of people to voluntarily write and review the online encyclopaedia's entries: a real testament to human self-actualisation. Would your customers willingly spend their free time on your organisation? The online examples are plentiful, from Task Rabbit (handyman help), Udemy (online learning) and UrbanSitter (child care), where the businesses are built around giving people a way to make a living on their terms, but there are also many great examples from the maker and DIY communities, where the very philosophy is about being a creator. Take the LEGO Ideas platform David Hall spoke about. Their community of builders can post an idea for a new LEGO product, and if it gains more than 10,000 votes in support, it will become reality. One per cent of the revenue is shared with the idea creator, and over 20 crowdsourced concepts have been produced (as of 2017) since its launch. As a kid, I'd have had a dream come true to see my LEGO model in the stores and a sell-out success for LEGO.[4]

"*You create*" can also offer parts of an organisation's product or service portfolio up for user's imagination, creation or takeover. One example is from a notoriously conservative industry: banking. You might not remember how cumbersome it was to transfer money (depending on your age), but, trust me, filling out a transfer note or filling in account numbers, addresses and other information was a nightmare.

The Nordics' second biggest bank, Danske Bank, created an app, MobilePay, where people easily can transfer money between friends and family as well as pay in stores – all you needed was the recipient's phone number. People felt money transfer had become as easy as the swipe of a button. The co-operative Spanish phone company, Suop, also turned to their most engaged customers to help with basic customer service in return for rewards. In the Nordics, there's been a historic tradition for co-operatives (businesses owned and run by its customers) and in 2007 a supermarket chain called Københavns Fødevarefœl-lesskab (Yeah, don't even try to pronounce it, but it roughly translates to "*Copenhagen Food Community*") was launched. Part of keeping food prices down was to require that members contribute working hours in the supermarket. The initiative was inspired by a similar supermarket from Brooklyn, New York, called Park Slope Food Coop. But the main driver for its members is not the prices but the community feeling and the supermarket's strong environmental and ethical stance.

Open up your product

How can the product or service empower, enable or transform people?
How can the product or service lower the bar of access or offer people access where there was none before?
Can the product or service be made by people?
Can you turn people's capabilities, means or passions into a service or product?
Are there parts of the production process where people can have a say?
How can you give people increasing control over a product or service?
How can you make people have a say earlier in the product innovation?

Transformative placement: a Tupperware party on speed

"*More trucks on the road*"[5] was Coca-Cola CMO's Marcos de Quinto's answer to slowing sales as he began his global role in 2015. And there is without doubt strength in being where people are, whenever and wherever. But the reach of Coca-Cola will still be limited as it depends on traditional resources such as trucks and drivers, physical locations, whereas a transformative organisation potentially can turn every individual into an access point, a distributor, a point of sales or service provider. When Marriott was bragging about its growth of hotel rooms in 2014, Airbnb CEO Brian Chesky famously tweeted: "*Marriott wants to add 30,000 rooms this year. We will add that in the next two weeks.*"[6] Think about how you can turn people into a distributor or provider of your service or product. Take Unilever's Project Shakti,[7] which enables rural women to become entrepreneurs by distributing goods to hard-to-access rural communities. The project began in 2001 and has since grown exponentially. Over 100,000 Shakti entrepreneurs distribute Unilever's products in India, Nigeria, Ethiopia, Pakistan, Guatemala, Myanmar and Colombia, and, while creating an income, it's also improving women's standing in society. It's like a Tupperware party on speed. The same thinking went into David Hakkens's Plastic project.

Transformative placement

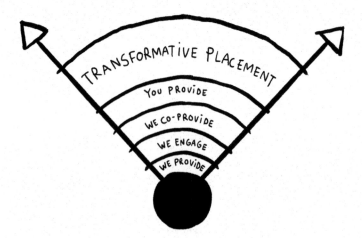

We provide

The distribution or placement of the product or service is through traditional channels like own stores, offices or retail outlets.

We engage

Digital has changed people's expectations, and the default today is where I want and when I want it. Admittedly, I can get frustrated if I don't have my online order within 48 hours, and my patience for food delivery doesn't stretch much beyond 30 minutes. At the same time, organisations have increasingly experimented with delivering unique experiences to people outside the regular outlets, raising the bar for what is possible. Take the previously mentioned food box subscription company Aarstiderne: they are hosting community dinners where people can get closer to the produce and get their hands dirty harvesting or planting (and obviously subscribing). For city populations on the rise, it's a popular and eye-opening experience. I was horrified to read a survey[8] showing a third of British children don't know where milk comes from and think cheese comes from a plant, not an animal. Talk about a good possibility to engage (or educate) people in a different setting.

"*We engage*" is an organisation's attempts to give people a say in how they want the product or service delivered and often covers events and promotions. Pop-up shops, essentially temporary sales or service outlets, is one way that organisations are creating a deeper engagement with people. The book publisher Penguin set up a pop-up bookshop in London on International Women's Day offering titles by female writers and, according to Penguin, honouring "*the way that women contribute, often under the radar, to every facet of society.*"[9]

But you might also offer people other novel ways of discovering your product. One example is Domino's, which is on a continuous mission to make pizza as fast and as convenient to order as the speed of thought: one of their initiatives has been a small pizza card box with a button; push it and a pizza is coming your way. In the United States, their steadfast commitment to fast delivery is said to be one of the key reasons they have beaten Pizza Hut to the King of Pizza's title, now holding the biggest market share in the United States.[10]

We co-provide

Co-creations are the equivalent of turning to people to determine or to give input on the distribution channel, and, as brick-and-mortar stores are challenged by online sales, it's helpful to turn to people to find the best possible delivery option. Ignoring people's changing needs can be fatal. Most logistics companies today offer several delivery options such as community stores as the pickup point for people's deliveries, offering an extra income for the stores, creating logistics savings for the companies and offering people easy and local pickup. But it's engaging people in those choices that makes the difference.

I earlier mentioned how logistics company DHL[11] engaged their customers in co-creation efforts that sparked the idea of a Parcelcopter – a test drone delivery service project based in Germany. According to Forbes, the test results are promising: customer satisfaction scores rose to over 80%, on-time delivery performance increased to 97% and, importantly, customer churn decreased.

You provide

Your customers or other stakeholders offer an unprecedented reach if you can turn them into the vehicles of delivery for your product or service. As in the case of the Swedish number where ordinary Swedes picked up the phone to promote the country. You turn people into creators. It wouldn't be fair to write about "*You provide,*" where you turn your stakeholders into the very vehicle of service or product delivery, without mentioning Tupperware parties. In the 1950s, Tupperware,[12] the US company behind those colourful plastic containers began offering busy housewives a flexible opportunity to earn an extra dime by using their network or community as a sales channel by hosting Tupperware Parties, essentially a product demonstration combined with a social function. To this day, Tupperware has no brick-and-mortar stores but is instead represented by three million people as a sales channel and generates more than $2.07 billion (2018).

If you truly know what matters to people, placement can be a strong competitive advantage, which BMW realised as they challenged the rental market with their DriveNow program launched in most of the larger cities in Europe. Rather than asking people to come to a rental station to pick up the car, they offer an app, where the users can see the nearest parked BMW, open it with an app, drive it and leave it wherever they see fit. It's a smart distribution model in which people decide where to pick up and park the cars, which handily will be where the demand is highest.

Or why not make your customers help other customers? The discount supermarket chain REMA 1000 launched in 2016 an app, Vigo, where one can earn an extra penny by picking up groceries for a neighbour. At launch, it was aiming for 10,000 users registered in Denmark, a small market of about six million inhabitants, and surpassed the goal by 80%.[13] Fostering community cohesion is a simple idea, but maybe, more importantly, it offers an extra hand to people who might either be too busy (such as a large family) or senior citizens or those who are too challenged to get to the supermarket – all representing revenue that would be lost to REMA 1000 if the service didn't exist.

Open up your placement

Can you turn people into service providers or product distributors?
Could any of your stakeholders be of help in delivering your product or service?
Think about your current locations and what businesses or entities are nearby. Could they be turned into a distributor?
Do your customers already frequently use products or services of other organisations that you could collaborate with?
Are your stakeholders often in a certain place you can utilise as a distribution point?
Think about people's day from morning to evening. Does that open new possibilities for distribution?
Is there any specific time of year when it would make sense to turn people into service or product providers?
Do people have any passions or hobbies that could be turned into delivery possibilities?
Have you asked people how or where they want your products or services delivered?

Transformative promotion: the voice of many

I began working in advertising when I was 22 years old, and one of the things that's always kept me curious about the trade has been what makes a successful ad. What makes one ad get millions of shares and others disappear with the blink of an eye? What's the secret behind that engagement?

Without doubt, the recent decades of advertising tactics are to blame for people's increasing annoyance with ads and for the rise in the use of ad blockers, but the ads that still stick around year after year are those that speak to a human truth or a strong insight. It's advertising by people for people – and in this merciless digital landscape, if you want to get a chance to engage people, you better make advertising that matters. As a brand, you should get people to talk about you or, even better, for you. Transformative promotion turns the usual marketing model on its head, and the audience becomes the messenger, making them speak, propelling their ambitions.

As soon as you spot a transformative promotion, you can tell the difference. It's a distinctive strategy because it's not about a campaign or a promo; it's bigger than that, it's a platform. Campaigns are often characterised by a set-in-stone message, a set campaign period, KPIs and a clearly defined target group whereas platforms are like fertile land for organic growth, where people can play a part but, moreover, make the effort their own with an often reciprocal benefit for organisation and individual.

Transformative Promotion

We promote

The centralised mass-marketing model, as we know it, consists of an organisation communicating its message to a target group through typically mass-media. A famous example mentioned in chapter 2 is Budweiser's "Whass Up."

We engage

In the digital marketplace, "*engagement*" outweighed "*views,*" and organisations began to engage people often with a simple task to "*like,*" "*share,*" "*sign-up-for-this-or-that*" or take part in a competition. I've dubbed this step "*We engage*" as an organisation gives people a possibility to engage, such as with a click. The logic is that the more time people spend on your marketing initiative, the more affinity there is. One example previously mentioned was the famous Burger King Subservient Chicken, where people on a dedicated website could write commands, and a chicken character would perform pre-made actions of what you wrote in often humorous ways.

We co-promote

When you as a brand rely on people to engage with your message to obtain reach or affinity, the natural evolution is, of course, towards a greater people focus, and "*We co-promote*" is about involving people in co-creating the campaign with you as a brand. Think about what matters to people and how you can offer them a co-creation possibility. One brilliant example is from the game FIFA 2014 World Cup where Nike partnered with Google to create the campaign Nike Phenomenal Shot. Haven't we all at one time marvelled at that one perfect goal? When a Nike athlete scored a goal in the game, an ad was delivered to the fan in real time. Now the fan could co-create the best goals from the match from rotating the players in 3D, framing them for shots that can be personalised with filters, captions and stickers. Once the fan was done with co-creating his or her "*Phenomenal Shot,*" it could be shared on social media – hopefully, impressing friends or fellow gamers.

You promote

Very few organisations dare to give up the creation of the promotion to people, but nothing beats unleashing an army of individuals fighting for what they believe in, what they love, and doing what they can to make the promotion a success. American Express's Small Business Saturday's stellar growth or the unparalleled spread globally of the Ice Bucket Challenge shows what happens when you turn your stakeholders from co-promoters into the campaign creators!

In the "*You promote*" step, the brand creates the platform, the fertile ground and the game plan, and the stakeholders have the freedom to make it their own, like the millions of people, celebrities or brands who put their very own fingerprint on what Movember means to them, rather than opting for pre-edited choices. In 2017 Playstation wanted to take part in the Movember movement, produced a limited-edition controller that lights up and called the effect "*Mo-Glow.*" They also gave one of their most famous game characters a "*Movember Moustache Makeover.*" Rather than limiting the promotion efforts to your organisation's resources, you are unleashing the power, creativity and reach of your stakeholders. In Chapter 10, I describe what makes the "*You promote*" effort unique, and I call this a "*platform*" as it's essentially about creating a game-like platform for people to participate and make it their own, compared to a campaign that's predefined and centralised.

Open up your promotion

How can you turn people into the messengers?
How can the promotion be part of people's own transformation?
Is your promotion like a game, which can be easily replicated time and time again?
Are people free to recreate the campaign?
How much can you open up your campaign for people's creativity?
Are there other stakeholders that, with advantage, can reuse your campaign efforts?
How can people help others towards transformation?
Can people's passions be part of the campaign?

Transformative price: a choice worth paying for

Let me share a story about price. In New York's Central Park in 2016, an elderly man was selling Banksy paintings for $60 apiece. His booth was right next to others selling everything from second-hand books to flowers, fruits and vegetables, as well as other art posters. During the entire day, only three paintings were sold, but what looked like any other booth turned out to be another provocative stunt by the world-famous street artist Banksy himself. The works of art were real, and their lucky new owners had scored a bargain worth tens of thousands of dollars.

This stunt illustrates the essence of branding: the difference between perceived value and real value. Branding works to build perceived value and to tell people why product X is worth more, highlighting its appearance or its basic product attributes. But today the price of your product or service is being scrutinised like an ant under a magnifying class. As every product is a click of a button away, so is a price comparison.

When did you last make a big purchase without doing a quick search online? Or posting a Facebook update: "*Any good recommendations for a travel company to Vietnam?*" The transparent market is making our purchase decisions more informed and conscious. That's good news for organisations delivering real value (or shared value) rather than perceived value.

Price and quality no longer stand alone

In a transparent market, products and services are increasingly quantified and compared on a multitude of parameters. Price and quality no longer stand alone; social, environmental, health and other value-added factors are put into play from the supermarket shelves to the global stock exchanges. This puts unprecedented pressure on organisations that are engaging in business as usual.

The online clothing store Honest By has chosen to be open about even the smallest details of its production, as well as about its products' social and environmental impact. However, Honest By has taken it one step further by showing, for example, exactly how much it pays for each material going into a pair of shoes and the profit Honest By makes. Just five years ago, this would have sounded ludicrous. Today, it makes good business sense.

A real change story about passion, fun and excitement

Since giving birth to my daughter, I lost my ability to dance. It has been my passion since I was a kid aside from drawing. I gained a lot of weight, went through horrible times, and I was getting depressed. The other year, the company I work for announced a contest of various talents. Only employees can join. One of my co-workers knew I used to dance in school and referred me to her friend. When her friend called if I could join their group, I was hesitant at first. Then came practice day. I said I will try. I had to swallow all the self-pity I had for years. I nervously went to the first practice day and learned the steps. Thankfully, they liked my performance and I got in. It took a lot of courage and determination to change my mindset. I started to think that if I don't do it now, I won't have another chance. I took the opportunity to remember who I was.[14]

– *Reng Abrantes, Senior Clerk, on Quora.com*

Transparency is the new reality. So, what's the price one is willing to pay for one product compared to another? This is determined by the perceived value of the product or service and is typically made up of many differ-ent factors such as perceived quality, functionalities, service, warranty, durability and the like, but there's only one who'll be able to tell whether that price is worth paying: you as a customer. And putting the pricing in people's hands can make sense especially when dealing with a product or service with an increasingly low marginal cost and in an increasingly competitive online environment. The other day, I was in a store to buy a loudspeaker for the office and I couldn't really find the price tag and asked the store assistant, if $100 could be the right price? He immediately responded by asking whether I thought that was too much and whether I had seen the price cheaper elsewhere. I hadn't researched anything and simply couldn't see the advertised price in the store, but without hesitation he googled the speaker and found a price $10 lower than the advertised store price and so that was the price I was offered. I gladly accepted and felt the store was on my side. I felt I got the speakers at market price. The other end of the scale is to ask people what they're truly willing to pay for your product or service ("*You decide*"). But be careful when turning to people to set the price as value is about perception like in the Banksy story, and you might risk devaluing your product.

Transformative price

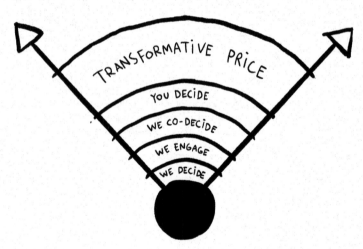

We decide

To get the pricing right, most organisations look to their competition, do surveys or try to evaluate people's willingness to pay and then decide where to put its price point. This is the "*We decide*" approach where the organisation ultimately sets the price point; for example, when Lufthansa feels threatened by low-cost carriers like Norwegian, Ryanair, Easyjet and others, they launch a new airline aimed at the low-cost segment: Germanwings.

We engage

"*We engage*" can cover a wide range of engagements around price from discounts, sales, competitions, customer queries and the like, but ultimately you as an organisation are setting the price. One example could be a Pay Your Age promotion when you receive a discount based on your age as done by the likes of Build-A-Bear and Nordic optician chain Synoptik. You're engaging people around price and can appeal to different segments or build loyalty by rewarding your best customers with discounts or perks. As customer choice is important it might make sense to break up your product or service into several price points, making it more accessible. Many airlines today have broken their products and services down into an array of options, a price list. Take Ryanair where the most basic option is the flight only, and everything else – from fast track, hand luggage and so on – adds to the basic price. Ryanair is giving people the choice and can appeal to a budget traveller who just wants to get from A to B as cheaply as possible or to an executive who might want to add perks like premium seat selection, fast track, premium boarding, food and other extras.

We co-decide

A good deal needs two satisfied parties. Why not ask people what they're willing to pay? Let's stay in the airline industry for the sake of an example. Across much of the Star Alliance network, including brands like United and Lufthansa, a betting function for class upgrades has been rolled out. As a customer, you can bid what you want to pay for an upgrade, with options going from a minimum to a maximum depending on the flight. Around 24 hours before take-off, you'll know whether the airline has accepted your offer. You feel there's potentially a bargain to be made and if you're a loyal customer of the alliance, your bid counts as higher.

One American fashion retailer, Everlane, turned to people to co-decide on the pricing of everything from scarves to dresses during a promotion. One would think everyone would choose the lowest price, but Everlane thought more highly of people and had a point to make about the company's radical transparency and the importance of workers' right echoing its mission: "*At Everlane, we want the right choice to be as easy as putting on a great T-shirt,*"[15] CEO and founder Michael Preysman told Inc. in an interview: "*By giving our customers three choices we are able to give them a true sense of value on each item and help inform their decision.*"[16] Online, the shoppers are presented with three prices for each item on sale. Take, for example, a Slim Trouser that was originally $98 and can now be chosen for $47, $56, or $89,[17] but the lowest price doesn't come for free because the shopper is presented with a moral dilemma as the lowest discounted option doesn't turn a profit for Everlane. It's a way of showing people full transparency of the costs going into creating their products, which is one of the cornerstones of what's fuelled Everlane's growth. Everlane trusts people to make the right choice and isn't that the first step in any effort to gain trust?

You decide

Can you ultimately make people set the price for your product or service? Think about it, how would you remunerate your own time and effort? People are increasingly expecting to have a say in what they're willing to buy or sell for, and digital platforms have given people new opportunities. At most sharing or reselling platforms, you can set the price on your product or service yourself, like on Airbnb where you determine what the price should be per day for the place you are renting out. Demand and supply will balance the price, but it's ultimately up to you to set the price and either decline or accept the deal.

English rock band Radiohead was one of the first big artists in 2007 to offer their record for whatever their fans wanted to pay for it. More than 1.8 million decided to download the album, and 40% paid an average of $2.26, generating more cash than any earlier digital sales for the band, ever.[18] Another example is Bandcamp, which supports fair pay for artists and allows millions of up-and-coming musical artists the opportunity to create and share their music with fans for a recurring, self-determined, monthly fee. It's important to consider the ups and downs of a "*You decide*" pricing strategy, because very few organisations have the brand affinity that Radiohead has. If your product or service has a low price point or comes with a high moral price, you can more easily ask people what they will be willing to pay. Take the example of umbrellas in London, which cost less on sunny days compared to when it rains. Why not ask people in that situation?

Open up your pricing

How can you make people have a say in pricing?
Can you divide your service or product into different pricing options?
How can you make your pricing more transparent to add value?
Have you asked people what price they'll be willing to pay?
Does any of your competitors give people a choice in pricing?
What's the lowest or highest price point you have tried?
How do you determine your price today?
How creative are you with your pricing strategy?

Transformative promise: WHO can you help people become?

The transformative promise is different from the other transformative market forces as it has to do with the organisation's raison d'être. It's what should be the truest purpose of any organisation: to enable better lives for people. That's also why the transformative promise is placed as the steering column or the axes on which the other 4Ts evolve. If you don't get your transformative promise right, your efforts are not authentic, and what could be a ripple effect for your marketing efforts from circle to circle, from "*We do*" to "*You do*" will simply be a lofty overpromise.

Previously I mentioned the health insurance company Discovery as an example of an organisation on a mission to enable people to live healthier lives (which is good for business), but digital has brought forth many new interesting players. One example of an organisation that's built around transforming its users is the website and app SuperBetter. Designed on gamification principles, the app's mission is to make its users stronger physically, mentally, emotionally and socially and to make you as a user achieve the goals that matter most to you. According to SuperBetter, they already helped half a million people so far achieve personal growth and tackle real-life challenges. The transformative promise of SuperBetter connects with people and has even achieved creating a community of people helping one another reach the goals they aspire towards. Yet another case to prove the power of a transformative promise.

Open up your promise

Does your promise focus on "*We*" or "*Me*"?
Is your promise a motivational cry to people? Do this? Become this?
Does your promise aspire towards a change in people's status quo?
Does your promise move people towards accomplishing their goals or dreams?
Do you activate your promise across the marketing mix?
Does everyone in your organisation know the promise by heart?
Is your marketing true to your promise when you look at your pricing, placement, promotion and products?

Finding mutual benefits

If you could change something about your organisation, what would it be? Let me ask you another question. If you could change something about yourself, what would it be? These are two important questions when looking how to engage people across the marketing mix. As an organisation, you should aim for the sweet spot where you can involve people and create value for both them and your organisation. Think about the earlier mentioned money transfer app from Danske Bank called MobilePay. For the bank's customers, it used to be a nuisance to transfer money from one account to another or to pay a friend back ten bucks. For the bank as well, it would involve labour-intensive work. Danske Bank created value for its customers while lowering the work for themselves but, more importantly, differentiating themselves from other banks in the Nordic. Or take the phone company Suop that turned its most techy customers' capabilities into advice and service for other customers, which probably will beat any other telco's customer service simply because Suop's techy customers do what they do because they care. Begin by putting yourself in people's shoes across the customer journey from consideration to purchasing to the post-purchasing evaluation phase. Where can you give people more control or choice? How can you make people become the creators? A move from "*We do*" as an organisation to "*You do*" as a customer.

Do you really know what you want?

A word of caution. It doesn't always go well when you trust people to make the call. When Justin Bieber asked his fans in 2010 where he should perform, the Internet decided North Korea. Or take Mountain Dew, which in 2012 asked people to help name its new soda flavour; the most popular contribution ended up being: "*Hitler did nothing wrong.*" Oh yes, the online community can be creative, and so they were when a new research submarine needed a name in 2016 in the UK. Meet the sub *Boaty McBoatface*. The vessel was eventually named RRS *Sir David Attenborough*. You'll not always get the answer you expect as an organisation when you ask people. That said, if you're looking to engage people, to get closer to people, to get inside their heads and hearts, you'll have to open the door to them.

Do you really know what you want in your life? Or what's best for you? Most of the time, probably not. And the amount of data that's collected about you or me on a daily basis raises the bar that an algorithm or artificial intelligence is getting it right before you or I do. I've experienced it on my own body, when I ran a recruitment app that would analyse my Facebook feed and give me a personality test. One of the outcomes was that the analysis claimed that I liked emojis, you know those symbols that have become commonplace in any digital dialogue: the smiling face, a heart or a cake. Even my mum uses them. And I really don't like emojis. I think they devalue the written language. I instantly went on Facebook, and, to my even bigger surprise, I did see that I actually had used them quite often in status updates and in messenger. The app knew me better than I knew myself. That being said, sometimes you need to shape that clay elephant or build that Billy bookcase to value the outcome. Choices are important as we feel in control, which the self-determination theory has shown to be important. In a marketplace where you as a customer are used to mass-marketing and where brand and product are king, it's a welcome change when you are placed in the driver's seat. After all, the only person you will become is the one you decide to be.

Key takeaways

1   **Transformative products**: There are many advantages, from insights to loyalty, to be harvested from giving people a bigger say in shaping products and services.

2   **Transformative placement**: As traditional distribution channels are being challenged on- and offline, everyone can potentially be a channel.

3   **Transformative promotion**: Mass-communication is dead, new participatory formats are gaining impact.

4   **Transformative prices**: It's worth giving people a bigger say over your prices to build trust, engagement and differentiation.

5   **Transformative promise**: It's the steering column of the model, the promise to people that should inspire all other efforts.

Questions to ask yourself

1   Can you think of an example from your organisation where you have successfully enabled people to participate or create?

2   Have you ever asked your customers for help or advice?

3   Do you think certain of your customer segments would be more open to participation?

4   Looking at the Wheel of Transformability, how do you evaluate your organisation's performance across "*We do*" to "*You do*"?

5   What are your reasons for applying or not applying a transform-ability strategy across one or more areas of the marketing mix?

10 A transformative platform

Trust is key and trust comes from opening up and collaborating with people.[1]

– Jaime Pla, CEO, Suop

JAIME PLA

Give people a blank canvas, and you'll discover an artist

Social media has become the toilet musings of the 21st century, a canvas for self-reflection, self-expression or shameless self-promotion, a place to look for everything from love to a lost cat. People own the media space, people hold the microphone, and as trust in big business, institutions, media and public figures is on a downward spiral, people choose to trust their peers and even strangers on the Internet. As described in the beginning, we're entering a third media phase, where it's about the power of the individual spreading messages within a spiderweb of other individuals, from many to many.

It's an opportunity: people's hopes, aspirations, fears and dreams are a treasure chest of engagement possibilities when you as an organisation or leader dare to give people a platform.

An ex-colleague of mine, Søren, caught my attention recently when he shared his personal struggle on Facebook, describing how after 20 years of eating and drinking completely as he saw fit, he suddenly took a look at himself in the mirror weighing 124 kilos and feared he might never get to see his two children grow up. Søren had tried many times before to change his diet or to exercise but always fell back into old habits. He found the helping hand he needed on Facebook.

"*The solution was to externalise my internal goal,*" he explained when I met up with him over a dinner in Copenhagen.

I'm a huge FC Copenhagen (Danish football club) fan, and I made a public declaration on Facebook that if I hadn't lost 10 kilos within six months, I'd pledge to wear my arch rival's team jersey. But not just that, I would wear the jersey with my all-time most despised player's name on it for a week. With this declaration, counting calories and a strict policy on carbohydrate consumption I am now – one year on – 24 kilos lighter and on a continuous journey of transformation. Literally.[2]

Søren understood he needed a little help by putting pressure on himself from his peers if he was to accomplish his goal. This is the little clay elephant of the Internet, as social media enables people to express themselves, to be creative, to be smart, to become better. How can you through your campaign transform people? It's up to your organisation to give them either a motivational push or a platform to take matters into their own hands moving across the transformative promotion from "*We promote*" to "*You promote.*"

I kick balls, deal with it!

Sport England, a public body in England, wanted to promote sport amongst women and in 2015 launched a campaign "*This Girl Can*"[3] consisting of TV ads, cinema, outdoor and social media advertising. I mentioned the campaign earlier in chapter 7 where it was tested up against more classic purposeful campaigns. The campaign wanted to break down barriers to women doing sports. Most women might not view themselves as the athletes portrayed in the majority of magazines or advertisements. The campaign instead encouraged all women to become active no matter how they do it, how they look or even how sweaty they get as long as their heart rate goes up.

One of the ads featured a sweating woman in a gym class with the caption: "*Sweating like a pig, feeling like a fox.*" Another one featured a woman with boxing gloves with the caption: "*Under these gloves is a beautiful manicure.*" But one of my favourites was a woman on a football field doing tricks with a ball with the caption: "*I kick balls. Deal with it.*"

And the campaign's insightful, motivational cry got people talking and hearts beating. On social media, the campaign reached more than 23 million people with women of all ages sharing their #ThisGirl-Can moments. The campaign did change behaviours, with 4.9 million women taking some kind of action as a result of it. Further, 3.3 million did some exercise as a result of the campaign, and 1.5 million started exercising. These women wanted to be more active, all they needed was just that little motivational push. The results speak for themselves, but the early mentioned test, comparing transformational and purposeful campaigns in chapter 7, also did show "*This girl can*" as the 2nd most effective test commercial in making people feel "*motivated and energised*". When so many organisations claim to be world bettering, there is no stronger proof than feeling the change within your own body. Too few campaigns dare to ask us to change: WHO do you help me become?

From "The best a man can get" to "The best a man can be"

"*The best a man can get.*" You most likely recognise the sentence as Gillette's advertising slogan, hammered into every man's head since its reveal during a 1990 Super Bowl commercial break to pitch Gillette's new type of blades. It was all about the product, and stayed that way until 2018, when Gillette's market shares were challenged by more agile online players like Dollar Shave Club and Harry's – as well as a change in grooming trends for men towards more facial hair or "*hipster-beards.*"

Through a campaign launched in late 2018, Gillette suddenly flipped its own slogan to "*The best a man can be,*" issuing a head-on challenge to stereotypes around men distancing itself from the toxic masculinity that formed a cornerstone of the #MeToo movement.

Damon Jones, Vice President, Global Communications and Advocacy at Procter & Gamble (P&G), explained in an interview with Forbes:

> I want to challenge people just to take a minute and have that "moment in the mirror". For guys, this might even be when you're shaving in the morning, ask yourself, "Are my actions what I want them to be? When people are watching me, what am I saying? Am I doing the things that really reflect me at my best?" If guys reflect on that, we think that will have a more positive impact on society.[4]

Gillette wanted to encourage men to change how men talk to one another and how they behave; as part of the campaign, Gillette donated $1 million per year to non-profit organisations in the United States that work with men to tackle some of these issues. The campaign created a lot of controversy and conversation.

The CEO of P&G, David S. Taylor, reiterated the brand's commitment to fighting toxic male stereotypes in media interviews. The brand challenged men to find the best version of themselves, and although it's still too early to see whether Gillette can make a brand or toxic masculinity turnaround at the time of writing, they did get everyone talking about an ad which only ran online. Marc, the Chief Brand Officer at P&G, told me why he thinks this shift was important:

> *For Gillette, which has arguably shaped masculinity for 110 years, it was a good time to come up with a more modern view of the best men can be. We believed it was important to role-model positive behavior for the next generation. That is why we're involved in these kinds of things, even if we get some heat, because we can have an impact. Brands matter. It is important that we step up and use our voice in a positive way.*

But as an organisation you can go further and make people shape or create the campaign. Think about the previously mentioned Small Business Saturday case from American Express where whole communities came together and invested time and effort into promoting one day of local shopping. This is what I call a transformative platform, the "*You promote*" step. What we help create or shape we value more, as demonstrated by the IKEA effect: people placed higher value on the shelf they assembled themselves than on the one they could easily have bought pre-made. I argue that the same applies to campaigns.

Make your activities open for play

"*Campaign*" and "*targeting*" illustrate the militaristic command-and-control language of traditional marketing that still dominates most of the media landscape. It clashes with a bottom-up, pluralistic and open media space where people embrace the opportunities of an Internet for them and by them, from citizen journalism to off-the-shelf e-commerce platforms for Average Joe with something to sell.

Most marketers these days are desperate for what they call "*engagement,*" which, translated into industry terms, means someone in the target group clicking, viewing, commenting or sharing their content – and this is often where the engagement stops. But there is rising realisation that digital is not delivering as much engagement as most hoped for. According to an Economist Group survey,[5] 58% of marketers say that their content does not provide enough opportunity for engagement. As previously argued, maybe it's not that people don't want to engage with content but rather that most content doesn't offer enough possibility for engagement.

Great communication has always been made with a stringent eye on engagement even in the pre-digital days. One of the Hall of Fame VW ads of the sixties, made by advertising legend and co-founder of DDB Doyle Dane Bernbach, illustrates this well. The black-and-white print ad features a picture of a VW Beetle shot slightly from the side with the headlights almost looking curiously at you as a viewer, and underneath it the headline, set in bold san serif font, reads: Lemon. The combination of the curious headline and rather plain image pulls in the reader in order to tell a story about how the featured car was rejected by inspector Kurt Kroner because of a flaw on the chrome piece of the glove box, which is part of a bigger story positioning VW above other cars in the US market because of its relentless sense of detail. As the ad goes: "*This preoccupation with detail means the VW lasts longer and requires less maintenance, by and large, than other cars.*" Concluding with a memorable tag line: "*We pluck the lemons; you get the plums.*"[6]

Great storytelling is like a circle where you leave out a piece for the recipient to think, fantasise or laugh. You're leaving open a piece of the puzzle to inspire curiosity, an extra heartbeat or brain activity. Communication should not be like a prefab, pre-sliced, bland bread ready to chuck down but rather be open for you to bake your own favourite bread.

Behaviour change as a metric

You don't have to look very long at the statistics to see that more and more people are living in bigger and bigger cities and, as a consequence, feeling more alienated from the outdoors. If you're REI, that's a golden opportunity to help people reconnect with the outdoors. We all know that feeling and are probably instinctively driven towards it. In an interview with *Adweek*, Chief Creative Officer Ben Steele explains its aim to motivate its co-op members:

> I'm going to make the outdoors a bigger part of my life. I'm going to protect public lands, because they're places that I care about. I'm going to step forward for things that I believe. At the risk of sounding grand about it, we're looking for impact at the societal level. That's evidence of a movement.[7]

And REI definitely understands people's motives and aspirations: in 2015, they launched the platform #OptOutside as a challenge to the biggest shopping day in the United States, Black Friday. REI closed its doors in all stores and across digital, paid employers for the day off, and instead encouraged people to enjoy the outdoors. In 2016, REI doubled its efforts, and more than 450 non-profit, government and corporate partners joined to inspire millions of people to hit the trails, parks and waterway. Participation jumped from 1.4 million in 2015 to 15 million in 2018, and although the campaign doesn't create the same press coverage anymore, online traffic and social continue to rise. It's a tenfold increase in participation in just three years.

Ben is not in doubt what's working:

> *You see a narrative of a life outdoors from the people who are actually living it, from someone who is summiting big mountains to someone who is stepping onto a trail for the first time. We have 16 million members around the world. The notion that we could invent something more compelling around the outdoors than they could, would be foolish.*

The numbers are there to prove his point, but REI views the success metrics as bigger than simply engagement: as Ben points out, it's *"less about sales and more about a healthy brand, a brand that's got a relationship with customers, that's got a healthy relationship with its employees, where you see engagement on both fronts. And for that, we feel it's been a huge success."*

And he also stresses the importance of the transformation the campaign is trying to achieve: *"One special metric, too, is behaviour change – which goes beyond brand affinity and into deeper aspects of the outdoor life."*

It seems evident that there is a correlation between how REI is pushing people to discover the outdoors and its sales. REI is a cooperative model, and customers can pay $20 to become lifetime members and part-owners of the company.[8] The first year REI ran #OptOutside saw its largest ever membership growth, increasing revenue by 9.3% to $2.4 billion. In 2018, REI hit the $2.62 billion mark in sales, a 2.5% increase from 2017. *"The ability to claim that moment and say, this is about our values and not about transactions, is still pretty differentiating,"* says Ben. *"This is going to sound New Agey, but I think it's a time for people to pause and be intentional about, How do I spend my time? Who am I with? Where am I going? Am I in the places that matter most to me? Or am I just going with the flow?"*

REI's members are not buying the outdoor apparel but are in fact on a transformational journey. It's the being they're buying. Compare REI's efforts to what another player in the outdoor apparel industry, Patagonia, decided to do. On Black Friday, Patagonia pledged to donate 100% of its global sales to grassroots environmental organisations working in local communities. Patagonia's contribution is truly applaudable – and something that's been a core part of its efforts, but it didn't generate the same attention, participation or behaviour change. Patagonia took the activist approach whereas REI made people the outdoor activists and champions. If you're not an iconic brand like Patagonia, it's a treacherous strategy to focus on your organisation as the agent of change rather than on people. REI successfully made people the creators of the campaign, amplifying the message, reach and number of people exploring the outdoors.

Zach Taylor, park manager at Staunton State Park, shared his experience of Black Friday to the local Denver paper, *Denverite*: "*At 11 a.m. on Black Friday, there was an hour-long wait – not to get into Best Buy or Walmart, but to get into Roxborough State Park.*"[9] According to Zach there was a record 620 cars whereas the previous record was about 550 cars, and over 35,000 people spent Black Friday outdoors in California State Parks. The effort doesn't stop here, and at the end of 2018, REI committed to turning #OptOutside into a year-long initiative called #ThriveOutside, together with the Outdoor Foundation, the charitable arm of the Outdoor Industry Association. The goal is to get more Americans to discover the health and well-being benefits of an active life outdoors.[10]

#OptOutside 2015-2018

2015: Participation, 1.4 million. Organisations, 170
2016: Participation, 6 million. Organisations, 475
2017: Participation, 8 million. Organisations, 700
2018: Participation, 15 million. Organisations, +700

Creativity unleashed

To create a platform, the most enabling step of a transformative promotion, it's not enough to leave the circle open for people to fill in the blank; you need to give people the whole circle to play within. The communication is people-centric, not product- or brand-centric. Transformative organisations communicate differently, moving away from the "*We promote*" to enabling the individual: "*You promote.*" I began to observe certain patterns and realised this was not a campaign, but something that in its own right deserved a name: a transformative platform. It's structured much like a game, just waiting for people to come and play again and again.

Def.: a transformative platform

A communication enabler that allows people to create campaigns or initiatives within a shared framework with a shared goal.

These platforms are rewriting the relationship between organisation and people and turning people into their own creators of content. No mass-market content here! The organisation is empowering an army of the willing to join in a shared mission! It's like a Wikipedia of campaigns, where everyone with a passion gets to create the content. I discovered eight attributes characteristic of a platform:

A transformative platform is:

Transformative: Set a clear, shared transformative goal.
Guided: Make a set of guidelines or directions.
Motivational: Aim for action.
Creative: Make it open for creativity.
Replicable: Create for re-creation.
Common: Make it open for everyone.
Accessible: Make the tools or mechanisms easily available.
Relevant: Make it relevant for your brand.

Transformative: set a clear, shared goal or target

You can view the creative development of a platform like designing a game, where you as a game master set certain rules for how to play the game or, in this instance to be part of the platform. As in games, there needs to be something you play to achieve, a mission, and the goal has to be **transformative** for those who take part. Moving people from one state of being to another, from an intent to self-actualisation, from an old-me to a better-me. Take a platform like the Ice Bucket Challenge from 2014. The goal was to raise awareness and money for motor neuron disease, also called amyotrophic lateral sclerosis (ALS). This is why you as an organisation encourage people to do what they do. But never forget to take people's perspective. What's their drive to take part? What transformation do they get out of it?

In the cold dip of the Ice Bucket Challenge there is a learning experience, you're challenging yourself, and that's an important element of a platform. There is a change in the status quo. A wished-for outcome, result or state of mind should be realised or encouraged. As a creator, you learned something, tried something or had a laugh. There is a transformation happening. You're being rewarded for doing, what you're doing. But the benefit needs to be clear for the organisation as well. In this instance, as a creator I show to my friends I dare. For ALS, they get both great exposure and raise funds. To make the platform transforma-tive, it's worth looking to the Arrow to make the benefit focused on the individual's transformation, the WHO.

Take the example of Small Business Saturday, you feel good about yourself when you support your local community stores. I guess, most of us, by the end of the day, feel bad when we don't do it. That was exactly the transformation, the WHO, that Small Business Saturday was aiming for: that feeling of being a conscious local.

The campaign had a shared goal or wishful outcome for people and for brand. For American Express, it was a continuation of its societal contribution going back to restoring the Statue of Liberty, but the busi-ness case was also clear with an uptick in credit card sales while build-ing loyalty with small businesses.

It's important to craft your transformation with care, begin with peo-ple and find the sweet spot for the organisation. Have in mind what would be the aspiration, passion or excitement for people. Typically, campaigns have resorted to rewards or monetary gains (extrinsic), but non-monetary benefits (intrinsic) like personal achievement or learning add more value. Create a platform for people's self-actualisation. Let them be the doers, the creatives, the chief creative campaign officers.

Guided: make a set of guidelines or rules

There also needs to be a set of guidelines or rules for how to play. In the Ice Bucket Challenge, the rules or the HOW is simply a dare game where you have to document that you exposed yourself to cold water or ice and you can pass the challenge on to two friends. If they don't dare, they'll have to donate to ALS, which a lot of people chose to do any-way after the cold dip. The rules or guidelines give people the recipe for how to take part and participate. That said, the rules need to be open enough for people to shape their participation, to feel enabled, to give them a sense of self-determination and an "*I promote*" feeling. It's about them creating. We want to build, share and create to feel fulfilled; it's inherent in us, and, as an organisation, you should make it possible. When done right, the guidelines behind a platform unleash people's creativity, passion and capabilities, potentially creating an exponential reach for your organisation – many to many. If you do a quick search for Small Business Saturday, you'll see the ingenuity of the many people, organisa-tions and businesses supporting and writing about it from individuals in the community doing reviews of local places to creating local events.

Let me for clarity give you another example. When I grew up in Den-mark in the 1980s, dinner consisted of over-boiled potatoes and vegeta-bles, pork fried in chunks of butter until it was as dry as a shoe sole and brown fat gravy of the prefabricated variety. We dined like any other Danish family, and we didn't know any better. In 2004, 12 Nordic chefs presented "*The Manifesto for the New Nordic Kitchen*" to rediscover the lost connection with our local traditions and food, and they put some guidelines in place like: "*To express the purity, freshness, simplicity and ethics that we would like to associate with our region*" and "*To reflect the different seasons in the meals.*"[11] They invited everyone on-board from food producers to politicians and challenged the status quo. It was like a constitution by chefs as the founding fathers for a completely new world of local gastronomic delight. In just a few years, the manifesto was part of turning the Danish food desert into a world-renowned culinary region that's changed the way Danes shop, eat and dine, cemented by Noma earning the title of world's best restaurant for four years. The manifesto empowered chefs around Denmark and showed them a different direction forward, and the result is a complete revival of local food across the country. The guidelines served as a platform for the chefs themselves to create their own version of Nordic delight. The guidelines were open enough for the chefs to add their own creativity, uniqueness and craft. None of us like to be told what to do, but I guess you, like me, are always open for a challenge or to prove someone right or wrong.

Motivational: aim for action

"*Start collaborating, boost plastic recycling,*" "*Shop small,*" "*#OptOutside,*" the rallying cries behind enabling platforms (respectively, Precious Plastic, American Express and REI) are clear and motivational. When your organisation has set a clear transformational goal on people's behalf, the next logic step is to make it happen. The WHEN in the Arrow. The clearer you are, when you want people to act, the higher chance of success. Like a game can have a set time, it's useful to think about when best to motivate people during the year, during the day or when in a specific state of mind. The Movember platform runs and creates awareness around testicular cancer in November, American Small Business Saturday is always the Saturday after the US Thanksgiving and REI always asks people to #OptOutside during Black Friday.

Always make sure to make your request simple and motivational. That doesn't mean you can't offer multiple ways for people to participate – remember it's on their terms, right? Small Business Saturday offers multiple possibilities for engagement from "*Getting your business involved,*" "*Rallying your community*" to simply "*Shopping small.*" They're offering tools for businesses and for people who want to rally the community.

Creative: make it open for creativity

The Ice Bucket Challenge unleashed an unbelievable amount of creativity, passion, fun and commitment from ordinary people to celebrities to make the challenge their own. The tech giant Bill Gates didn't just dump a bucket of ice over his head but built a sophisticated contraption to get the job done. The hip-hop artist Macklemore turned the challenge into an

80-second music video, and Amazon's Jeff Bezos did a stand-up routine with an ice-cold ending. As in a game, a platform opens up for an infinite number of ways to play. Think about the simple design of the board game Ludo and the infinite ways the game plays out. Always make sure there is plenty of room for creativity. Think about the feeling people have when they have been part of making or creating something like refurbishing an apartment or building an enclosure in the garden. That project will become their little darling.

Remember Dave Hakkens from Precious Plastic? His philosophy was all about opening up for the ingenuity and creativity of everyone to create their own DIY-plastic machines and products – and so they did. In Indonesia, the Precious Plastic community was launched in 2018 during a festival, and on their blog, they shared how they saw themselves as a "*community of communities,*" and one could feel the enthusiasm from one of their posts:

> *I hope that this year is a great year for growth in the Precious Plastic Indonesia Community and that we can start making bigger changes in Indonesia. And yes, I hope that one day there won't be any plastic waste around . . . but for now this is a good way to help make something nice from rubbish.*[12]

In Indonesia they create their way.

It's important to ask yourself how many possibilities for interaction your platform offers. Make sure people have plenty of creative possibilities and ways to express or challenge themselves.

Replicable: create for re-creation

A platform is created with an eye for infinite recreation, as was evident with ALS. The thrust behind the initiative is in the hands of people. One example is a Danish Cancer Charity, Kræftens Bekæmpelse, which has launched a tool where everyone can run a fundraiser for the organisation that is often centred on a loved one diagnosed with cancer or deceased.

Think about the return on investment for a platform, compared to normal fundraising activities where you run campaign efforts or go door to door to ask one individual at a time to donate.

On a platform, you give individuals the possibility to create their own fundraisers, often generating many times more the return. Hey, after all, we trust our friends more than some non-profit or organisation. Sometimes, it doesn't demand much to make it replicable. In November 2017, *The Times of India* launched #NoConditionsApply campaign.[13] The campaign took on a 400-year-old Hindu tradition where married women put a red dot on their forehead during a religious festival. *The Times of India* encouraged married women to wear two red dots, one for them and one for a woman who is not allowed in the celebration in order to promote inclusiveness and celebrate all the single women, divorcées, lesbians, widows, sexual workers who can't take part.

Common: make it open for everyone

Platforms are open for everyone – or at least everyone who is aligned with the goal. ALS did truly create an exponential reach with a reported $220 million worldwide in donations in just eight weeks, and public awareness rose dramatically with the challenge turning into the fifth most popular Google search for all of 2014.[14] The power behind a platform is that you can turn individuals into an army behind your effort.

Accessible: make the tools or mechanisms easily available

To make a platform accessible for everyone as an organisation, you're often dependent on resources like time or effort, tools or a mechanism in one shape or another, but it always needs to be easy or with the lowest barrier possible. It might be a website, an app, a DIY kit or something most people have readily available, like a bucket and some ice. Or an extra red dot as in the case of #NoConditionsApply. In a game design, this would be, for example, the board, the tokens or the question cards.

In Colombia, the Environmental Agency saw an increasing threat to local fish species from the alien dragon fish. Methods to catch the dragon fish were expensive and something most fishermen couldn't afford. So the Agency turned to a do-it-yourself model, where they devised a number of ways for the fishermen themselves to create tools to catch the dragon fish out of readily available and cheap materials like old soda bottles. The concept of "*Priceless Traps*" was born, enabling fisherman to take matters into their own hands and potentially saving hundreds of thousands of fish. The model was self-sustaining rather than being dependent on continuous government grants. Always think about how you can keep the barrier for participation as low as possible.

Relevant: make it relevant for your brand

Lastly, remember to keep your platform relevant to your brand. Small Business Saturday by American Express is a continuation of the company's earlier societal efforts, and it addresses how credit cards can make a positive contribution in society. It was on brand. Think about how often you see a campaign or an initiative, but you can't remember the brand behind it. Most often, it's a lack of relevance between the issue or the goal of the campaign and the specific brand.

There is no recipe for success

The eight attributes are no guarantee of success – if only marketing was that simple – but they can serve as a checklist when creating your next platform. Look at the most successful platform in recent history, the

#MeToo movement. It doesn't have a clear goal, and the guidelines, if any, are rather loose, but it's a decentralised platform, where everyone can voice up and turn a broad message of female empowerment into their own rallying cry. It gives women across the world a possibility to use their creativity and voice to make the platform the very loudest it can be!

From my years of experience with campaigning, I noticed one interesting thing: how organisations stood in the way of their own progress. The ability to act, the ability to create change was centralised and thus dependent on resources, staff, campaigns funds and other input. When digging deeper, I found certain initiatives outperformed others in growth or reach; they had a transformability factor. They were not campaigns, they were platforms that empowered people and made them the change agents unleashing exponential reach.

A campaign is centralised, and, although some offer co-creation possibilities – "*We co-promote*" – it still feels like a brand-driven initiative. A platform enables all the participants to create or take part on their own terms, generating a strong-willed army of individuals on a mission. It's one-to-many and many-to-one. It doesn't feel or smell of marketing as it's far from top-down but rather bottom-up. An organisation's role is to create a platform that truly enables individuals and ultimately unites them behind a shared transformative goal.

A real change story about societal contribution

Volunteering is a rewarding commitment. It is important because it helps you become an enriched person. I have volunteered for years now, mostly at school, and I love it so much! If you volunteer at someplace you love or a fond interest, then it makes it so much enjoyable. I volunteer at a library as well and being an avid reader it makes me so happy to be surrounded by books. It is important because it improves social skills, helps us become more responsible, teaches empathy, and is just time well-spent. Of all my hobbies, volunteering is my favourite because it shows that I am helping and contributing in my community in some way and that makes my heart happy.[15]

– *Salmeen H, on Quora.com*

People made Small Business Saturday great

There are clear parallels to be found behind the success of REI's #OptOutside campaign and the spread of Small Business Saturday, as both prove the exponential growth potential of a transformative platform. The "*You promote*" step. As an organisation, you're not standing in the way of your own success but allowing others to create and help expand the reach and impact. As previously described, Small Business Saturday[16] began in 2010 on the back of the financial crisis and created an enormous buzz both online and in the press. The day has seen a continuous growth year on year among US consumers, and in 2013, the campaign was launched in the UK. Both in the UK and the United States, hundreds of organisations and businesses have joined the day, and in 2017 the US Senate passed a resolution to officially recognize Small Business Saturday as an official day to support small businesses.

The campaign has succeeded in putting small businesses front of mind for Brits and Americans alike and creating a meaningful alternative to other shopping days. According to a survey in the United States in 2018 by the National Retail Federation, 67 million people planned to shop on Small Business Saturday, and 78% of those said they would do so "*specifically to support small businesses.*" By comparison, 34 million people plan to shop on Thanksgiving, 116 million plan to shop on Black Friday and 75 million are expected to shop online on Cyber Monday. For a day that didn't exist eight years ago, that's quite an accomplishment and shows that if you dare to give people a stage, they'll rally with you for what they believe in, for what they shape.

Small Business Saturday

US spend in small businesses

2010: No public info
2011: No public info
2012: $5.5 billion
2013: $5.7 billion
2014: $14.3 billion
2015: $16.2 billion
2016: $15.4 billion
2017: $12.9 billion
2018: $17.8 billion

Small Business Saturday

UK spend in small businesses

2013: £468 million
2014: £504 million
2015: £623 million
2016: £717 million
2017: £748 million
2018: £812 million

Make sure you get every step right!

Before you run to your company's CFO betting all of your marketing budget on transformative platforms, let me reiterate: there are no recipes for success. In marketing, campaigns often don't go the way we plan them after all, it's about humans, and we're not even good at creating change in our own lives.

Let me give you an example of a campaign by the innovative Swedish airbag bicycle helmet company Hövding called "*Give a Beep.*" The effort could have achieved even greater results but stood in its own way. You most likely have heard of Hövding, invented by two Scandinavian students of Industrial Design, Anna Haupt and Terese Alstin? Their solution is an inflatable helmet much like an airbag activated on impact and camouflaged nicely in a scarf or what might just look like the collar of your jacket or sweater. I would definitely have loved Hövding when I was a kid, and all bicycle helmets made you look as though you were wearing a big white bucket on your head. In your early teenage years, you definitely didn't want to look like Darth Vader or be called Lord Bucket when you're bicycling to school.

But that's not the story here. I want to share how Hövding wanted to promote safer bicycling in London. Their mission statement is rather long but worth having a look at:

> At Hövding, we consider cyclists to be everyday heroes and we see it as our mission to keep them safe. We are very proud of the fact that Hövding over the years have helped protect more than 800 cyclists in accidents. Because we believe the world will become a better place if more people choose the bicycle – for inner city environment, health and climate reasons.[17]

So they're on a mission to get more people to "*choose the bicycle,*" but they also view people as everyday heroes. One of the ways they have brought their promise alive was to turn people into activists by providing a platform, called "*Give a beep,*" for safer bicycling in London in 2016.[18] Hövding reinvented the old bicycle bell and turned it into a smart Flic button. Hundreds of cycling influencers got the smart button and with an easy click could register their specific frustration (or danger) hot spots in the London traffic. Each use of the smart bell was noted on an interactive heat map of London. Simultaneously an automated email was sent to the Mayor of London to motivate him to act. Hövding gave people the possibility of taking part in making biking safer and not just helping themselves to a safer bike ride through London, and in helping fellow Londoners, eventually pushing more people to bicycle when they feel safe enough.

The campaign did generate an impact and it was **transformative, guided, relevant** and **motivational**, but on the four other criteria for a platform it struggled: "*Give a Beep*" was less **accessible** as it was dependent on the Flic button, making it less **creative**, less **replicable** and less **common**. If the campaign was to spread, more Flic buttons would have to be distributed at a high cost for Hövding. What could potentially have turned every cyclist into a springboard for greater bicycle safety in London with the right tool instead created a barrier for its own success and impact.

Platform checklist

Transformative: Is there a clear shared goal?
Guided: Are there guidelines and directions?
Motivational: Is there a cry for action?
Creative: Is it open for creation?
Replicable: Is the initiative replicable?
Common: Can everyone participate?
Accessible: Is it easy to participate?
Relevant: Is your brand's role relevant?

Make people matter

When it comes to doing what you care about or enjoy, time (or any kind of resource) is less of an issue. No matter if you are "*a Brooklynite that cares about his neighbourhood and its stores*" (Small Business Saturday), "*a city dweller with a craving for the outdoors*" (REI), "*a beard-growing hipster giving a damn and not afraid to show it*" (Movember) or "*a woman that prefers munching over a Marathon, but feels bad about it*" (#ThisGirlCan), a door waits to be kicked in or gradually opened. This is your life-changing chance and business opportunity as an organisation. REI succeeded in creating outdoor champions, many millions of them. Twitter user @Tom2Michael posted a picture with his smiling family posing during their trek: "*Caught the last bit of light above #Boise, as we #OptOutside for #BlackFriday. #rei #hiking @rei #foothills.*" The fulfilled Twitter user and his equally-so family are heaven for any organisation wanting to make a meaningful difference in people's lives. If you want to create change at scale, you have to begin by moving one person.

Key takeaways

1   Most marketing activities don't offer enough opportunities for engagement; never be afraid to open up for people's creative input and urge to create.

2   A transformative platform is a marketing enabler made available by an organisation that allows people to create or recreate campaigns or initiatives for a shared transformative goal.

3   A transformative platform has eight characteristics: transformative, guided, motivational, creative, replicable, common, accessible and relevant.

4   A transformative platform is the "*You promote*" step in the Wheel of Transformability.

5   Platforms unlock marketing growth, personal betterment and reach by turning an individual's passion and resources into part of the promotion.

Questions to ask yourself

1   Do people talk about your product or your point of view as an organisation?

2   How much opportunity for engagement does your current campaigns offer?

3   Looking at the eight characteristics for a platform, how many of them do you recognise from your recent campaigns?

4   Can you think of any transformative platforms you have observed recently?

5   How can you use a platform approach to unlock growth and reach?

11 Unlocking the potential of all people

I think that focus should be more about what can be done instead of what can be told. I really don't care about psychological manipulation that's happening all the time. Personally, I love the idea of having a positive impact budget instead of a marketing budget.[1]

– Jukka Peltola, CEO, Goodio

JUKKA PELTOLA

Your stakeholders are your licence to operate

All your stakeholders matter, from your customers, employees, communities, legislators, investors and suppliers to non-profits. Their thoughts, their ideas, their opinions about your organisation are what build your relevance, build your brand. After all, behind any title from chairperson to a farmer is a human being with dreams, aspirations and fears. The stakeholder-centric approach is becoming evident not just from the threat of tweets and shit-storms from opinionated employees or suppliers but from the very top of the power pyramid: the investors. Usually investors were silent partners especially as long as their investments paid off, but money doesn't speak loud enough in itself.

In 2018 Larry Fink, the CEO of the world's biggest asset manager, Black Rock, representing $6 trillion, wrote in his annual letter: "*Without a sense of purpose, no company, either public or private, can achieve its full potential. It will ultimately lose the license to operate from key stakeholders.*"[2] The message is resoundingly clear: no organisation is an island, and its legitimacy is in the hands of you and me and its many other stakeholders. This makes it increasingly important for you as an organisation to get as close to as many of your individual stakeholders as possible.

Put the stake into stakeholders

Apple is one the most valuable brands in the world, but that doesn't make them immune to the ramifications of its stakeholders. A shit-storm in 2010 cut off brand value when it was revealed that the working conditions at one of Apple's contracted suppliers, Foxconn, were so appalling the workers were killing themselves.[3]

In recent years, there has been a shift towards looking at all the company's stakeholders from a transactional point of view to one of collaboration and partnership. If you are familiar with the United Nation's 17 Sustainable Development Goals (SDGs) that's a number of goals and targets to unlock a more sustainable future in 2030, then you'll also know that goal 17 is collaboration. Systemic challenges like plastic waste, climate change, lack of talent or poverty are best dealt with together– even if that means bringing competitors into the equation. In 2010, GlaxoSmithKline and Novartis joined 11 other companies, governments and foundations to launch a coordinated effort toward eliminating ten forgotten tropical diseases by 2020. Their efforts saw increased R&D funds dedicated, expanding drug donations and the sharing of expertise. For the partners, it was a possibility not only to deliver on their mission but also to increase innovation, grow new markets and build better relationships across the value chain.

There is often a mutual benefit in working with your stakeholders. The British retailer Marks & Spencer has, in collaboration with its suppliers, created a tier system that pushes each supplier on a journey towards better social and environmental performance. The programme has financial returns for both the retailer and the suppliers. Today, traditional competitors like low-cost supermarkets Tesco and Aldi can work together on initiatives where there is a shared benefit, such as the plastic pact, Wrap, in the UK where the partnership aims to reinvent, rethink and redefine how plastic is used.

Engaging your stakeholders is not just about minimising risk but about tapping into the potential benefits for your organisation and its stakeholders. Stakeholders have a stake in your company's success and can be a valuable part of your organisation. Like your customers, they too have personal ambitions waiting to be turned into reality! Rather than treating your stakeholders like business partners, there's reciprocal value in enabling them to do more! It makes sense: you work harder for the business you have a stake in. This is where enablement comes into play. The US dairy producer Chobani chose to take a different route when it went public and gave its 2,000 full-time employees, no matter their job role or seniority level, an ownership stake worth up to 10% of the company. For Chobani, it was a way of saying thanks to all its employees as the current and future employees are the path to its continuous success.

Unilever is one of the companies that have pledged to support smallhold farmers. Through their Lipton tea brand,[4] they're supporting 750,000 smallholdings, mostly in Africa and Asia where more than one million people are thought to work. Unilever is also investing heavily in training the farmers and investing in capacity building, but it's an exercise that's just as much a matter of securing their tea business for the future. Climate change, water scarcity and competition for land from other crops are threatening their livelihood and profitability. For Unilever,[5] engaging farmers means higher yields, more secure supply and ultimately better profitability for both parties.

Another company that's taking a skill- and capability-building approach is the Guatemalan electricity company Mayan Power and Light: it's launched a clean-tech technical training programme educating female students about electrical circuitry, solar power, sales and marketing, so that they can install solar power systems and run microbusinesses. But the programme goes further than education and provides financial security to the women and their families while providing clean affordable energy to their communities. The more you empower others, the more you'll find yourself surrounded by people who support you the most.

Both REI and American Express have with great success enabled stakeholders to jump on board their initiatives #OptOutside and Small Business Saturday, with both brands seeing an increase in organisations joining. In a four-year period, REI[6] went from 170 to more than 700 organisations backing up its efforts, and many of the state parks waived entrance and parking fees to encourage visits. The CEO Jerry Stritzke stated in 2016:

> (P)eople who build their lives around the outdoors really embraced the idea of reclaiming Black Friday. It took on a life of its own and became about much more than REI. Opt Outside should be a platform for the non-profits and public servants who are on the front lines of the outdoor community. They're the ones who make the outdoors accessible for everyone. That's why, from today onward, we're going to lift them up as the official spokespeople for Opt Outside.[7]

REI succeeded in creating a movement for people who loved the outdoors and empowered its stakeholders to join on the shared mission.

Unlocking value together

The transformability steps from "*We do*," "*We engage*," "*We collaborate*" to "*You do*" can also be used to unlock value among stakeholders and turn them into a resource in the marketing mix. As a farmer, where do you feel more motivated: when you're simply selling your fresh produce at market price or when you're collaborating with Unilever to increase the yield? This is the "*We Collaborate*" step. Or take the example of REI's #OptOutside campaign and its collaboration with state parks: rather than REI donating money, they're partners with the parks on a mission to spread the love of the outdoors. Your stakeholders have aspirations and dreams; help them come true. As an organisation, the more you enable your stakeholders, the more you can leverage their passion, means and capabilities as a resource in the marketing mix, from product to promotion. The steps go from no-engagement "*We do*" to increasingly enabling stakeholders with "*We engage,*" "*We collaborate*" to ultimately putting the efforts in your stakeholders' hands with the enabling "*You do.*"

Enabling your stakeholders

We do: When you as an organisation are in control of the whole effort.

We engage: When you as an organisation engage your stakeholders around the effort.

We collaborate: When you offer your stakeholders the chance to co-create or customise the effort.

You do: When you enable your stakeholders to create the effort.

We do

This is when the organisation and stakeholder have a purely transactional relationship and where the organisation is calling the shots – typical business and supplier relationship.

We engage

The organisation is engaging the stakeholder. This can be through many different means such as questionnaires or surveys – or, for example, an event for the stakeholders.

We collaborate

The organisation collaborates with the stakeholder on certain projects or initiatives, such as the cross-sector collaboration The Plastic Pact, Wrap, or Marks & Spencer's tier collaboration with its suppliers.

I do

The organisation leverages the stakeholder's means and capabilities as a resource in the marketing mix, from product to promotion. One example is how many of the big logistics companies have today turned to community stores to be the pickup point for people's deliveries, offering an extra income for the stores, creating logistics savings for the companies and offering customers easy local pickup points.

Bring everyone's best to the table

There is a host of advantages in bringing your stakeholders closer, and it's not simply a communication- or relationship-building exercise. Your stakeholders can unlock new business models and drive growth, as demonstrated by the South African health insurance company Discovery, which, as part of its Vitality programme to keep people healthier, collaborated with local gyms and supermarkets to nudge them to exercise more and eat healthier. The business case and benefits for the health insurance company, the gym, retailer and its customers are clear. Each stakeholder can bring a unique perspective and capabilities to the table.

Or think about the historic collaboration between businesses and non-profits. The non-profits have vast knowledge of complex issues, social obstacles and on-the-ground experience, but if combined with the skill sets of business, such as strong consumer insights, research and development and business model focus, there is a win–win for both parties.

What if you can't stand the fact that tourism is one of the most polluting industries in the world and you hate the commotion and cheap sales tricks of industry giants like Hotels.com or Booking.com? Christian Møller Holst, the co-founder of travel booking platform Goodwings, set out to make a real difference by turning each hotel stay into lasting impact.

Rather than relying on the usual industry practise of heavy marketing budgets, he partnered with non-profits to use their extensive network with companies to create a truly collaborative model. The non-profits are Goodwings ambassadors opening the doors at its corporate partners with a simple pitch; book your travels through Goodwings at no extra cost, and you're helping generate funds for our causes. It's brothers in arms fighting to make a difference, and travellers can feel and see the tangible impact Goodwings and its many partners are making. It's not a charitable add-on – it's a collaborative business model. Within just one year of its launch, Goodwings was working with 90 NGOs across 45 countries, including organisations such as World Wide Fund for Nature, Plastic Change and the World Diabetes Foundation.

Analyse and evaluate your stakeholders' means and capabilities, talk to them, go on a journey of discovery to find the sweet spot for collaboration or transformability. You can with advantage use the Wheel of Transformability to see where you together can harvest benefits – or maybe even a chance to turn your stakeholders into service providers, part of the promotion or creators of the product. Take the previously earlier example of Mayan Power and Light; they educate skilled potential employees but also generate a decentralised model for selling their products through women and scaling up the access to clean electricity across Guatemala. Mayan Power and Light gets a farther reaching distribution, but the women and their communities win as well.

Always remember a people-first perspective, when you're looking to enable your stakeholders, in order to make sure it's ultimately anchored in a benefit for those you want to target. Unilever's smallhold farmers have a clear advantage from the partnership: they get long-term profitability and higher yields. As people are aspiring towards a good life and their consumption patterns are changing, you can with advantage explore what the sustainability agenda can bring to your organisation or its stakeholders within topics such as health, liveability, community, environment and economic empowerment. According to an MIT Sloan Management Review,[8] 90% of businesses agree that collaboration is needed to face sustainability issues but that the potential is untapped as only 47% state that their companies collaborate on sustainability. How can you, together with your stakeholders, make people's lives better?

Brothers in arms fighting for the same goals

When you as an organisation have a clear ambition, a transformative promise, stakeholders with a similar agenda gets attracted or are more easily engaged. The French supermarket Carrefour[9] took on a big challenge to change European regulation in order to support more diverse fruits and vegetables. An absurd law supported by the agro-chemical lobby prevents people from getting access to all but 3% of fruits and vegetables. The other 97% are illegal because a producer can only grow what is registered in the Official Catalogue of Author-ised Species. Carrefour turned to the farmers and its customers to help rally for change. In 2017, Carrefour opened the Black Supermarket where it would sell illegal fruits and vegetables to rally for biodiversity. The efforts were supported by a petition and a campaign celebrating "*illegal*" farmers as national heroes. Carrefour even signed five-year supply contracts with the farmers and invited opinion leaders to wit-ness the act. Eventually the campaign succeeded in changing the EU regulation giving access to more varieties and in 2021 full access. In a press release, Carrefour explained the importance of the victory: "*New varieties are now sold in our stores: it's a source of pleasure for our customers and of enormous pride for us. . . . This practice is essen-tial for maintaining the planet's biodiversity.*"[10] No fewer than 85,000 consumers signed the petition to support Carrefour's efforts, and sup-pliers to Carrefour became proud farmers fighting for something they all believed in: biodiversity.

We engage

Engaging stakeholders is becoming the new normal as tightening legal requirements demand continuous dialogue. But reaching out to stakeholders is also an important first step in voicing up for an agenda you believe in as an organisation. One example is how IKEA's former chief sustainability officer Steve Howard in 2017 called on govern-ments to deliver, "long, loud and legal"[11] policies to aid compa-nies with the transition to a low-carbon economy. If you want your stakeholders to change, you'll have to begin with voicing up what you want from them.

We collaborate

There are many ways to collaborate with your stakeholders. One obvi-ous way is to find a like-minded organisation where there's a shared goal. Up comes co-branding or cause marketing, when it's a brand collaborating with a non-profit.

Back in 2015, the US supermarket chain Target partnered with UNICEF on a campaign called Kid Power. Target sold kid-friendly fitness track-ers to encourage kids to become more active (which is much needed across the Western world), and each completed activity would make Target donate food packets to underprivileged children around the world. UNICEF is getting much needed help with fighting malnutrition while Target is helping US kids to be more active.

Taking a collaborative approach is really about seeing your organisation's potential in a different light and exploring new business opportunities. Let me share an example where a fairer model has evolved viewing suppliers as people. There's been a surge for fair trade products across markets as it's been an easy value proposition for people to understand, but as people and producers get more educated, a new category called "*direct trade*" is on the rise. "*The most important resource a customer, coffee brand or even the roaster has in the coffee industry is the relationship with a farmer,*"[12] said Thrive Farmers' co-founder, Ken Lander, to Sustainable Brands from his small coffee farm tucked away in the village of San Rafael de Abangares, Costa Rica. Thrive Farmers works with farmers in a direct relationship with no intermediaries. Thrive views its suppliers differently and in a manifesto on Thrive's website explains the philosophy: "*Our farmers aren't suppliers – they're people. And what they cultivate isn't a commodity – it's a livelihood.*" On average, Thrive's farmers earn more "*to live for*" than would be offered through Fair Trade programmes, for example, ultimately giving you as a customer a better taste in your mouth the next time you sip a cup of coffee.

A real change story about emotional well-being

For most of my life, I had a fairly low self-esteem and confidence. I would make myself face my fears, public speak in groups, be an extravert when needed. I would study up on what I had to talk about and know what I was talking about and able to answer questions. I learnt to put on my "Mr Confident" face, even when my legs were shaking. I kept moving and was animated and developed a sense of humour. Others close to me asked how I did it. I just told them "I made a choice, committed to it and gave it my all.[13]

– *Shane Butcher, Life Transitioner in Alternate Worlds (1966–present), on Quora.com*

You do

As you've seen from the many other cases shared throughout the book, something incredibly powerful happens when you give people the opportunity to be in control and to realise their goals or dreams. That's no different when we look towards the many stakeholders around an organisation. One of the most successful retail and hospitality concepts in terms of growth has been the franchise model. For the young Swede Maria de la Croix, that model wasn't working, and she co-founded Wheelys Café, previously mentioned, where everyone can purchase a coffee bicycle, live out their dream and become their own organic barista or simply their own boss: "*I loved the idea of enabling people to do their own thing,*" Maria[14] explained to me in a late evening Skype call. And from an economic standpoint, it seems to make more sense: "*We found out that those who own the Wheelys café and sell coffee by themselves also get more money. When you work for yourself you strive to do best all the time.*"

Giving all stakeholders a say

When someone believes in you or trusts you, it's incredibly empowering. Think about the millions of people who every day choose to step into a stranger's car using Lyft or Uber – or decide to rent their apartment to someone from a country they never even heard of. All thanks to a simple social contract of reciprocity: you rate me, I rate you – or I trust you, you trust me. I know, yes, it can be nerve-racking to give up control, but you can put some checks and balances in place. When the travel booking platform Goodwings turned their non-profit partners into the acquisition engine, they also waived goodbye to conventional advertising. The ability to drive traffic to the site and ultimately drive money to the non-profits rested almost purely in the hands of Goodwings's non-profit partners. In its initial year, Goodwings signed up more than 90 non-profits across the world. In an interview with Goodwings's founder Christian, he said, "*(I)t's not a free ride for the non-profits,*"[15] Goodwings had put metrics in place for the partners to live up to. Goodwings is an inspiring example not only of how you can turn your stakeholders into an important element of your marketing mix but also of how you can manage expectations and set metrics for success because you're co-dependent.

There are many ways to categorise the stakeholders of any given organisation, so do take this as a guideline and look at the stakeholders that are relevant for your organisation. You can also take a look at the Wheel of Transformability to see where a potential stakeholder can leverage means and capabilities as a resource in the marketing mix, from product to promotion.

Transforming stakeholders

Beyond Billy: the IKEA mission

I've mentioned the IKEA Billy bookcase, shared the story behind IKEA's flat-packs and the interesting aspects of the IKEA effect, but IKEA is in itself an organisation on a journey towards playing a bigger role in people's lives. IKEA's vision is to create a better everyday life for many people. I sat down with Joanna Yarrow,[16] who's its head of Sustainable and Healthy Living, in Hyllie, a suburb to Malmø, at the global marketing headquarters of IKEA. It's just over the bridge from where I live in Copenhagen. While sipping coffee from the canteen, we're talking and enjoying a view over the green grass roofs of the office building, which has won acclaim as Scandinavia's most sustainable building.

Early in the 80s, IKEA began looking at the impact of their business, mostly stemming from issues in the supply chain, and in 2012 they launched their People Planet Positive ambition, setting concrete targets across their business towards 2020. They knew their customers were a key part of the equation as the biggest impact most often happens in the hands of its customers, so IKEA had to get their customers on-board. One example Joanna shared was renewable energy, where IKEA committed to producing all their operations energy renewably by 2020. Today it has over 414 wind turbines and 75.000 solar panels meeting 83% of its energy needs, and it's on target to become a green energy supplier in 2020.[17] But IKEA also looked to influence its customers' energy consumption. In 2014, they introduced hydro solar in the UK, and today its hydro solar products are in seven markets, with a view to global presence by 2025. In 2018, IKEA made an important commitment on its customers' behalf, pledging to inspire and enable one billion people to live a better life at home, within the limits of the planet's resources. Joanna explained that the pledge is seen as a business opportunity but also as a necessity. IKEA has to play a role in customers' lives going forward by helping people to grow their own food and by providing solutions to help people save energy and water and reduce waste.

To accomplish this audacious goal, IKEA had to take a different approach. From the Sustainable Living at Home research, they knew over 90% of people wanted to live a more sustainable life, but only 3% could tell what that actually means in practice. They also discovered that the meaning of a home was rapidly changing across markets, as Joanna explained:

> *Physical home structures are changing, household configurations are changing, the ways we live and work in cities are also changing. Our everyday life would traditionally have played out within the four walls of our home, but it's becoming a lot more fluid. It's because we are more confined in our space at home, we might have multi-generational living, we might work remotely, so it's becoming much more blended. We can't just limit ourselves to what happens within the four walls, so we need to think broader than the home and more about people's everyday life, wherever it plays out.*

Joanna shared how IKEA is very aware of the shift that's happening in marketing, and during her six years with IKEA it's become increasingly important to involve people. Joanna revealed how their one-billion strategy was shaped by deeper customer interaction. In 2014, they launched a programme in the UK across 5,000 households with a mix of co-workers and customers to better understand how to help people live more sustainably. They called the programme "*Living Lagom.*" Haven't heard about Lagom? It's another one of those trending Scandinavian words like *lykke* or *hygge*," but "*Lagom*" means "*not too little, not too much, just right.*" The programme offered the participants the chance to test IKEA products that help save energy and water, reduce waste and promote a healthy lifestyle. Joanna explains:

> *First of all, the starting point was that we were trying to understand their lives and together with them explore sustainable living where they were setting goals on their terms. For example, one guy might want to lose weight, someone else might want to save money, others might want to have more time with their kids. They had different topics like energy, water, waste or food that they decided to focus on. I think that was the personalisation, and starting from them and the reality of their lives and their needs was a trigger. I don't wake up in the morning thinking "How am I going to cut my carbon footprint" today. I'm thinking what's my daughter going to have for breakfast? How am I going to get to work?*

IKEA made the customers themselves dictate their targets, and Joanna described how they became a little community that shared solutions with one another. She had no doubt about the key to their high engagement: "*A real energiser for participants was the idea that they had the opportunity to potentially shape our business.*"

Joanna sees Lagom as a microcosm of what IKEA want to achieve by reaching one billion people, something they'll begin rolling out through the 124 million IKEA family members worldwide (a customer membership programme). It's a mix of getting people to live more sustainably and healthy but also delivering the products and services to enable that change. That's the real business opportunity, and, as Joanna points out, they want the sustainable range to grow four times as fast as the rest of the business. IKEA has done it before. Joanna gave the concrete example of the switch to 100% LED lighting across its range, which benefitted the business and obviously saved customers on their electricity bills. IKEA could use the scale of its operations to make LED lighting the most affordable in the market, drive rapid change and completely disrupt the lighting market.

Products and services obviously play an important part in getting people to live more sustainably. Joanna explains:

> What do we need to do as a retailer is help people rethink their relationship with stuff. . . . We have our colleagues in range and supply who are working towards the goal that by 2030 everything will be made from renewable or recyclable material and everything will be designed in order to have a second life. But what else can we do as a retailer to support people to consume in a sustainable way? To extend product life, to refurbish, to repair, to rent, to lease all these different things, etc. It's an important area for us.

It's not only the way people aspire to live or how life within the four walls is changing – retail itself is also changing. In 2019, IKEA opened up a new store concept in Greenwich, London.[18] It's a central location and much more integrated with the community featuring green spaces, a roof garden, flexible work areas and workshops, a roof pavilion and a learning lab where customers can explore how to prolong the life of products, grow food, upcycle and make their homes more sustainable. Joanna explained how today's IKEA has to change and be in a constant dialogue with its customers and community and give them a real say, which is a radical departure from earlier business practices:

> We have had 75 years of success with a linear, standardised business model. So, we offer a global standardisation: you go into any household in the UK and you're going to see the same products. You'll get to have the same customer experience, you go into a shop that looks exactly the same. That has been key to our success.

The retail and product strategy were also followed up by a 2019 communication effort. The A Better World Starts at Home campaign aims to kick-start IKEA's work towards inspiring and enabling one billion people to live a better life within the planet's limits and is planned to run over three years. The first part of the campaign focused on climate, highlighting climate-friendly products and behaviours and telling the story of the *"Accidental Environmentalist"* – people unknowingly cutting their carbon emissions through everyday actions supported by IKEA products. The campaign also drove people to an IKEA Better Living app, where customers as well as co-workers can see the environmental impacts of their everyday actions, compete in challenges to have the biggest positive impact, or take on one of 75 climate- or health-improving actions. *"We said okay, we want to inspire, we want to help people to understand that there is this connection between their lives and the big issues they care about,"* explained Joanna. *"We want them to see IKEA as a brand that can help them. We also want to demonstrate the effect of when we all do these things at scale."*

IKEA knows people want to live more sustainably because the vast majority have been telling them again and again through research and the Lagom program, and although the one billion target is ambitious, it's broken down into concrete tasks. There are areas and actions that everyone within the business and its customers can relate to, focused around simple everyday actions towards a better life at home. IKEA supports the effort with products and services that are specifically designed to help you live more sustainably and reduce the impact of your everyday life as well as through new retail spaces, campaign activities and apps. The IKEA mission is not just something written on the wall as you enter the headquarters in Hyllie; they're aiming to enable it, and its success is dependent on a shared journey with its customers: *"Much more a relationship,"* as Joanna described it. Going forward, it will be exciting to see whether IKEA can successfully keep an eye on its long-term ambition and push their customers towards that momentous change. Time and numbers will tell.

A goal bigger than yourself

As I mentioned in the beginning, no organisation is an island and as soon as you recognise that your success is dependent on your web of stakeholders, you might as well give them a real stake.

And writing about islands, a small bank from an island in the Baltic Sea, Ålandsbanken (Bank of Åland), succeeded in creating what most banks would only dream of: global impact. You've probably never heard about the bank, but Bank of Åland is on a mission so important it turned to explain its competitors, other banks, why they should join too. When you shop, you might think about the environmental impact of your purchases, but during a busy day every day, it's difficult to gain an overview of what's good and bad and ultimately change behaviour. In 2016, the Bank of Åland, with a number of other non-financial partners, decided to create an overview –Aland Index – which shows you the environmental impact of what you buy as a carbon footprint estimate. If you buy a shoe, the Index gives you an estimate of the carbon footprint.

Periodically, you receive an overview of the carbon footprint of all your purchases as if it were a bank statement. The Bank of Åland[19] made the Index readily available for any other bank that is ready to adopt. In 2018, the Bank of Åland was in negotiations with more than ten banks worldwide with a potential of reaching 16,235,000 customers and influencing their everyday decisions through their card transactions. The UN has invited the bank to present its solution at its headquarters, and the Index been endorsed by the Finnish environmental minister. And, maybe more importantly, the Index works. The carbon footprint amongst users had decreased on average 2.7% in March 2018 compared to March 2017, with some categories seeing a dramatic change in behaviour: taxi use was down by an average of 11%. It does help when you motivate people to change and give them the tools – and if you dare to involve your stakeholders and even competitors, the impact can be exponential. That reminds me of an often cited African proverb that aptly sums up the potential: "*If you want to go fast, go alone. If you want to go far, go together.*"

Key takeaways

1   No organisation is an island. Engaging your stakeholders, from suppliers to investors, is mandatory for an organisation.

2   The Wheel of Transformability can be used to unlock value among stakeholders and turn them into a resource in the marketing mix, but always take a people-first perspective.

3   Each of your stakeholders offers an untapped potential from new insights, fresh partnerships, extra resources to new distribution possibilities. Take a look at your many stakeholders to discover the transformability potential.

4   A clear and strong transformative promise can attract like-minded stakeholders to join a shared journey.

5   Don't be afraid to set success metrics and align expectations with your stakeholders.

Questions to ask yourself

1   Are you experiencing an increasing need or demand for dialogue with key stakeholders?

2   How much do you engage your stakeholders today? Do you have a clear picture of your stakeholder's dreams, fears and aspirations?

3   What stakeholders are pivotal to your organisation's success? Can you with advantage give them more control?

4   What stakeholders are faced with similar challenges as your organisation? Could there potentially be a collaboration or alignment of efforts?

5   What stakeholders are you in contact with the least? Why?

12 It's time to . . .

In a capitalist world that's so much about excess, it's about time for companies to chart a different path that's about human enlightenment. The last frontier in purpose – how can we achieve the inner betterment of people? If we don't succeed with improving our minds and behaviours, we won't succeed with the greater challenge of discovering better ways of living in our communities and in society at large.[1]

– Tom Daly and Max Vallot, Co-founders, District Vision

TOM DALY

MAX VALLOT

Safe return doubtful

"*Men wanted,*"[2] reads the headline of the often quoted ad that British explorer Ernest Shackleton allegedly printed in the *Times* in 1913. It continues, "*for hazardous Journey, small wages, bitter cold, long months of complete darkness, constant danger, safe return doubtful, honour and recognition in case of success.*"

More than a century later, the job advert still hits the spot because it speaks to a universal human aspiration. In an uncertain business environment, the only certainty is our humanity, our human physiology and psyche. And as a species, we're the dominating force on our planet, shaping its flora and fauna from the deepest trenches in the ocean to our planet's outer layers (by the way, the ozone layer is not saying thank you). We live in a truly anthropogenic period, where humankind is the all-dominating force. Business is without doubt becoming even more personalised, automated and artificial intelligence led in a desperation to reach us, but it's still undeniably simple. It's all about being human. Don't obsess with the next big thing in technology, but look for the smaller things happening as life goes by day to day.

We all aspire to something. We all get up in the morning wishing today will be better than yesterday. It's a continuous hope for personal transformation, a cornerstone of philosophy and the world's religions. As in the religious story of Adam and Eve, there are plenty of obstacles or snakes in our way, challenging our humanity. For organisations or leaders, this should be a constant burning flame, a transformative promise or North Star: how to help people achieve those dreams or aspirations, or, essentially and simply, how to cope with being human, with all the flaws that entails.

Any organisational structure getting too big loses the sense of the individual and its needs. It's time to recalibrate that focus because the ultimate goal of business is to serve you and me. Never one over the other. I easy to get lost in technology, tools or innovations, all of which are happening with unprecedented speed, but our human limitations and ingenuity are the single constant. It's time to create a human re-evolution, another human enlightenment, where we strive to bring the best out in our humanity. Toilet musings and grey clay elephants are still the most powerful weapons in business and leadership: embrace those ambitions or fears wholeheartedly, and be insanely inquisitive about people's daily lives.

In the last decade or so, people have been able to explore alternative worlds through gaming, virtual reality, role playing, online connectedness and digital forums. All individuals can chip in what they believe is a better life and can take part in its ongoing creation. This opens the door for a new, modern interpretation of what life should be like (and the businesses enabling it), based on collaboration and democratic processes – where you have a say rather than submitting to the vision of a single, eccentric tyrant (or organisation). In a transparent, pro-social, democratised marketplace, there's no room for the self-serving, and power is ultimately earned and given by your stakeholders. We as people demand to have a say about the future. After all, it's our future.

Advertising is not working for me

Advertising will be forced to change, and we're already seeing the ramifications. The increasing amount of information that is readily available in more and more aspects of our lives is pushing the frontiers further; in a transparent market, the facts are not as easily distorted or decorated. Personalised data can ultimately lead to better informed decisions, potentially overruling emotions and intuition and nudging consumers towards their ideal way of living, be that staying healthy and motivated through a tech device like Fitbit or offering your children the most nutritious food. Information delivered by expert recommendations like GoodGuide, real-time comparisons like PriceRunner, consumer labels like the Energy Label or peer-to-peer consumer recommendations will add (and already are adding) more transparency to choices than ever before.

We're just scratching the surface. New technologies will take this information and make it increasingly accessible. Think of, for example, intelligent displays on the shelf (or built into products) recommending you products based on your known preferences or on an analysis of your physical and mental well-being. P&G, Philips and many others are exploring the IoT (Internet of things), where your devices are connected to the Internet, like an Oral-B toothbrush which tracks your toothbrushing and suggests improvements. Organisations need to embrace a rapidly and radically changing world order or be exposed as nothing but screaming quacks selling snake oil who are destined to be chased out of town.

As an organisation, you'll have to give people a reason to opt in to your messages. Retail will inevitably change from being sales channels to multifunctional spaces for community, experiences, exercise and learning. Life is difficult, some will even say it sucks, and the brands that can help people cope will always have a role to play. But this is not about paying lip service to people's self-actualisation or transformation: as you see from the cases we've looked at, it comes down to truly changing behaviours. This puts an unprecedented pressure on organisations to deliver transformational value through brand, service and product – and isn't this in reality what the capitalist society should be all about? A competition that improves services and products, propelling us forward, rather than a beauty contest based on incremental or advertised made-up differences, which leaves us stagnating?

There is an enormous energy and potential in unleashing human ambitions, creativity and resources everywhere in society. As marketing and brands are the most influential cultural shaper, there is a significant, mutually beneficial, interdependent role to be explored.

Life online and offline is merging

The expansion of digitalisation into every aspect of our lives can either be one of the greatest possibilities to unlock human ingenuity, collaboration and potential or, as it's quickly becoming, a bloody digital battlefield where commercial interests are mining our data to target us with personalised messages at every corner, like a stalker on electric rollerblades. How free is the Internet, when every Google search is for sale?

Or your social media feed is packed with advertised products instead of your friends' smiling babies and big brown-eyed dogs?

Of course, data can serve humanity and potentially prevent everything from suicides to an overcooked meal, but it's you and I producing the data that supplies the content on Facebook or the blog post on LinkedIn. Yet we have only little to no control over our work or our data – we're sucked into the system, and we're not getting remunerated or heard. As more and more of our time is spent digitally, it's important to have space for us all to freely learn, connect, laugh, love and work online. It's important that we choose who we want to share our data with, just as we choose our friends in the physical world. It's important we get paid for what we produce digitally, especially when others earn on our efforts through ads. We wouldn't put up with working for free at the office, why should we digitally? As an organisation, you cannot ignore these questions. You have to truly enable your community both offline and online. No hidden cookies.

Work to live or live to work?

The search for self-actualisation will only be a stronger driving force as robots, AI, automation and digitalisation are taking over what used to be our most defining role as an individual: our work. Through working with the unemployed, I've witnessed first-hand the damaging effects of how people without a job quickly begin to feel useless or without meaning in life. How does one find meaning outside of work? Switzerland was the first nation to put forward a vote for citizen pay in 2016. The idea is that every citizen should receive a benefit from the state, whether they have a job or not. The notion was unsuccessful as the vote didn't get enough support.

In 2017,[3] Finland launched a two-year trial among 2,000 unemployed people aged 25 to 58 in which they received a monthly payment of €560 with no obligation either to seek or accept employment. In the test, even employed people received the same amount. The trial didn't push more people into work, but it did raise satisfaction levels among the unemployed.

The social consequences of digitalisation can be brutal. It's estimated that by 2030, 80% of households in United States and Japan will own robots for elderly care, personal assistance and companionship. When work is not defining you in society, people will increasingly look to realise themselves through creativity, through friendships or maybe through mindfulness?

In ancient Greece, the rich aristocrats had plenty of time on their hands, as slaves and servants were taking care of their basic needs. This sparked an upheaval in philosophy, politics and arts, laying the groundwork for our modern society and an aspiration towards the ideal body and mind. Are we seeing a similar quest for the perfect life, for human enlightenment, in our own times?

The future of better me

As technology and biology morph, our minds and bodies are no longer a limitation to self-actualisation. And today, we're just scratching the surface.

We can upgrade our bodies' functionality: Swedish train service SJ allows people to use biometric implants as tickets; artist Neil Harbisson, who was born colour-blind, invented The Human Antenna to transpose colours to vibrations using a simple head-mounted camera extension. Or take a simple everyday example: think about how our concept of knowledge has changed since all the world's knowledge is simply one click away. We don't need to know all the world's countries by heart or the periodic table.

Our ideas about education have changed too, as we now have the capacity to embark on a lifelong educational journey, learning the skills to think critically rather than relying on established knowledge, structures and professions.

In the intersection between tech and self-improvement, new players are emerging all the time, utilising VR, AR or AI to help people realise their goals. Indian start-up Boltt is combining wearable devices in shoes and wristbands to track personal data and through an AI-powered personal coach offering real-time advice across multiple self-improvement areas from fitness and nutrition to sleep.

And where our bodies are holding us back from achieving more, body hackers are pushing the boundaries and exploring new ways to fuse technology and biology, raising ethical questions and sparking an organisation such as the Cyborg Foundation, set up to protect soon-to-be cyborg rights. It's like a cycle race, but instead of performance-enhancing drugs, the whole body and mind make up the canvas for hacking and improving. Brace yourself for a fast-as-lightning Cyborg Lance Armstrong! There are exciting possibilities for those who dare to dream big on people's behalf when neither body nor mind seems to be a barrier for ingenuity – as long as we can work out how to answer the acute ethical questions involved.

Transforming whom?

Sadly, economic growth still rules: it's an utterly perverse fact that the world's eight richest people (Bill Gates, Amancio Ortega, Warren Buffett, Carlos Slim Helú, Jeff Bezos, Mark Zuckerberg, Larry Ellison and

Michael Bloomberg) on this planet hold the same amount of wealth as the faceless, voiceless poorest half.[4] And big business is getting gargantuan (especially in developed markets) as companies are pushed toward mergers, consolidations, acquisitions and growth. In 2018 (and on the 64th list), Fortune 500 companies represent two-thirds of the United States's GDP.[5] These enormous homogeneous structures make our societies less pluralistic, less diverse, less creative and less resilient as they convey one way of thinking, one way of doing things, one culture, one shopping basket. The potential higher short-term yield of monoculture in business comes with a devastating price on diversity, health and our planet – just as monoculture does when it comes to farming.

According to research by the International Monetary Fund,[6] the result of more power in fewer hands means higher consumer prices and greater corporate markups, with an average upswing of 43% since the 1980s.

The environmental and social implications are a whole other sad story.

People generally hate big business. According to Gallup, Americans continue to show negative attitudes toward big business and prefer small business. Gallup's[7] research from 2017 shows that 70% of Americans have "*a great deal*" or "*quite a lot*" of confidence in small business, more than three times the 21% confidence rating for big business. There is a wealth, trust and power gap that needs to be addressed more seriously, if we are to create a fair and sustainable society – and if you as an organisation want to have a role in our lives going forward.

The redefinition of business

Corporations will eventually have to be redefined. Corporate talk about serving a higher purpose than simply earning money rings hollow if the underlying corporate structure is not truly serving people. Organisations like B-Corps and the cooperative movement are gaining popularity across the globe, and we'll see other corporate structures evolve, potentially posing a real challenge to big business benefiting the privileged few with an empty promise of prosperity for the many.

The unhinged wealth and growth of tech companies – many powered by the very same ideas I talk about in terms of democratising access and turning people into the producers, such as Facebook where we as users make the content – pose fundamental questions to the sustainability of these platforms. As Facebook is equivalent to the biggest country of the world with 1.3 billion users (2018 numbers), how does it guarantee the wealth and well-being of those who actually contribute to its continuous success? And although the philosophical foundation of Facebook has been expressed by Mark Zuckerberg to be all about giving the power back to the community, it quickly ends up being empty words when the company itself centralises power and wealth in Cupertino, California.

Who should ultimately own Facebook, as it has become a public commons just as Google is in regards to search? Should it be public infrastructure in the digital domain much like a bridge or a hospital? When shareholders snap the whip to maximise profit, how does our collective contribution to the platform become heard? Platforms like Kickstarter with 15 million users have become a B-Corp and pledged to be there for users in the long term rather than cashing in on the stock market, which is a great step, but is it going far enough? When talking about these emerging, transformative organisations, it's difficult not to ask oneself if that can ever truly be realised when the ownership structure is not addressed. Or for that matter, if one can really talk about the concept of *"shared value,"* as if a company's stakeholders really get their fair share? Ask the woman in India sewing shoes or a store attendant, if either feels that shared value?

All of these questions are uncomfortable to ask, but this agenda is unstoppable, so it's important we all chip in to find a fair path forward. I'm not talking about some elitist communist pipe dream. The reality of a decentralised system cannot be ignored, breaking down or making old power structures obsolete. People can have a say, and in the political world, there are experiments with direct democracy that will surely eventually influence the leadership of countries as well as companies. Most people pay their fair and equal share of taxes but not companies. The tax question is important as its people's contribution, as well as companies' contribution, to a democratic, prosperous, healthy and fair society.

Ownership will have to be readdressed, and the conversation will quickly turn towards fair, transparent and participatory structures. The sick economic and social divide we're witnessing today is not the answer. Can we really talk about democracy, when even in developed democracies those with money or network have easier access to those in power?

If citizens or stakeholders should be taken seriously, shouldn't everybody owning a stake in the company's or nation's success be valued and heard? From employees to an increasingly participatory citizen or customer?

Being brought up in Denmark, I've witnessed first-hand how equal access to education can benefit society at large – and not just the privileged – because the education system is paid for and supported from kindergarten to university by the Danes' tax contribution. There is no such thing as an American Dream; that's an illusion at best, if it is not supported by equal access to education in order to truly foster social mobility and personal growth. Similarly, business has to be redefined to serve society and all its stakeholders more broadly. Corporate profit should never capitalise on the health and wealth of stakeholders. I'm not advocating for Utopia; I do believe capitalism has an important role to play. We simply need to rethink how it can universally benefit everyone, and, as our democratic forefathers cried during the French revolution, I believe this comes from equality, fraternity and liberty. Those were words in 1789 that can come true today.

Responsibility or possibility?

Traditionally, organisations have looked at creating higher societal value as a corporate social responsibility, but with rising sustainability challenges facing these organisations, there's been a move away from risk management to chasing new business opportunities. A carmaker today can't ignore the rising urban populations but has to rethink how transportation needs are met.

There is a business opportunity. A lot of these challenges are systemic, which have pushed for increasing collaboration between old competitors. The United Nations Sustainable Development Goals (SDGs) opened up new opportunities for organisations to collaborate on issues. Collaboration is in fact SDG number 17. This is an important step in, together, launching efforts and tackling shared challenges.

A study by Accenture for UN Global Compact,[8] the world's largest CEO study on sustainability to date across more than 1,000 top executives from 27 industries and across 103 countries, concludes that: "*Without radical, structural change to markets and systems, CEOs believe, business may be unable to lead the way toward the peak of a sustainable economy.*" In the same survey, 93% of the CEOs responded that sustainability issues are important to very important for the future success of their business. The recognition of action is absolutely there; the million-dollar question is how do we create the change at the speed and scale needed?

Power in numbers

Undoubtedly, we as a society are faced with massive socio-economic and environmental challenges that all call for urgent action. In the book *The Trajectory of the Anthropocene: The Great Acceleration,*[9] the development is described as an increased acceleration with an exponential rise across urban populations, energy, tourism, forest loss, carbon emissions, water usage, loss of fish stocks . . . and I could go on. This rapid growth will have to be balanced out by an equally swift, large-scale, counter development. Is business suited to meet those challenges and swiftly enough? We definitely shouldn't ignore the billions of people whose lives have to change maybe more dramatically than we right now imagine.

In a report from the Stockholm Resilience Centre from 2018,[10] the challenge is aptly described: "*A key challenge lies in the psychology of worldviews. While the adoption of the SDGs is such a positive global act – a true turning point for the entire agenda on world development – we still remain in a world view where 'Everybody knows, but nobody wants to understand' the magnitude of the transformation that is needed.*" If you want change to happen, it's about time you make people themselves responsible with a rallying cry of "*you create the change.*"

We need to fundamentally change our current centralised, feudal-like system which currently creates wealth and power centres benefiting those at the top at a high cost for those at the bottom, rather than enabling prosperous, equal societies.

As we're increasingly moving towards decentralisation, where everything from energy to food can be produced locally or even by individuals, such as solar energy, the centralised model is under pressure. Old monopolies are trying to hold on to their slipping power grip over food, energy, banking and so on.

In Holland, a scalable city, ReGen Villages, is being built as an attempt to explore a different city structure. ReGen Villages is 100% self-sufficient in energy and 100% self-sufficient in food. What does that potentially mean to the energy companies and the supermarket chains? Or take Blockchain's so far unsuccessful attempt to challenge the power grip of financial institutions? Is the wolf watching the sheep, or should the sheep be looking out for one another? As an organisation, you can either fight against decentralisation, or you can aim to build platforms to unleash the creativity, skills and resources of the billions – and that's where I believe change grows in speed and scale.

The elephant in the room: consumption!

One of my bigger beefs with my work in advertising has been the relentless focus on driving consumption: growth, growth and growth at any cost.

In a resource-constrained world, it's pivotal that we create a new way forward, and younger generations are calling for change. I believe the best way to succeed is by creating change one person at a time rather than overreaching for a Superman-like save-our-planet strategy. Let's anchor this change on an individual level and bridge the gap between a world bettering aspiration and personal action. There is a reason the New Year's pledge for most of us ends up being a new start to old, bad habits. You are your own biggest enemy of change.

Today's needs and wants have become too fickle and fast-changing to understand, from a sudden embrace of a plant-based diet, or car ownership being turned on its head, or a love–hate relationship with juice and its natural high-calorie content. Jeff Bezos, Amazon CEO, is obsessed with customers, and his philosophy "*Start with the customer and work backward*"[11] is built into the organisation, from press releases always featuring customer quotes to Amazon meetings reportedly always featuring an empty chair for the customer. Understanding consumption today demands an increasingly customer-centric approach, but I'll go further and claim it's about a life-centric approach.

Four good tips going forward
1. Always put people's lives, well-being and happiness first.
2. Aim for a transformative promise to put people in charge of the change.
3. Turn people into your innovation and marketing engine.
4. Enable people to go further than they ever could've imagined.

Turning people into agents of change

There is massive untapped potential in companies or any organisation for enabling people to become agents of change towards a better life. Think about it. Fast-consumer-goods conglomerate P&G touches 4.6 billion people daily with their products[12]. Coca-Cola 1.9 billion. Facebook 1.5 billion. Think about the change they can unlock if they can get just every third household in this world to use just a little less water when cleaning dishes or promoting better recycling habits. From Starbucks to Patagonia, companies are becoming louder and more activist, but the real potential for change lies in turning each and every one of us into everyday creators of a better life. Activism most often ends up being counterproductive to change as it is exclusive rather than inclusive. And I definitely think it's counterproductive to the sustainability or climate movement as inclusion is paramount to the change we need. Let's say you were good at biology in school; you shouldn't point fingers, ridicule or exclude those who didn't get it but rather help. Why do we point fingers at those who still don't act on or get climate change? Changes should never be for the few but for the many. When Google co-founder Sergey Brin,[13] following the election of the divisive US President Donald Trump, spoke about how he was "*upset*" and "*sad*" and saw the election as being contrary to Google's values. His reaction sparked outrage because obviously not everyone inside and outside Google shared Sergey's views and instead embraced the new president. For organisations and leaders, taking an activist stand can alienate people. The same obviously goes with the role your organisation wants to play in people's lives. Think about Nike's focus on athletes and performance versus RYU's embracement of whatever people's life goals are. Some people might feel alienated by Nike's focus as they don't feel (or look) like an athlete.

People are sceptical towards organisations and can be even more sceptical about organisations doing a value crusade, interfering in our lives and telling us to do this or that. Nobody likes to be told to smoke less, exercise more, eat less sugar or get out of the house and meet some people! Real leadership is not about being a missionary but about walking behind people and enabling them to make the change. Don't dictate, enable, transform. Always start with WHO you can help me become.

Are people the hero?

"*What's the business case for ending life on earth?*"[14] asks the late Interface founder and sustainability champion Roy Anderson.

Although that is a significant question, you as a leader or an organisation have to begin with people. Not with planet. If you try to save the world, your broad goal will blind you and others, but if you enable one person to make a difference, that person knows five other people that know five other people and so on. The steps of many will turn into a leap for mankind. I'm not saying you shouldn't be allowed to dream *big*, but if you don't succeed in nudging people, the dream might quickly turn into a nightmare – or a hero trap! As an organisation, the change begins with a transformative promise. The running shoes don't run by themselves. The waistline on your pants doesn't shrink automatically. The organic apple doesn't just jump into the shopping basket. Communication is a powerful tool, and, as the unhinged dream machine of advertising promising us greater lives if we consume while nearing the last stop, it's time to unlock real change, real action.

Products designed to become obsolete. An overload of food grown to be thrown away. Superfluous packaging. Explosive amounts of ignored advertising. Mass-production to mass-media to mass-movements was only a short-term strategy: mass is becoming a losing system. In industrial times, you'd be the low-paid worker doing grinding labour on the assembly line; today you have an opportunity to be your own boss with life's endless possibilities as your factory floor. Everyone is free to converse, do business and find love on their own terms.

Now, what role does your organisation want to play in my life? An organisation that doesn't promise a positive personal or societal benefit is as useless as a clown on a spacecraft. There simply will be few or no organisations without a life bettering promise in a post-capitalist world; the question is simply who's getting it right?

In my dialogue with all these different transformative businesses, from Wheelys Café to IKEA, I realised there were certain common denominators from freedom to a dialogue with the community, interdependence, but more importantly, organisations are no longer simply a set of characteristics, a position or the outcome of your customers dialogue. They're a vehicle. Yes, a vehicle.

Once you allow your organisation to become a vehicle, the magic happens; there is no limits for what wonderful places you can discover together. And time is not on humankind's side if we are to solve the social and environmental mess, we ourselves have created. You need to create change now. Not tomorrow. As a leader or an organisation, you need to set in motion a personal imperative for change.

What I picked up again and again in my conversations was that organisations should bring you on a personal journey, should transform you – it's not simply a transactional role but transformational. Time for organisations to chart a different path. It's the last purpose frontier – how can organisation realise the inner betterment of people? If you don't succeed in improving people's minds and behaviours, you won't succeed with the greater challenge of creating better ways of living in our communities, in society at large or in the challenged ecosystems we're dependent on.

As some societies have reached a more than sufficient level of material wealth, it's time for us to start focusing on inner human wealth: happiness, better connections with the community, less stress, fulfilled citizens. Materialism is a losing strategy. The happiness of buying new shoes is a short-lived dopamine kick, whereas finding better ways of living in balance with yourself adds lifelong value. It's time to create the right human and planetary balance. It's time to create a new leadership that enables people to move towards change. There is simply no one else to blame for the lack of change than yourself.

It's time to . . .

You fill in the blank.

Key takeaways

1 Corporate purpose has to be redefined to enable the many rather than serving the few.

2 Globally increasing living standards and materialism fatigue, combined with digitalisation, automation, robotics and bio-tech, are strengthening the development towards a market driven by self-actualisation.

3 The corporate model has to be reinvented to better serve people rather than short-term profit. Models like B Corps and cooperatives are a step in the right direction.

4 In a fast-changing marketplace, customer-centricity is a minimum; it's about people's lives. Let people have a bigger say.

5 A better life is not something you give; it's something people create for themselves.

Questions to ask yourself

1 Reading this book, how do you think these trends will develop? How do you think they will be strengthened? Weakened? Why?

2 In an everything-is-possible world, what would be your all-transformative promise?

3 What are the three key takeaways in this book that mattered the most to you or your organisation?

4 How do you share these learnings with your organisation or with your peers?

5 After reading, what is the one thing you'll have to act on now?

Appendix

The transformative toolbox

Brand or campaign activities are one thing; another is the organisation behind them, and the totality of actions and impact. This section gathers all the models we've discussed in the book with case study examples, plus some extras, so that you can use it as a handy quick reference guide for your future output.

The models unlocking transformation

1.0 The Arrow

WHAT product do you sell or service do you deliver?
This is the product you sell or the service you deliver, for example, running shoes.

HOW are you unique in delivering your product or service?
This is what makes your offering stand out, for example, convenience.

WHO can you help people become?
This is the personal transformation you enable, for example, a mindful runner.

WHEN do you enable this change?
This is your call to arms: a specific time of day, a situation, a life-phase or a state of mind.

2.0 The transformative promise

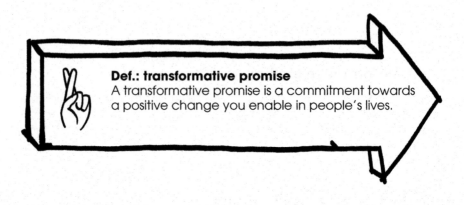

Def.: transformative promise
A transformative promise is a commitment towards a positive change you enable in people's lives.

How to shape a transformative promise

1 **People-centric**
   Is the promise focused on an obstacle or benefit?
2 **Transformative**
   Does the promise focus on a personal change or transformation?
3 **Specific**
   Does the promise focus on a specific challenge or opportunity?
4 **Active**
   Is the promise an active encouragement?
5 **Operational**
   How is the promise enabling people across the business?

3.0 The WHO void

Def.: WHO void

A differentiating position in the market where you
can play a transformative role in people's lives.

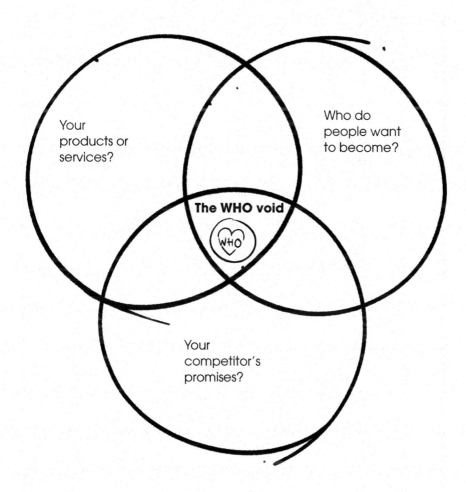

4.0 The People Transformation Canvas

The Brand Transformation Canvas

Home: Providing people with a safe and secure environment for themselves and significant others.

Example: Lifestyle brand, KonMari, is on a mission towards simpler living: Tidy your space, transform your life.

Romance: Enhancing the ability of people to find love and discover new meaningful connections.

Example: Dating platform Bumble challenges female users to make the first move, basically eliminating the bro-culture of other dating platforms.

Family: Nurturing deeper connections with family members.

Example: The upscale hotel Wyndham offers a digital-detox program, called Reconnected, addressing the vital need for quality family time over screen time.

Friends: Improving friendships and connections and giving a sense of belonging.

Example: Kind Snacks says, "Co the kind thing for your body, your taste buds & your world."

Mindfulness: Unlocking the possibility for people to discover a new deeper meaning of altruism, self-esteem, forgiveness, ethics, dignity and respect.

Example: The app Calm is on a mission to make people happier and healthier through mindfulness.

Work: Adding to people's professional development.

Example: LinkedIn says, "To connect the world's professionals to make them more productive and successful."

Finances: Providing people with the skills and resources to feel economically secure.

Example: Next bank enables young people to achieve their financial goals no matter what they are.

Health: Improving people's physical health and well-being.

Example: Discovery incentivises people to become healthier.

Personal development: Making people understand their motivations and fears and helping them achieve their goals.

Example: RYU says, "We're here to help you achieve more than your gym goals, RYU is here for your life goals."

Passion, fun and excitement: Helping people explore new horizons, new experiences and follow their passions.

Example: Red Bull's relentless focus on "giving wings" to daredevils.

Societal contribution: Providing people with a possibility to contribute to something greater than themselves and experience community care and service.

Example: Precious Plastic's fight against plastic pollution.

Emotional well-being: Giving people increased confidence, security, vitality and emotional well-being.

Example: Always is committed to empower young girls and women around the world.

5.0 The Wheel of Transformability

Def.: transformability

The ability of an organisation to enable people to leverage their passions, means and capabilities as a resource in the marketing mix, from product to promotion.

The Wheel of Transformability

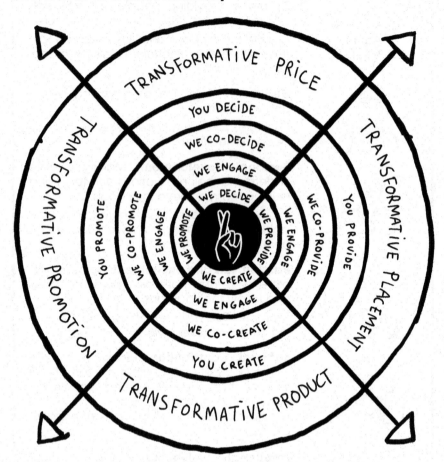

Each of the 5Ts represents an opportunity to enable an organisation's stakeholders, and each of them individually or in combination offers a growth potential for people and organisation: transformability.

6.0 Open up your product

Open up your product

How can the product or service empower, enable or transform people?
How can the product or service lower the bar of access or offer people access where there was none before?
Can the product or service be made by people?
Can you turn your customers' capabilities, means or passions into a service or product?
Are there parts of the production process where people can have a say?
How can you give people increasing control over a product or service?
How can you make people have a say earlier in the product innovation?

7.0 Open up your placement

Open up your placement

Can you turn people into service providers or product distributors?
Could any of your stakeholders be of help in delivering your product or service?
Think about your current locations: what businesses or entities are nearby, and could they be turned into distributors?
Do your customers already frequently use products or services of organisations that you could collaborate with?
Are your stakeholders often in a certain place you can utilise as a distribution point?
Think about people's day from morning to evening; does that open new possibilities for distribution?
Are there any specific time of year when it would make sense to turn people into service or product providers?

8.0 Open up your promotion

Open up your promotion

How can you turn people into the messenger?
How can the promotion be part of people's own transformation?
Is your promotion like a game, which can be easily replicated time and time again?
Are people free to re-create the campaign?
How much can you open up your campaign for people's creativity?
Are there other stakeholders that, with advantage, can reuse your campaign efforts?
How can your customers help others towards transformation?

9.0 Open up your pricing

Open up your pricing

How can you let people have a say when it comes to pricing?
Can you divide your service or product into different pricing options?
How can you make your pricing more transparent to add value?
Have you asked people what price they'd be willing to pay?
Does any of your competitors give people a choice over pricing?
What's the lowest or highest price point you have tried?
How creative are you with your pricing strategy?

10.0 Transformative platform

Def.: a transformative platform

A communication enabler that allows people to create campaigns or initiatives within a shared framework with a shared goal.

A transformative platform is:

Transformative: Set a clear, shared transformative goal.
Guided: Make a set of guidelines or directions.
Motivational: Aim for action.
Creative: Make it open for creativity.
Replicable: Create for re-creation.
Common: Make it open for everyone.
Accessible: Make the tools or mechanisms easily available.
Relevant: Make it relevant for your brand.

11.0 Checklist for a transformative organisation

Transformative promise

Delivers on a specific promise to transform people's lives.
Example: Canadian lifestyle brands RYU's mission states, "We're here to help you achieve more than your gym goals, RYU is here for your life goals." They enable people to achieve these goals across the organisation from staff, multifunctional stores to discounts.

Organisational-wide enabler

Leverages the power and capabilities of the organisation to fulfil its promise and enable its stakeholders internally and externally.
Example: Discovery is working with stakeholders like supermarkets and gyms to incentivise healthier living through, for example, discounts on healthy food.

Regenerative operations

Operates in a way that enables the well-being, resilience and flourishing of stakeholders, society and environment.
Example: The meal subscription service Aarstiderne is constantly increasing the share of its produce from regenerative, biodynamic farming.

Transformative products and services

Delivers products and services that enable people and ultimately realises its transformative promise.
Example: Organisations successful at transforming people as much as possible across the Wheel of Transformability like, for example, Spanish phone company Suop turning customers into service operators.

Transparent, open and participatory organisation

Ensures a transparent, open and participatory way of running its business where its stakeholders have a significant say.
Example: A co-operative model like outdoor retailer REI that ensures its customers have a say, or Dave Hakkens's open-source mindset behind Precious Plastic.

12.0 Unlocking action

Make WHEN happen with the S.M.A.R.T. formula

When planning behaviour change, it's good to keep an eye on the S.M.A.R.T. model. George T. Doran established the model in 1981 to create a tool for project management to ensure that the objectives of a project were realistic. S.M.A.R.T. stands for Specific, Measurable, Attainable, Relevant and Time-bound.

Specific

As a goal, "*limit water usage*" might sound good, but what does it really mean? How are you going to act on it on a day-to-day basis? Begin with one concrete goal, like take a shorter shower. When you put goals in place, always be specific, so you can hold people – and people can hold themselves – accountable. Example: Ariel launched their washing powder for cold washing cycles and asked people to wash at 30°C.

Measurable

If your goal is not measurable, how are you going to know if you succeeded? You might want to put a time limit on it – like four minutes maximum for the shower. There's been plenty of discussion around the effectiveness of marketing in relation to the investment: ROI = return on investment. The discussion around ROI = return on impact is only developing now. How are you improving people's lives or society as a whole? Discovery can track their customer's progress through the Vitality app, viewing healthier food bought, gym visits and the like – data the company can use to improve its impact.

Attainable

You need to be realistic on people's behalf. Is this really an attainable goal? Nike's mission statement is to "*bring inspiration and innovation to every athlete* in the world.*" Pay attention to the asterisk after "athlete." The story goes that it was added by co-founder Bill Bowerman, who explained that "*if you have a body, you are an athlete.*" This is an important part of Nike's mission: whether you're Wilson Kipketer, an amateur runner or just someone who likes to wear comfortable sweat pants, there is potentially Nike gear for you at Walmart.

Relevant

It might be difficult to evaluate whether the goal is relevant for the individual you have in mind, but nonetheless it's a great reality check. It might sound like common sense, but I promise you, I've experienced tons of times when an organisation put an ask in place that didn't make the best use of people's skills or interests. Movember made testicular cancer relevant to men by speaking in a tone of voice they understood and creating activities that were fun and cool for them to participate in.

Time-bound

Everybody could run a marathon, if time were no issue. Therefore, it's essential to put a time limit in place. How much time should this project or effort run for? Is time a parameter of success? When Microsoft's Bill Gates entered the do-good space with the Bill & Melinda Gates Foundation, he set out to eradicate polio by 2020. Deadlines work because people commit to a time-bound goal and can plan accordingly.

S.M.A.R.T.: five questions to ask yourself

Specific: Can you put a specific, quantitative target in place for the behaviour change?

Measurable: Can you measure the progress towards that target?

Attainable: Is the target realistic for people?

Relevant: Does the target really connect with people?

Time-bound: When will the goal be reached?

13.0 The sustainable development goals turned personal

Translating global challenges into personal opportunities to make change

In 2015 the United Nations set 17 global goals and 169 targets for creating a better and more sustainable future called the Sustainable Development Goals covering global challenges such as poverty, inequality, climate, environmental degradation, prosperity, and peace and justice. The goals opened up the landscape for everyone to play a part and speak a shared language, be they governments, companies, non-profits or individuals. A coalition of organisations set out to translate each of the wide-ranging, global goals into something you and I can do in our everyday life, called The Good Life Goals.[1] It's worth sharing to illustrate how you as an organisation can make it possible for people to participate. Remember, people really want organisations to show them the way and give them a chance to make an impact. You can see more on the goals if you google The Good Life Goals, but here is an overview of one action per goal.

The Good Life Goals

1   Help end poverty
Buy from companies that pay people fairly.

2   Eat better
Buy local, seasonal and fairly traded food.

3   Stay well
Wash your hands and exercise regularly.

4   Learn and teach
Keep learning throughout life.

5   Treat everyone equally
Raise kids to expect equality.

6   Save water
Don't flush any trash or toxic chemicals.

7   Use clean energy
Buy from companies powered by renewable energy.

8   Do good work
Support local businesses at home and abroad.

9   Make smart choices
Stay smart and kind online.

10 Be fair
Buy from companies that pay taxes and treat people fairly.

11 Love where you live
Learn about and take part in local decisions.

12 Live better
Waste less food and use leftovers.

13 Act on climate
Eat more plants and cut down on meat.

14 Clean the seas
Remember that litter ends up in the water.

15 Love nature
Discover the wonders of the natural world.

16 Make peace
Be kind and tolerant.

17 Come together
Get involved and volunteer in your community.

References

Introduction

1 Phone interview with Marc Pritchard, Chief Brand Officer, Procter & Gamble.
2 Faber, R. (2019, May 3). What Have You Done to Drastically Reduce Your Spending Habits? *Quora.* Retrieved October 22, 2019, from www.quora.com/What-have-you-done-to-drastically-reduce-your-spending-habits
3 Jackson, M. (1987). Man in the Mirror. *Bad.* Retrieved October 23, 2019, from https://music.apple.com/us/album/man-in-the-mirror/559334659?i=559334757

Chapter 1

1 In person interview with Joanna Yarrow, Head of Sustainable & Healthy Living, INGKA Group (IKEA).
2 Ghonim, W. (2012). *Revolution 2.0.* Boston: Houghton Mifflin Harcourt.
3 Bloomberg. Are You a Robot? Retrieved October 22, 2019a, from www.bloomberg.com/news/articles/2017-02-28/in-video-uber-ceo-argues-with-driver-over-falling-fares
4 Kantor, J. Harvey Weinstein Paid Off Sexual Harassment Accusers for Decades. *The New York Times.* Retrieved October 22, 2019, from www.nytimes.com/2017/10/05/us/harvey-weinstein-harassment-allegations.html
5 Murphy, B. Google and Facebook Now Make More from Ads Than Every Newspaper, Magazine, and Radio Network in the World Combined. *Inc. com.* Retrieved October 22, 2019, from www.inc.com/bill-murphy-jr/google-and-facebook-now-make-more-from-ads-than-every-newspaper-magazine-and-rad.html
6 These Are the Fortune 500's 10 Most Profitable Companies. (2017, June 7). *Fortune.* Retrieved October 22, 2019, from http://fortune.com/2017/06/07/fortune-500-companies-profit-apple-berkshire-hathaway/
7 Retrieved from www.edelman.com/sites/g/files/aatuss191/files/2019-02/2019_Edelman_Trust_Barometer_Global_Report_2.pdf?utm_source=website&utm_medium=global_report&utm_campaign=downloads, p. 34
8 Lynch, J. The 20 Most-Watched TV Episodes of All Time. *Business Insider.* Retrieved October 22, 2019, from www.businessinsider.com/most-watched-episodes-2016-9?IR=T
9 Friedman, T. L. (2007). *The World Is Flat 3.0.* New York: Picador.

10 Death to the Mass. (2016, May 23). *Medium*. Retrieved October 22, 2019, from https://medium.com/whither-news/death-to-the-mass-eb33c08dc3b6; https://medium.com/@jeffjarvis

11 This Is What "Charlie Bit My Finger" Brothers Look Like Now. (2017, May 22). *Metro*. Retrieved October 22, 2019, from https://metro.co.uk/2017/05/22/this-is-what-charlie- from-charlie-bit-my-finger-looks-like-now-6650977/?ito=cbshare

12 HDCYT. (2007, May 22). Charlie Bit My Finger – Again ! *YouTube*. Retrieved October 22, 2019, from www.youtube.com/watch?v=_OBlgSz8sSM

13 Godin, S. (2011). *Tribes*. New York: Hachette.

14 Sinek, S. (2011). *Start with Why*. London: Penguin.

15 Earned Brand. (2018). *Edelman*. Retrieved October 22, 2019, from www.edelman.com/earned-brand

16 American Express. Retrieved October 23, 2019, from https://about.americanexpress.com

17 Top 15 Ad Campaigns of the 21st Century. Retrieved October 22, 2019, from https://adage.com/lp/top15/#intro

18 Phone interview with Marc Pritchard, Chief Brand Officer, Procter & Gamble.

19 Consumer Electronics Giant Samsung Just Became the World's Spendiest Advertiser, Bypassing Procter & Gamble. *TechCrunch*. (2018, December 4). Retrieved October 22, 2019, from https://techcrunch.com/2018/12/04/consumer-electronics-giant-samsung- just-became-the-worlds-spendiest-advertiser-bypassing-proctor-gamble/

20 Swaine, J. (2014, March 2). Vice's Shane Smith: "Young People Are Angry and Leaving TV in Droves." *The Guardian*. Retrieved October 22, 2019, from www.theguardian.com/media/2014/mar/02/vice-media-shane-smith-north-korea

21 *Phonebloks*. Retrieved October 23, 2019a, from https://phonebloks.com

22 Skype interview with Dave Hakkens, designer & founder, Precious Plastics & Phonebloks

23 Hornback, T. (2018, May 8). Where Do You Call Home? *Quora*. Retrieved October 22, 2019, from www.quora.com/Where-do-you-feel-most-at-home

24 The Disruptors – the New Space Race. *BBC News*. Retrieved October 22, 2019, from www.bbc.co.uk/news/resources/idt-sh/disruptors_the_new_space_race

25 Pearson, B. (2018, July 13). Etsy Has Raised Its Artisan Fees: 5 Ways the Shopper Experience Could Change. *Forbes*. Retrieved October 22, 2019, from www.forbes.com/sites/bryanpearson/2018/07/13/etsy-has-raised-its-artisan-fees-5-ways-in-which-the-shopper-experience-could-change/#61761476b734

26 Frier, S. (2013, November 12). Etsy Tops $1 Billion in 2013 Product Sales on Mobile Lift. Retrieved October 22, 2019, from www.bloomberg.com/news/articles/2013-11-12/etsy-tops-1-billion-in-2013-product-sales-on-mobile-lift

27 Which Big Brands Are Courting the Maker Movement, and Why. *Adweek*. (2014, March 17). Retrieved October 22, 2019, from www.adweek.com/brand-marketing/which-big-brands-are-courting-maker-movement-and-why-156315/

28 Global DIY Market Value 2012–2018. *Statista*. Retrieved October 22, 2019, from www.statista.com/statistics/374093/global-diy-market-value/

29 Digital Disruption Will Wipe Out 40% of Fortune 500 Firms in Next 10 Years, Say C-Suite Execs. *Information Age*. Retrieved October 22, 2019a, from www.informa tion-age.com/65-c-suite-execs-believe-four-ten-fortune-500-firms-wont-exist-10-years-123464546/

30 Tyrangiel, J. (2006, December 25). Andy Was Right. TIME.com. Retrieved October 23, 2019, from http://content.time.com/time/magazine/article/0,9171,1570780,00.html

Chapter 2

1 Skype interview with Maria de la Croix, co-founder, Wheelys Café.
2 Kross, K. (1992). *Jump: Totally Krossed Out*. Retrieved October 23, 2019, from https://music.apple.com/us/album/jump/170146852?i=170147030
3 The Changing Relationship Between People and Goods. (2017, January 1). *Sitra Study*. Retrieved October 22, 2019, from https://media.sitra.fi/2017/05/05143553/Selvi tyksia122.pdf
4 Sharing Economy Statistics. *Statista*. Retrieved October 22, 2019, from www.statista.com/statistics/289856/number-sharing-economy-users-us/
5 PWC. *The Sharing Economy*. Retrieved October 22, 2019, from www.pwc.com/us/en/technology/publications/assets/pwc-consumer-intelligence-series-the-sharing-econ omy.pdf
6 Enabling the Good Life Report. *SB Insights*. Retrieved October 22, 2019, from https://insights.sustainablebrands.com/full-report/
7 How Millennials Are Changing the Face of Marketing Forever. Retrieved October 22, 2019, from www.bcg.com/publications/2014/marketing-center-consumer-customer-insight-how-millennials-changing-marketing-forever.aspx
8 Morgan, B. (2015, June 1). NOwnership, No Problem: Why Millennials Value Experiences over Owning Things. *Forbes*. Retrieved October 22, 2019, from www.forbes.com/sites/blakemorgan/2015/06/01/nownershipnoproblem-nowners-millennials-value-experiences-over-ownership/#49761f295406
9 Interview with Dr Jaak Panksepp, author of *Affective Neuroscience: The Foundations of Human and Animal Emotions*. Campbell, G. (2010, January 13). *Brain Science Podcast*. Retrieved October 22, 2019, from http://docartemis.com/Transcripts/65-brainscience-Panksepp2.pdf
10 Brickman, P., Coates, D., & Janoff-Bulman, R. (1978). Lottery Winners and Accident Victims: Is Happiness Relative? *Journal of Personality and Social Psychology*. Vol. 36, No. 8, 917–927. Northwestern University, University of Massachusetts. Retrieved from https://pdfs.semanticscholar.org/fbcf/098df289397dd4842756a9ee6634ee138d9b.pdf
11 Aarstiderne. Retrieved October 23, 2019, from www.aarstiderne.com/hello-again
12 The Good Life 2.0 Playbook, Why Don't We Redefine the Good Life? *World Business Council for Sustainable Development (WBCSD)*. Retrieved October 22, 2019, from www.wbcsd.org/Overview/News-Insights/WBCSD-insights/Why-don-t-we-Re define-the-Good-Life
13 2017 Cone Gen Z CSR Study: How to Speak Z – Cone Communications. (2017, September 13). Retrieved October 22, 2019, from www.conecomm.com/research-blog/ 2017-genz-csr-study#download-the-research
14 Millennial and Gen Z study by Deloitte from 2018. Retrieved from https://www2.deloitte.com/content/dam/Deloitte/lu/Documents/about-deloitte/gx-2018-millen nial-survey-report.pdf
15 Virden, L. (2018, August 16). What Is the Hardest Thing You Ever Had to Go Through? *Quora*. Retrieved October 22, 2019, from www.quora.com/What-is-the- hardest-thing-you-ever-had-to-go-through
16 4-Day Work Week – Why IIH Nordic Invented the 4DWW. *IIH Nordic*. Retrieved October 22, 2019, from https://iihnordic.com/about-us/4-days-work-week/

17 Graham-McLay, C. (2018, July 19). A 4-Day Workweek? A Test Run Shows a Surprising Result. *The New York Times.* Retrieved October 22, 2019, from www.nytimes.com/2018/07/19/world/asia/four-day-workweek-new-zealand.html

18 Love Your Job Not Your Company. *The India Times.* (2015, October 7). Retrieved October 23, 2019, from https://timesofindia.indiatimes.com/life-style/relationships/soul-curry/Love-your-job-not-your-company/articleshow/47429782.cms

19 What Are Digital Nomads and What Do They Do? *MBO Partners.* Retrieved October 22, 2019, from www.mbopartners.com/state-of-independence/research-trends-digital-nomads

20 Mission Statement. *Starbucks Coffee Company.* Retrieved October 23, 2019a, from www.starbucks.com/about-us/company-information/mission-statement

21 Join a Movement. *Wheelys Café.* Retrieved October 23, 2019, from https://wheelyscafe.com/movement/

22 *Suop.* Retrieved October 23, 2019, from www.suop.es

23 Skype interview with Jaime Pla, CEO, Suop

24 Overcoming the Existential Crisis in Consumer Goods. (2018, March 7). *Bain.* Retrieved October 22, 2019, from www.bain.com/insights/overcoming-the-existential-crisis- in-consumer-goods/

25 How Big Consumer Companies Can Fight Back. Retrieved October 22, 2019, from www.bcg.com/publications/2017/strategy-products-how-big-consumer-companies-can-fight-back.aspx

26 Consumer Goods: Big Brands Battle with the "Little Guys." (2018, February 28). *Financial Times.* Retrieved October 22, 2019, from www.ft.com/content/4aa58b22- 1a81-11e8-aaca-4574d7dabfb6

27 Moynihan, R. These Are the 20 Most Popular Brands Around the World. *Business Insider.* Retrieved October 22, 2019, from www.businessinsider.com/here-are-worlds- 20-best-selling-brands-2018-6?r=US&IR=T&IR=T

28 Seven Hills | Paul Lindley Says Goodbye To Ella's Kitchen As The Business Achieves 12-years Of Double Digit Growth. Retrieved February 8, 2020, from https://www.wearesevenhills.com/paul-lindley-says-goodbye-to-ellas-kitchen-as-the-business-achieves-12-years-of-double-digit-growth/

29 B Corp Analysis Reveals Purpose-Led Businesses Grow 28 Times Faster Than National Average. *Sustainable Brands.* Retrieved October 23, 2019a, from https://sustainable brands.com/read/business-case/b-corp-analysis-reveals-purpose-led-businesses-grow-28-times-faster-than-national-average

Chapter 3

1 Skype interview with David Hall, Senior Director, Brand, LEGO.

2 Norton, Michael I., Mochon, Daniel, & Ariely, Dan. The "IKEA Effect": When Labor Leads to Love. *Harvard Business School.* Retrieved January 30, 2020 from www.hbs.edu/faculty/Publication%20Files/11-091.pdf

3 Sundbo, J., & Sørensen, F. (Eds.). The Experience Economy: Past, Present and Future. *Handbook on the Experience Economy.* Cheltenham: Edward Elgar, p. 269.

4 Shell, E. R. (2009). *Cheap: The High Cost of Discount Culture.* June 29, 2010. London: Penguin Books.

5 Maslow, A. (1954). *Motivation and Personality.* New York: Harper.

6 Chaykowski, K. (2017, January 8). Meet Headspace, the App That Made Meditation a $250 Million Business. *Forbes.* Retrieved October 22, 2019, from www.

forbes.com/sites/kathleenchaykowski/2017/01/08/meet-headspace-the-app-that-made-medita tion-a-250-million-business/#79cb60071f1b

7 District Vision. Retrieved October 23, 2019, from www.districtvision.com

8 Harron, M. (2000). *American Psycho* (G. Turner, Ed.).

9 Amabile, Teresa M. *Motivation and Creativity: Effects of Motivational Orientation on Creative Writers*. Retrieved from https://files.eric.ed.gov/fulltext/ED240445.pdf

10 Selfdeterminationtheory.org to Human Motivation & Personality. Retrieved October 22, 2019a, from http://selfdeterminationtheory.org

11 Story shared by Greta Valvonytė, space and sustainability enthusiast.

12 Millennials Disruption Index. Retrieved from www.millennialdisruptionin-dex.com/

13 The Psychological Effects of Empowerment Strategies on Consumers' Product Demand. Retrieved January 30, 2020 from www.researchgate.net/publication/228221625_The_Psychological_Effects_of_Empower-ment_Strategies_on_Consumers'_Product_Demand

14 Gilliam, T. (1975). *Monty Python and the Holy Grail* (T. Jonas, Ed.).

Chapter 4

1 Skype interview with Dave Hakkens, designer and founder, Precious Plastics & Phonebloks.

2 Glossier. Retrieved October 23, 2019, from www.glossier.com

3 How to Build a Brand in 2017: Tips from Glossier CEO Emily Weiss. (2017, February 17). *TechCrunch*. Retrieved October 22, 2019, from https://techcrunch.com/2017/02/17/beauty-guru-emily-weiss-on-building-a-brand-from-scratch-in-2017/

4 Mandell, J. (2018, February 22). Glossier Just Got $52 Million in Fresh Capital, Bringing Total Funding to $86 Million. *Forbes*. Retrieved October 22, 2019, from www. forbes.com/sites/jannamandell/2018/02/22/glossier-just-got-52-million-in-fresh- capital-bringing-total-funding-to-86-million/#280f328712b6

5 Feloni, R. How Lego Came Back from the Brink of Bankruptcy. *Business Insider*. Retrieved October 22, 2019, from www.businessinsider.com/how-lego-made-a-huge-turn around-2014-2?r=US&IR=T&IR=T

6 Skype interview with David Hall, Senior Director, Brand, LEGO.

7 Farrell, S. (2014, September 4). Rise of the Bricks – Lego Movie Lays Foundations for Big Profit Rise. *The Guardian*. Retrieved October 22, 2019, from www.theguardian.com/lifeandstyle/2014/sep/04/rise-bricks-lego-builds-profits-lego-movie

8 How Discovery Keeps Innovating. *McKinsey & Company*. Retrieved October 22, 2019, from www.mckinsey.com/industries/healthcare-systems-and-services/our-insights/how- discovery-keeps-innovating

9 The Impact of Wellness Engagement on Morbidity and Mortality – A Big Data Case Study. Retrieved from www.actuaries.org/PRESIDENTS/Docu-ments/CapeTown2/Wellness_Mortality_BigData_Stipp.pdf

10 Can Insurance Companies Incentivize Their Customers to Be Healthier? *Harvard Business Review*. Retrieved October 22, 2019a, from https://hbr.org/2017/06/can-insurance-companies-incentivize-their-custom-ers-to-be-healthier?utm_campaign=hbr&utm_source=twitter&utm_medium=social

11 Story shared by Sarunas Kazlauskas, photographer.

12 Harron, M. (2000). *American Psycho* (G. Turner, Ed.).

13 A Brief History of Brands and the Evolution of Place Branding. Retrieved from http://webbut.unitbv.ro/bulletin/Series%20VII/BULETIN%20I/22_Briciu.pdf

14 Definition of Character by Lexico. *Lexico Dictionaries | English*. Retrieved October 22, 2019, from https://en.oxforddictionaries.com/definition/character

15 Kind Snacks. Retrieved October 23, 2019, from www.kindsnacks.com/our-mission.html

16 Skype interview with Daniel Lubetzky, founder and executive chairman, Kind Snacks.

17 Powell, Roo. (2014, June 26). "Like a Girl" Is No Longer an Insult in Inspiring Ad from P&G's Always. Retrieved October 23, 2019, from www.adweek.com/creativity/girl-no-longer-insult-inspiring-ad-pgs-always-158601/

Chapter 5

1 Skype interview with Marcello Leone, CEO, RYU.

2 Enabling the Good Life Report – SB Insights. *SB Insights*. Retrieved October 22, 2019, from https://insights.sustainablebrands.com/full-report/

3 How Brands Can Earn Trust. *Edelman*. Retrieved October 24, 2019, from www.edel man.com/research/how-brands-can-earn-trust

4 There's More to Under Armour CEO's Resignation from Trump's Council. Retrieved October 24, 2019, from https://finance.yahoo.com/news/theres-armour-ceo-kevin- planks-resignation-trump-council-132459708.html?guccounter=1&guce_referrer=aH   R0cHM6Ly93d3cuZ29vZ2xlLmNvbS88&guce_referrer_sig=AQAAAKDaLFDuiHlq   PF18HM8-qsv-0W-rz9TuN9e0aSFIPGDKeUqaydsXcoqNypE761Xc8Snu1YO   292bYG-4ODBe3u947wm41Nq1MJbmi87kzD9ZQ_IBun_qmpAAuaeeh-FGnSHcQI nQOwen4t2muOWkmnra3Vi-3eTgMnCpi3HbedTTk

5 Nike "Proud" of Kaepernick Ad as Campaign Drives "Record Engagement." *Marketing Week*. Retrieved October 24, 2019, from www.market-ingweek.com/nike- proud-of-colin-kaepernick-ad-campaign/

6 Colorado Store That Quit Selling Nike Products Over Kaepernick Ad Goes Out of Business. (2019, February 14). *Fox News*. Retrieved October 24, 2019, from www.foxnews.com/us/colorado-store-that-quit-selling-nike-products-over-kaepernick-ad-goes-out-of-business

7 Makortoff, K. (2015, September 29). Volkswagen Cut from Top Sustainability Index. *CNBC.com*. Retrieved October 24, 2019, from www.cnbc.com/2015/09/29/volkswa gen-cut-from-dow-jones-sustainability-rank-ing.html

8 Millennial and Gen Z Study by Deloitte from 2018. Retrieved from https://www2.deloitte.com/content/dam/Deloitte/lu/Documents/about-deloitte/gx-2018-millen nial-survey-report.pdf

9 After 50 Years, Avis Drops Iconic "We Try Harder" Tagline. Retrieved October 24, 2019a, from https://adage.com/article/news/50-years-avis-drops-iconic-harder-tagline/236887?fbclid=IwAR2qfpwffWi937xDr mSpTQe6dJr07viygsNv6qrFqVO1RE6TIxHWwwKAY8o

10 In-person interview with Søren Ejlersen, Co-founder, Aarstiderne

11 Interview: Martin Scorsese. (2003, January 3). *The Guardian*. Retrieved October 25, 2019, from www.theguardian.com/culture/2003/jan/03/artsfeatures.martinscorsese

12 About Us – Discovery. Retrieved October 25, 2019, from www.discovery.co.za/corporate/about-us

13 KIND Snacks. Retrieved October 25, 2019, from www.kindsnacks.com/our-mission.html

14 Startup Spotlight: Blinkist (Berlin) Summarises Books for You. *Tech. eu*. Retrieved October 25, 2019, from https://tech.eu/features/4592/startup-spotlight-blinkist/
15 Story shared by Sarah Lindgren, Journalist
16 In-person interview with Jukka Peltola, CEO, GOODIO
17 Mui, C. (2012, January 18). How Kodak Failed. *Forbes*. Retrieved October 25, 2019, from www.forbes.com/sites/chunkamui/2012/01/18/how-kodak-failed/#2cb5cbb96f27
18 Crowe, C. (1996). *Jerry Maguire*.

Chapter 6

1 In-person interview with Søren Ejlersen, co-founder, Aarstiderne.
2 Bradesco Bank – Next. *IxD Awards*. Retrieved October 22, 2019, from http://awards.ixda.org/entry/2019/bradesco-bank-next/
3 Dan, A. (2013, July 8). The Heart of Effective Advertising Is a Powerful Insight. *Forbes*. Retrieved October 25, 2019, from www.forbes.com/sites/avidan/2013/07/08/the- heart-of-effective-advertising-is-a-powerful-insight/#6dcce07921d5
4 Cheng, A. (2018, October 19). Procter & Gamble Is Surging, and Beauty Brands SK-II and Olay Are Leading the Way. *Forbes*. Retrieved October 25, 2019, from www.forbes.com/sites/andriacheng/2018/10/19/beauty-brands-like-sk-ii-and-olay-are-leading-procter-gambles-growth/#66afae387398
5 Skype interview with Tom Daly and Max Vallot, co-founders, District Vision.
6 The New Science of Customer Emotions. *Harvard Business Review*. Retrieved October 25, 2019, from https://hbr.org/2015/11/the-new-science-of-customer-emotions
7 Danny Morel, Founder of Intero Real State & CEO Inc 500, on Quora.com
8 New Photo Contest for Local Guides in the Nordics and UK. Retrieved October 22, 2019, from www.localguidesconnect.com/t5/News-Updates/New-photo-contest-for-   Local-Guides-in-the-Nordics-and-UK/ba-p/220406
9 Skype interview with John Schoolcraft, Global Chief Creative Officer, Oatly.
10 Raphael, R. (2017, November 13). This New Hotel for Activists Encourages Community (and Pampering). *Fast Company*. Retrieved October 22, 2019, from www.fastcompany.com/40490911/this-new-hotel-for-activists-encourages-community-and-pampering
11 Enabling The Good Life Report. Retrieved from https://insights.sustainablebrands.com/full-report/

Chapter 7

1 Interview by e-mail Valérie Hernando-Presse, Global Marketing Director, Danone.
2 Ai Weiwei: Wonderful Dissident, Terrible Artist. *The New Republic*. Retrieved October 25, 2019, from https://newrepublic.com/article/112218/ai-wei-wei-wonderful-dissident- terrible-artist
3 More Than Half of Consumers Now Buy on Their Beliefs. *Edelman*. Retrieved October 25, 2019a, from www.edelman.com/news-awards/consumers-now-buy-on- beliefs-2017-earned-brand

4 Enabling the Good Life Report. *SB Insights*. Retrieved October 22, 2019, from https://insights.sustainablebrands.com/full-report/
5 Festinger, L. (1962, October). Cognitive Dissonance. *Scientific American*. Vol. 207, No. 4, pp. 93–106.
6 How Ariel Makes Consumers Save Energy by Switching from 40°/60° to 30°? Retrieved January 30, 1950 from www.nudgingforgood.com/wp-content/uploads/2015/11/Case-study-Ariel-Turn-to-30.pdf
7 UN Global Compact | CEO Study | Accenture. (2019, September 23). Retrieved October 25, 2019, from www.accenture.com/dk-en/insights/strategy/ungcceostudy
8 Skype interview with Marcello Leone, CEO, RYU.
9 RYU Apparel Reports First Quarter 2018 Results, 94% Revenue Increase. Retrieved October 22, 2019, from www.newswire.ca/news-releases/ryu-apparel-reports-first-quarter-2018-results-94-revenue-increase-683575541.html
10 Conscious Consumers Flocking to Pinterest for Sustainable Lifestyle Ideas. *Sustainable Brands*. Retrieved October 22, 2019, from https://sustainablebrands.com/read/behavior-change/conscious-consumers-flocking-to-pinterest-for-sustainable-lifestyle-ideas?platform=hootsuite
11 All Things Hair. *The Shorty Awards*. Retrieved October 22, 2019, from https://shortya wards.com/7th/all-things-hair
12 Nike on Demand | Work | R/GA. Retrieved October 22, 2019, from www.rga.com/work/case-studies/nike-on-demand-2
13 Lifebuoy Creates Innovative ROTI Reminder. *Unilever Global Company Website*. Retrieved October 22, 2019, from www.unilever.com/news/news-and-features/ Feature-article/2013/lifebuoy-creates-innova-tive-roti-reminder.html
14 Barbara Meuleman, studied at University of Bakersfield, California, on Quora.com.
15 Reiner, R. (1989). *When Harry Met Sally* (N. Ephron, Ed.).
16 Fitbit, Inc. – IR Overview. Retrieved October 22, 2019, from https://investor.fitbit.com
17 Purposeful Campaigns:
Budweiser: "Wind Never Felt Better."
Jst Awesome Commercials. (2019, September 26). Budweiser Super Bowl 2019 Commercial. Wind Never Felt Better. YouTube. Retrieved October 25, 2019, from www.youtube.com/watch?v=_Z7IBOqCtDo
T-Mobile "#Littleones."
SB15. (2018, March 7). Little Ones: T Mobile-2018 Big Game Ad. YouTube. Retrieved October 25, 2019, from www.youtube.com/watch?v=LvWTWo71YFM
DB Export: "Brewtrolium" M+AD. (2015, July 1). Brewtroleum. YouTube. Retrieved October 25, 2019, from www.youtube.com/watch?v=BHqnDdzb2xo
Hyundai: "Hope Detector."
Funny Commercials. (2018, February 5). Hyundai Super Bowl Commercial 2018 Hope Detector. YouTube. Retrieved October 25, 2019, from www.youtube.com/watch?v=yihgufUn86g&t=3s
Transformative campaigns:
Always: "Like a Girl."
Always. (2014, June 26). Always #LikeAGirl. YouTube. Retrieved October 25, 2019, from www.youtube.com/watch?v=XjJQBjWYDTs
Sport England: "This Girl Can."

The National Lottery. (2015, January 23). This Girl Can – What About You? YouTube. Retrieved October 25, 2019, from www.youtube.com/watch?v=jsP0W7-tEOc

Nike: "Dream Crazy"

NikeHongKong. (2018, September 6). Nike – Dream Crazy. YouTube. Retrieved October 25, 2019, from www.youtube.com/watch?v=E48hHS-5HyM

Land Rover: "Never Stop Discovering."

Ads seen on TV. (2018, May 17). Land Rover: Never Stop Discovering (2018). YouTube. Retrieved October 25, 2019, from www.youtube.com/watch?v=1MxUAPVSNp4

18 Huddleston, T. (2019, January 30). CNBC – Price of Super Bowl Commercial. *CNBC.com*. Retrieved October 22, 2019, from www.cnbc.com/2019/01/30/how-much-it-costs-to-air-a-commercial-during-super-bowl-liii.html

19 Transformative Versus Purposeful Campaigns. (2019, August). University of Bari, Luca Petruzzellis, Valentina Mazzoli, Luigi Piper and Thomas Kolster.

Chapter 8

1 Skype interview with Daniel Lubetzky, Founder and Executive Chairman, Kind Snacks.

2 (2015, October 27). Designers, Can You Solve The Mystery Hidden Inside This Photoshop File? Retrieved February 10, 2020, from https://www.adweek.com/creativity/designers-can-you-solve-mystery-hidden-inside-photoshop-file-167787/

3 Three Ways Companies Can Make Co-Creation Pay Off. *McKinsey & Company*. Retrieved October 22, 2019, from www.mckinsey.com/industries/consumer-packaged-goods/our-insights/three-ways-companies-can-make-co-creation-pay-off

4 Marcus, L. (2018, November 2). Made-to-Order KitKat Store Opens in Japan. *CNN Travel*. Retrieved October 22, 2019, from www.cnn.com/travel/article/kitkat-shop-osaka-japan/index.html

5 Liter of Light. Retrieved October 22, 2019, from https://literoflight.org/

6 PWC, the Sharing Economy. Retrieved October 22, 2019, from www.pwc.com/us/en/technology/publications/assets/pwc-consumer-intelli-gence-series-the-sharing-econ omy.pdf

7 IKEA Hackers – Clever Ideas and Hacks for Your IKEA. *IKEA Hackers*. Retrieved October 22, 2019, from www.ikeahackers.net/

8 Rochelle, H., on reddit.com, Rochelle, H. (2011, July 11). What's the Biggest Personal Change You've Ever Made? *Reddit*. Retrieved October 22, 2019, from www.reddit. com/r/InsightfulQuestions/comments/23jx51/whats_the_biggest_personal_change_ youve_ever_made/

9 My Starbucks Idea: Crowdsourcing for Customer Satisfaction and Innovation, Digital Innovation and Transformation. Retrieved October 26, 2019, from https:// digital.hbs.edu/platform-digit/submission/my-starbucks-idea-crowdsourcing-for-customer- satisfaction-and-innovation/

10 Precious Plastic. Retrieved October 26, 2019, from https://preciousplastic.com

11 Skype interview with Dave Hakkens, designer and founder, Precious Plastics & Phonebloks.

12 Logistics Trend Radar, Delivering Insight Today. Creating Value Tomorrow! Version 2016. Retrieved October 26, 2019, from www.dpdhl.com/content/dam/dpdhl/en/trends-in-logistics/assets/dhl-logistics-trend-radar-2016.pdf

13 2019 Edelman Trust Barometer Reveals "My Employer" Is the Most Trusted Institution. *Edelman.* Retrieved October 22, 2019, from www.edelman.com/news-awards/2019-edelman-trust-barometer-reveals-my-employer-most-trusted-institution

14 Turistföreningen, S. *The Swedish Number.* Retrieved October 22, 2019, from www.theswedishnumber.com

15 The Swedish Number. *Grey Advertising Global.* A WPP Company. Retrieved October 22, 2019, from http://grey.com/europe/work/key/swedish-number/id/12871/

Chapter 9

1 Skype interview with John Schoolcraft, Global Chief Creative Officer, Oatly.

2 Prahalad, C. K., & Ramaswamy, V. (2004). Co-Creation Experiences: The Next Practice in Value Creation. *Journal of Interactive Marketing.* Vol. 18, No. 3.

3 Rifkin, J. *The Zero Marginal Cost Society.* Retrieved October 22, 2019, from www.thez eromarginalcostsociety.com/

4 Lego Ideas – Home. Retrieved October 26, 2019, from https://ideas.lego.com

5 How Coke's New CMO Marcos De Quinto Can Make the Brand Sparkle. Retrieved October 26, 2019a, from www.campaignlive.co.uk/article/cokes-new-cmo-marcos- de-quinto-brand-sparkle/1329608

6 Featured Case – Airbnb: What's Next? *Thecasecentre.org.* Retrieved October 26, 2019, from www.thecasecentre.org/educators/ordering/selecting/featuredcases/Airbnb

7 Taking Action for Equality in Our Business and Beyond. *Unilever Global Company Website.* Retrieved October 22, 2019, from www.unilever.com/news/news-and-features/Feature-article/2019/taking-action-for-equality-in-our-business-and-beyond.html

8 Survey Shows a Third of British Children Don't Know Where Milk Comes from. Retrieved October 22, 2019, from www.farminguk.com/News/Survey-shows-a-third-of-British-children-don-t-know-where-milk-comes-from_46824.html

9 Penguin Pop-Up Shop to Be Stocked Solely by Women Writers. (2018, February 15). *The Bookseller.* Retrieved October 22, 2019, from www.thebookseller.com/news/penguin-launches-pop-shop-stocked-solely-women-writers-733796

10 Kelso, A. (2019, January 22). How Domino's Plans to Continue Dominating the Pizza Market. *Forbes.* Retrieved October 22, 2019, from www.forbes.com/sites/aliciakelso/2019/01/22/how-dominos-plans-to-gain-even-more-market-share/#392507225132

11 Logistics Trend Radar, Delivering Insight Today. Creating Value Tomorrow! Version 2016. Retrieved October 26, 2019, from www.dpdhl.com/content/dam/dpdhl/en/trends-in-logistics/assets/dhl-logistics-trend-radar-2016.pdf

12 Tupperware Brands Reports Fourth Quarter 2018 Results, Retrieved October 22, 2019, from https://ir.tupperwarebrands.com/~/media/Files/T/TupperWare-IR/Events/ 2019/4q-18-earnings-release.pdf; Annual Financials for Tupperware Brands Corp. Retrieved from www.marketwatch.com/investing/stock/tup/financials

13 Vigo the Rema App. Retrieved from January 31, 2020 from https://rema1000.dk/om-rema-1000/betalingskort/om-vigo/

14 Reng Abrantes, Senior Clerk, on Quora.com. Abrantes, R. (2018, October 4). What Is a Personal Challenge That You Had to Deal with for a Long Time but You Were Able to Successfully Overcome and What Do You Believe. *Quora*. Retrieved October 22, 2019, from www.quora.com/What-is-a-personal-challenge-that-you-had-to-deal-with-for-a-long-time-but-you-were-able-to-successfully-overcome-and-what-do-you-believe-is-the-key

15 Everlane. *Everlane*. Retrieved October 26, 2019, from www.everlane.com/about

16 Townsend, T. (2015, December 29). Everlane Is Letting Customers Choose Prices Through New Year's Eve. *Inc.com*. Retrieved October 26, 2019, from www.inc.com/tess-townsend/everlane-tells-customers-pay-what-you-want.html?cid=search

17 Schlossberg, M. One Retailer Is Letting Customers Decide How Much to Pay – but There's an Invisible Price If You Choose the Lowest Option. *Business Insider*. Retrieved October 22, 2019, from www.businessinsider.com/everlanes-pay-what-you- want-sale-2015-12?r=US&IR=T&IR=T

18 Press Release for Radiohead Fans, Does "Free" + "Download" = "Freeload"? Retrieved October 22, 2019, from www.comscore.com/Insights/Press-Releases/2007/11/Radio head-Downloads

Chapter 10

1 Skype interview with Jaime Pla, CEO, Suop.

2 Story shared by Søren Christensen, co-owner and strategy director at Robert/Boisen & Like-minded.

3 This Girl Can Does It Again. WARC. Retrieved October 26, 2019, from www.warc.com/newsandopinion/news/this_girl_can_does_it_again/39521

4 King, M. (2019, January 20). Gillette Responds to Controversial Advert Challenging Toxic Masculinity. *Forbes*. Retrieved October 22, 2019, from www.forbes.com/sites/michelleking/2019/01/20/gillette-responds-to-controversial-advert-challenging-toxic-masculinity/?ss=womenatforbes&utm_source=TWITTER&utm_medium=social&utm_content=2091084071&utm_campaign=sprinklrForbesWomanTwitter#5ddda5fa5bb7

5 A Five Reasons Interactive Content Drives Engagement. (2016, January 25). *MarketingProfs*. Retrieved October 26, 2019, from www.marketingprofs.com/opinions/2016/29198/five-reasons-interactive-content-drives-engagement

6 How Volkswagen Just Squandered 55 Years of Great Advertising. (2015, September 29). Retrieved October 26, 2019, from www.adweek.com/brand-marketing/how-volkswagen-just-squandered-55-years-great-advertising-167239/

7 Inside Year Three of #OptOutside with REI's Chief Creative Officer. (2017, November 20). Retrieved October 22, 2019, from www.adweek.com/creativity/inside-year-three-of-optoutside-with-reis-chief-creative-officer/

8 The History of #Optoutside. Retrieved from January 31, 2020 www.rei.com/blog/social/the-history-of-opt-outside

9 Coloradans Skipped Black Friday Shopping and Flooded State Parks. (2016, November 25). *Denverite*. Retrieved October 26, 2019, from https://denverite.com/2016/11/25/coloradans-skipping-black-friday-flooding-state-parks/

10 Beer, J. (2018, November 22). How REI Is Keeping the #OptOutside Magic Alive on Black Friday. *Fast Company*. Retrieved October 23,

2019, from www.fastcompany.com/90271139/how-rei-is-keeping-the-optoutside-magic-alive-on-black-friday

11 The New Nordic Food Manifesto. *Nordic Cooperation*. Retrieved October 26, 2019a, from www.norden.org/en/information/new-nordic-food-manifesto

12 Plastic, P. (2018, April 4). *Happiness Festival 2018*. Retrieved October 26, 2019, from https://preciousplasticindonesia.id/blog/2018-04/happiness-festival-2018/

13 Shindoor Khela #NoConditionsApply. *The Times of India*. Retrieved October 23, 2019, from https://timesofindia.indiatimes.com/Shindoor-Khela-NoConditionsApply/cam paignlanding/60791868.cms

14 Surowiecki, J. (2016, July 18). What Happened to the Ice Bucket Challenge? *The New Yorker*. Retrieved October 23, 2019, from www.newyorker.com/magazine/2016/07/25/als-and-the-ice-bucket-challenge

15 Salmeen, H. on Quora.com. (2017, May 4). What Is Volunteering, and Why Is It Important? *Quora*. Retrieved October 22, 2019, from www.quora.com/What- is-volunteering-and-why-is-it-important

16 Clifford, C. (2018, November 24). Small Business Saturday by the Numbers: 67 Million Expected to Shop, $85 Billion Spent. *CNBC.com*. Retrieved October 23, 2019, from www.cnbc.com/2018/11/21/small-business-saturday-67-million-expect-to-shop-85-billion-spent.html

17 Hövding. Retrieved October 26, 2019, from https://hovding.com

18 Give a Beep – Hövding. *Edelman Deportivo*. Retrieved October 26, 2019a, from www.edelmandeportivo.com/projects/give-a-beep/

Chapter 11

1 In-person interview with Jukka Peltola, CEO, Goodio.

2 Larry Fink's 2019 Letter to CEO's Purpose & Profit. *Black Rock*. Retrieved October 23, 2019, from www.blackrock.com/corporate/investor-relations/larry-fink-ceo-letter

3 Merchant, B. (2017, June 18). Life and Death in Apple's Forbidden City. *The Guardian*. Retrieved October 23, 2019, from www.theguardian.com/technology/2017/jun/18/foxconn-life-death-forbidden-city-longhua-suicide-apple-iphone-brian-merchant-one-device-extract

4 Ian Busch of Unilever Shares Thoughts on Sustainable Tea for International Tea Day. *Rainforest Alliance*. Retrieved October 23, 2019, from www.rainforest-alliance.org/busi ness/blog/2016/12/14/ian-busch-of-unilever-shares-thoughts-on-sustainable-tea-for-international-tea-day/

5 Connecting with Smallholder Farmers to Enhance Livelihoods. *Unilever*. Retrieved October 23, 2019, from www.unilever.com/sustainable-living/enhancing-livelihoods/inclusive-business/connecting-with-smallholder-farmers-to-enhance-livelihoods/

6 Beer, J. (2018, November 22). How REI Is Keeping the #OptOutside Magic Alive on Black Friday. *Fast Company*. Retrieved October 23, 2019, from www.fastcompany.com/90271139/how-rei-is-keeping-the-optoutside-magic-alive-on-black-friday

7 REI Brings Back #OptOutside – This Year More Than 275 Organizations Ask America "Will You Go Out with Us? *REI*. Retrieved October 23, 2019, from https://newsroom.rei.com/news/corporate/rei-brings-back-optoutside-this-year-more-than-275-organi zations-ask-america-will-you-go-out-with-us.html

8 Kiron, D., Nina, U., & Kruschwitz, N. (n.d.). Corporate Sustainability at a Crossroads. *MIT Sloan Management Review*. Retrieved October 23, 2019, from https://sloanreview.mit.edu/projects/corporate-sustainability-at-a-crossroads/

9 One French Supermarket Chain Uses Black Markets to Highlight the Absurdity of EU Food Regulations. (2018, May 24). Retrieved October 23, 2019, from www.adweek.com/brand-marketing/one-french-supermarket-chain-used-black-markets-to-highlight-the-absurdity-of-eu-food-regulations/

10 Forbidden Market – 7 Months After Launch. *Carrefour*. Retrieved October 23, 2019, from www.carrefour.com/current-news/forbidden-market-7-months-after-launch

11 IKEA Achieves Zero-Waste-to-Landfill Status in the UK. *Edie.net*. Retrieved October 27, 2019, from www.edie.net/news/5/Ikea-achieves-zero-waste-to-landfill-status-across-the-UK/

12 How Thrive Farmers Is Collaborating to Create Sea Change in the Coffee Industry. *Sustainable Brands*. Retrieved October 23, 2019, from https://sustainablebrands.com/read/organizational-change/how-thrive-farmers-is-collaborating-to-create-sea-change-in- the-coffee-industry

13 S. Butcher, Life Transitioner in Alternate Worlds (1966–present), on Quora.com. Butcher, S. (2018, October 21). What Is a Personal Challenge That You Had to Deal with for a Long Time But You Were Able to Successfully Overcome and What Do You Believe. *Quora*. Retrieved October 22, 2019, from www.quora.com/What-is-a-personal-challenge-that-you-had-to-deal-with-for-a-long-time-but-you-were-able-to-successfully-overcome-and-what-do-you-believe-is-the-key

14 Skype interview with Maria de la Croix, Co-founder, Wheelys Café.

15 In-person interview with founder and CEO is Christian Møller-Holst, Goodwings

16 In-person interview with Joanna Yarrow, Head of Sustainable and Healthy Living, INGKA Group (IKEA).

17 Yarrow, J. Head of Sustainable & Healthy Living, IKEA Group: "We Need to Develop a Positive Vision of How to Live a Good Life Within the Limits of the Planet." *Sustainable Brands Madrid*. Retrieved October 23, 2019a, from https://sustainablebrandsmadrid.com/blog/joanna-yarrow-head-of-sustainable-healthy-living-ikea-group-we-need-to-develop-a-positive-vision-of-how-to-live-a-good-life-within-the-limits-of-the-planet/

18 Jahshan, E. (2019, February 7). IKEA Officially Opens New Greenwich Store. *Retail Gazette*. Retrieved October 23, 2019, from www.retailgazette.co.uk/blog/2019/02/ikea-officially-opens-new-greenwich-store/

19 Aland Index. *The Baltic Sea Project*. Retrieved October 27, 2019a, from www.balticproject. org/en/aland-index

Chapter 12

1 Skype interview with Tom Daly and Max Vallot, Co-founders, District Vision.

2 Horn, J. (2013, May 15). Shackleton's Ad – Men Wanted for Hazardous Journey. *Discerning History*. Retrieved October 27, 2019, from http://discerninghistory.com/2013/05/shackletons-ad-men-wanted-for-hazerdous-journey/

3 Money for Nothing: Is Finland's Universal Basic Income Trial Too Good to Be True? Retrieved from January 31, 2020 from www.theguardian.com/inequality/2018/jan/12/money-for-nothing-is-finlands-universal-basic-income-trial-too-good-to-be-true

4 According to Oxfam's analysis, in 2018 26 people owned the same wealth as the 4.8 billion people who make up the poorest half of humanity, down from 43 people the year before. Retrieved January 31, 2020 from www.oxfamamerica.org/static/media/files/bp-public-good-or-private-wealth-210119-en.pdf

5 Fortune 500. Retrieved February 1, 2020 from http://fortune.com/fortune500/

6 Chart of the Week: The Rise of Corporate Giants. Retrieved February 1, 2020 from https://blogs.imf.org/2018/06/06/chart-of-the-week-the-rise-of-corporate-giants/

7 Business Gets Bigger Even as Americans Prefer Small. Retrieved January 31, 2020 from https://news.gallup.com/opinion/polling-matters/216674/business-gets-bigger-even-americans-prefer-small.aspx

8 The UN Global Compact-Accenture CEO Study on Sustainability 2013. Retrieved January 31, 2020 from www.unglobalcompact.org/library/451

9 McNeill, J. R. (2016). *The Great Acceleration*. Belknap Press, Harvard University Press.

10 Annual Report 2018. Stockholm Resilience Centre. Retrieved October 27, 2019, from www.stockholmresilience.org/news-events/general-news/2019-04-09-annual-report-2018.html

11 Koetsier, J. Why Every Amazon Meeting Has at Least 1 Empty Chair. Retrieved January 31, 2020 from www.inc.com/john-koetsier/why-every-amazon-meeting-has-at-least-one-empty-chair.html

12 P&G Policies and Practices. Retrieved January 31, 2020 from www.pg.com/en_AP/company/purpose_people/index.shtml

13 Google's Sergey Brin Calls 2016 Election "Offensive" in Leaked Video. *CNET*. Retrieved October 27, 2019, from www.cnet.com/news/google-co-founder-calls-2016- election-offensive-in-leaked-video/

14 Interface and Dutch Government Go Circular. Marjolein's Blog About Change for a More Sustainable World. (2019, February 10). Retrieved October 27, 2019, from https://changeincontext.com/interface-dutch-government-go-circular/

Appendix

1 The Good Life Goals by Futerra Sustainability Communications Ltd and 10-Year Framework of Programmes on Sustainable Lifestyles and Education Programme Is Licenced Under CC BY-ND 4.0. Retrieved February 1, 2020 from https://sdghub.com/goodlifegoals/

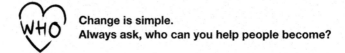

Change is simple.
Always ask, who can you help people become?

Index